Islam and Democracy

Islam and Democracy

John L. Esposito
John O. Voll

New York   Oxford
OXFORD UNIVERSITY PRESS
1996

Oxford University Press

Oxford   New York
Athens   Auckland   Bangkok
Calcutta   Cape Town   Dar es Salaam   Delhi
Florence   Hong Kong   Istanbul   Karachi
Kuala Lumpur   Madras   Madrid   Melbourne
Mexico City   Nairobi   Paris   Singapore
Taipei   Tokyo   Toronto

and associated companies in
Berlin   Ibadan

Published by Oxford University Press, Inc.
198 Madison Avenue, New York, New York 10016

Oxford is a registered trademark of Oxford University Press, Inc.

Library of Congress Cataloging-in-Publication Data
Esposito, John L.
Islam and democracy / John L. Esposito, John O. Voll.
p.   cm.
Includes bibliographical references.
ISBN 0-19-510296-7; 0-19-510816-7 (pbk.)
1. Islam and state.   2. Democracy—Religious aspects—Islam.   3. Islamic
countries—Politics and government.   I. Voll, John Obert, 1936– .   II. Title.
JC49.E76   1996
320.917'671'09045—dc20   95-42339

5   7   9   8   6   4

Printed in the United States of America
on acid-free paper

Acknowledgments

We have received assistance and cooperation from many people throughout the Islamic world and in the academic world in our research for this book. It is impossible to list them all here but we hope that they know how grateful we are for their help. We especially thank the National Endowment for the Humanities and the United States Institute for Peace for their support and advice. Positions taken in this book are, of course, not those of the NEH or the USIP but their help reflects the continuing significance of those institutions as indispensable sources of support for research in the social sciences and humanities. Parts of the first chapter appeared originally in *Middle East Quarterly* as an article, "Islam's Democratic Essence," and we express our thanks to the Middle East Forum for permission to use that material. We also express our gratitude to Georgetown University, the new academic home for both of us, and the staff of the Center for Muslim-Christian Understanding for their patience and help. Finally, we recognize that our wives, Jean and Sarah, provide the essential encouragement that we need in projects like this.

Washington, D.C.   J.L.E.
November, 1995   J.O.V.

Contents

Islam and Democracy

Introduction

Religious resurgence and democratization are two of the most important developments of the final decades of the twentieth century. In many areas, movements of religious revival coincide with and sometimes reinforce the formation of more democratic political systems. In other areas, the two dynamics are in conflict. In the Muslim world, these issues are raised with special force because of the strength of the Islamic resurgence and the intensity of the demands in recent years for greater popular participation in the political processes.

The Islamic Revolution that overthrew the Iranian monarchy in 1979 was one of the first popular revolutions against a modern authoritarian political system in the final quarter of the twentieth century. In the early 1990s, another Islamic movement, the Islamic Salvation Front (FIS), was suppressed after it dramatically challenged the authoritarian regime of the Front de Libération Nationale (FLN) in Algeria when the government had been forced to allow open elections. In many areas of the Muslim world, one of the crucial issues defining the political future is the relationship between the forces of Islamic resurgence and the development of democratic political systems.

Governments and political leaders throughout the Muslim world respond to popular sentiments for greater political participation and the activities of religious movements. Rulers and regimes are forced to choose among policies of repression and greater popular participation, with the threat that if they make the wrong choice they themselves could lose power, as did the Shah of Iran or the Algerian FLN. If they do not adjust rapidly enough, they could be overthrown; however, they also face the risk, if they open their political systems, of electoral defeat. Islamic movements and their leaders face similar critical choices between adaptation or violent opposition. All groups, whether Islamic or secular, that are seeking greater democratization must decide upon the most effective means for achieving their goals. These options represent power conflicts as existing regimes and popular opposition movements of many different kinds interact in complex ways. Competition, cooperation, and conflict are among the most important dimensions of

3

Muslim life in the first years of the fifteenth Islamic century and the final years of the twentieth century of the Common Era.

ISLAM AND POLITICS

Islamic politics are frequently described as in some way combining "religion and politics." In the words of modern Islamic movements, Islam is *din wa dawla*, that is, "religion and state." Many scholars, Muslim and non-Muslim, speak of Islam as a comprehensive way of life[1] and note the absence of ordained priesthoods and the formal institutions of a "church." However, even in medieval Islamic civilization, in the era of the great Muslim empires of the Umayyads and the Abbasids, nonstate structures with important functions in the life of religious faith and action developed. The emergence of the ulama, the "learned scholars of the faith," as a distinctive grouping within Islamic society, and the development of the great schools of Islamic law in a way independent of governmental control were important parts of the early Islamic experience. Later, great mystic brotherhoods developed as an important foundation for popular religious life. These institutions and social structures were not "churches," but they were autonomous and separate from the state, and sometimes in conflict with state institutions.[2]

Many different kinds of political systems existed within the Muslim world at the beginning of the modern era. Some of the largest states were ruled by sultans, great commanders of empires such as the Ottoman Empire in Europe and the Middle East and the Moghul Empire in India. In Shii Iran, the rulers were shahs; throughout the Muslim world there were smaller principalities ruled by local notables such as the Imam of Yemen and the chieftains of the Persian Gulf states. All these states faced the challenges of the sociopolitical changes of the modern transformation.

The structural evolution of states in the Muslim world involves both Islam and politics. Political systems were transformed by major reforming rulers such as Muhammad Ali at the beginning of the nineteenth century in Egypt and Mustafa Kemal Ataturk in Turkey in the years following World War I. Established institutions were modified, and reformers implemented programs of conscious change. The relationship between Islam and politics has been a major theme in these transformations of the past two and a half centuries. Important lines of tension existed among movements of modernizing reform and the older, established institutions and customs of premodern Muslim societies. The first major modernizer in the Ottoman Empire, Selim III, was overthrown in 1807 by a coalition of conservative and reactionary forces. The conservative ulama of Egypt sometimes resisted educational reform, in less dramatic fashion, especially changes in the great Islamic university of al-Azhar. In that context, there was an apparent tension between the forces of modernization, which were often explicitly seen as Westernization, and elements explicitly representing Islam, which was often seen as premodern, if not antimodern, forces. Conservatism and traditionalism tended to be identified with Islam, and adaptationism and modernizing reform tended to be identified with secularism and modern Western perspectives. Activist movements of religious revival were often viewed as efforts to slow the processes of modernization and as opponents of modernity.

In the twentieth century, new movements of Islamic affirmation and reassertion began to emerge. These were different in structure and approach from earlier Islamic movements and represent the emergence of an important new style of Islamic organization. The Muslim Brotherhood, established by Hasan al-Banna in Egypt in 1928, and the Jamaat-i Islami, established by Abu al-Ala Mawdudi in South Asia in 1941, are two important early examples of these new groups.[3] These movements did not receive their support from the conservative elements of society. Instead, the majority of the supporters had received modern-style educations and worked in the modern sectors of their societies. They did not call for a return to premodern conditions. Instead, their programs called for the establishment of structures that could function in an authentically Islamic way in the context of modernity.

During the first half of the twentieth century, new-style Islamic movements such as the Brotherhood and the Jama'at were visible but not very powerful. The main trends in political thought and action were in the direction of increasingly secular perspectives and programs. Although emerging nationalist movements had significant Muslim components, both in terms of members and of concepts, nationalism was not articulated in significantly Islamic terms. Similarly, in the period following World War II, when most Muslim countries that had come under European control were achieving political independence, the major ideologies of protest and of radical reform were shaped by Western democratic, socialist, and Marxist perspectives.

Independent states in societies with Muslim majorities joined the world of sovereign nation-states. Political systems, whether radical republics or conservative monarchies, developed structures that fell basically within the framework of the ideas of the modern nation-state.[4] This development defined the political context of the Muslim world in the second half of the twentieth century. It is as political units seen as nation-states that Muslims have operated in the international scene and in domestic politics.

Basic in this great transformation were issues of adapting existing Islamic concepts and structures to modern, Western-influenced sociopolitical realities. This took many forms. The intellectual efforts to construct an "Islamic modernism" had roots in the late nineteenth century, in the works of people like Muhammad Abduh in Egypt and Ahmad Khan in India. Islamic modernism became the dominant mode of theological thought throughout much of the Islamic world by the middle of the twentieth century. It provided a flexible intellectual foundation for the articulation of ideologies such as Islamic socialism.

There were also important institutional adaptations. When Libya was created as an independent state in 1951–1952, it was established as a monarchy, and the head of the Sanusiyyah, a great Sufi brotherhood, became the king of a new "nation-state." In Sudan, two of the largest older Muslim associations, the Khatmiyyah Tariqah and the Ansar (followers of the Mahdi), organized themselves into mass political parties. They were able to compete effectively in the elections of the parliamentary system that was created when Sudan became independent in 1956. In many other areas, similar reforms and adaptations of existing Islamically identified structures took place. The character of the role of Islam in politics was that of adapting existing structures and concepts to new conditions.

POLITICS AND NEW ISLAMIC MOVEMENTS

The role of Islam in politics began to change in important ways by the 1970s. Rather than simply being a reactive element within the political community, Islamic groups emerged as sources of new initiatives for political change and development. In the 1970s, many of the leaders and governments in the recently established nation-states faced serious difficulties. The hopes and aspirations of the era of nationalist struggles had sometimes given way to disappointments, political instability, and major economic problems. As a result, many people in the Muslim world, as elsewhere, began to question the effectiveness and validity of the prevailing ideologies. As growing numbers of people looked to Islam as a possible source of inspiration in times of difficulties, new-style Muslim organizations assumed new importance. Established organizations like the Muslim Brotherhood and the Jamaat-i Islami were joined by many newly formed organizations. These new associations were especially popular among students and younger modern-educated professionals in many different Muslim countries.

New Islamic organizations are a significant part of the Islamic resurgence of the final decades of the twentieth century. They are activist elements that are not simply responding to the initiatives of others. These movements represent the emergence of a major credible political and social alternative or orientation. The movements reflect the dual aspirations of modern-educated professionals in Muslim societies, who want greater participation in the political processes, and also want their societies to be more explicitly identifiable as Islamic. As a result, the new organizations bring together the two great trends of the late twentieth century: religious resurgence and democratization.

ISLAMIZATION AND DEMOCRATIZATION

The dual aspirations of Islamization and democratization set the framework for most of the critical issues in the contemporary Muslim world. When one looks at the issues of Islam and democracy, it becomes clear that the most important questions revolve around the compatibility of Islam and democracy and the role of the new-style movements in the political evolution of Muslim societies. The older kind of approach, which works to adapt existing structures to the conditions of modernity, is still significant. However, in the era of postmodern perspectives and institutions, the two most important issues relating to religious resurgence and political development are the potential democratic resources of the Islamic tradition and the ability of the new Islamic movements to operate effectively to meet the demand for both Islamic authenticity and popular democratic participation. As a result, although this study will note the role of older Muslim associations and institutions, it will concentrate primarily on the issues involving the role of the new-style Islamic associations and their relationship to the processes and experiences of democratization.

The starting point for this discussion will be the conceptual and ideological resources available for programs of democratization in the Islamic tradition. Like all of the major worldviews and religious traditions, Islam has a full spectrum of potential symbols and concepts for support of absolutism and hierarchy, as well as foundations for liberty and equality. However, in a context in which many non-Muslims question the existence of any conceptual or theological foundations for democracy in Islamic traditions, it is important to examine the conceptual resources within Islam for democratization. These include both the ideas and concepts of egalitarian participation and concepts of legitimate opposition. Without a relatively thorough discussion of these ideas and ideals, it is difficult to understand the programs and aspirations of the Islamic movements in the contemporary world.

It is important not to view the Islamic tradition in isolation. The experience of Muslims has many important similarities to the development of political institutions that build on the foundations of Greek and Christian traditions. The relationship between Islam and democracy is best understood in a perspective that views both the global context of democratization and the distinctive concepts and experiences of Muslims. The first two chapters of this volume provide an examination of these subjects, looking at the basic concepts in the Islamic tradition that can provide a foundation for democratization and for concepts of modern-style opposition. These discussions make it possible to see the context of the faith and practice of Islamic movements, whose experiences are the core of major political developments in the contemporary Muslim world.

Democratization in the Muslim world takes place within the framework of the existing state system. To a remarkable degree, the political boundaries established by the politics of imperialism and nationalism in the first half of the twentieth century remain the defining boundaries of the critical political arenas of the 1990s. The borders of independent "nation-states" are remarkably significant in defining the identity, leadership, and field of activities of new Islamic movements, even when a movement spreads beyond national boundaries. In specific cases such as the Mus-

lim Brotherhood, which originated in Egypt, but in which the name and some
sense of a shared tradition extend beyond the boundaries of a single state, it is possible, and necessary, to speak of the *Egyptian* Muslim Brotherhood, the *Sudanese*
Muslim Brotherhood, and the *Syrian* Muslim Brotherhood. The same is true for
the Jamaat -i Islami of Pakistan, Bangladesh, Afghanistan, India, or Kashmir. While
they may share a common primary founder, such as Hasan al-Banna of the Muslim Brotherhood or Mawlana Mawdudi of the Jamaat, differing national contexts
give rise to differences in agenda and methods among new Islamic movements.

The continuing importance around the world of nation-state borders is seen
when considering the processes of democratization in the late twentieth century.
In non-Muslim areas, only in Germany did the democratic revolution result not
only in the end of a political system within a state but the creation of a new and
larger state. State destruction, as seen in Yugoslavia and the Soviet Union, tended
to create new and smaller nation-states rather than units that transcended the old
nation-state. This was also true in the Islamic world. The overthrow of the monarchy in Iran by an *Islamic* revolutionary movement raised expectations that the revolution would spread. However, even the anti-government Shiites of southern Iraq
did not take the opportunity of the war between the Iraqi government and the
Islamic republic of Iran in the 1980s to revolt and join the Islamic revolution.
"National" identities were remarkably strong.

As a result, when one examines the experiences of the new Islamic movements
and their relationships with the processes of democratization, the cases are defined
by the experiences and boundaries of the existing nation-state system. Transnational activist movements have very limited visibility and appeal. It is the "national"
movements, which seek to Islamize the existing political units, that are of greatest
importance.

SPECTRUM OF EXPERIENCES

The Muslim world presents a broad spectrum of experiences in both religious
resurgence and democratization. Each state and society has a unique history as
well as characteristics it shares with other Muslim societies. In trying to discover
distinctive elements and common features, it is important to examine a number of different political contexts and how the various new-style Islamic movements operate within those contexts. It would be difficult to create in a single
volume a complete collection of case studies of all the new-style Islamic movements that exist in the 1990s.[5] However, some experiences provide important
insights into the spectrum of Islamic experiences, which in turn provides a basis
for a broader understanding of the relationships between the Islamic resurgence
and democratization.

Several factors are of critical importance in understanding the role of new
Islamic movements in the developing relationships between the Islamic resurgence

and democratization. The first is whether or not Islamic movements were legal or illegal as they emerged, and how that status may have changed over time. A second dimension is the degree to which the new movement was a movement of activist and possibly revolutionary opposition to the existing system, or to which a movement was willing to cooperate with existing political rulers. A third important aspect was the attitude of the political rulers toward the new style movements: Did the existing state seek to suppress Islamic movements or were there at least some opportunities for nonviolent political participation by Islamic movements? These basic conditions provide the framework within which Islamic movements interacted with state structures and existing political systems. This interaction is, in many ways, the key to understanding the relationship between the Islamic resurgence and democracy.

Islamic activist movements have come to power in two countries, Iran and Sudan. In Iran, the process involved a major populist revolution and the overthrow of an authoritarian, Westernizing political system. In Sudan, the Islamic movement had participated in many different ways in the evolving Sudanese political system, at times as an opposition party in a parliamentary system and at other times as an underground movement of opposition to a military regime. These two cases are often depicted as the prime examples of militant, revolutionary Islam. Discussion of Iran and Sudan is clearly necessary in a study of Islam and democracy at the end of the twentieth century.

In contrast to the Iranian and Sudanese experiences of revolutionary opposition and the subsequent creation of new political systems, in a number of other areas Islamic movements have been and continue to be active and participating parts of the political system. While they have by their participation helped to shape the political systems, these experiences represent a more pluralistic style of political operation. In these states, the new-style movements have been legally recognized and accepted by the governments even when the movements have been in opposition. It is not possible to present a discussion of Islam and democratization in the late twentieth century without examining the successful participation within existing systems represented by some of these experiences. That of the Jamaat-i Islami in Pakistan and Angkatan Belia Islam Malaysia (ABIM) in Malaysia represent important examples of this kind of experience and will be examined in detail in this book.

A third kind of experience is one in which the new-style Islamic movements are in some way illegal or reflect continuing movements of revolutionary opposition to the existing political system. There are many countries in which movements advocating active Islamic revival are illegal and suppressed. In Syria, the Muslim Brotherhood was crushed by the government in the early 1980s, with thousands killed. In Morocco, the major articulators of the Islamist perspective have been restricted. In Turkey, it is illegal to use Islam as a formal basis for identifying a political organization, although more Islamically oriented parties have had some success in recent years. However, two of the most important and visible cases of the new-style Islamic organizations operating, at least at times illegally, are in Algeria and Egypt. In both countries, the Islamist movements opted to participate in the political processes defined by the existing state. In Egypt, although some militant groups advocated the forceful overthrow of the state, the largest new-style organization, the Muslim Brotherhood, worked within the democratic structures in Egypt with varying degrees of success, even though the Brotherhood itself has not been recognized as a legal organization. In Algeria, when the FLN regime was forced to hold open elections, it was an Islamic movement, the Front Islamique du Salut (FIS), that won a major victory. The FIS was, however, prevented from taking control of the government when the Algerian military intervened and suspended the electoral process before it could be completed. Since that military intervention in early 1992, FIS has been in revolutionary opposition to the military regime.

These three major kinds of experiences reflect the great diversity in the Islamic world. The spectrum ranges from the Islamists in power in Iran and Sudan, to new-style movements that are active participants in existing systems (Malaysia and Pakistan), to movements that are illegal and sometimes violently suppressed opposition in countries like Algeria and Egypt. Although an examination of these cases will not provide a comprehensive presentation of every possibility, this broad spectrum of experiences does provide important insights into understanding the complex relationships between Islam and democracy in the contemporary world. It is not enough to look at Islamic movements simply as rejectionist and revolutionary opposition movements. It is also important to see how they operate as parts of heterogeneous systems and what the results have been when they come to power.

We start with a discussion of the general potential resources for democracy within Islamic experiences, and then examine how Islamic movements in different circumstances utilize those resources. In this way, it becomes possible to suggest generalizations about the relationships between Islam and democracy and Islamization and democratization. We hope that this volume will, beyond this, provide insight into the broader global phenomena of religious resurgence and democratization in the last years of the twentieth century.

ONE

Islam and Democracy

Heritage and Global Context

The resurgence of Islam and the desire for democratization in the Muslim world exist in a dynamic global context. Throughout the world, many peoples express similar desires, making religious resurgence and democratization two of the most important themes in contemporary world affairs. The assertion of special communal identities and the demand for increased popular political participation occur in a complex world environment in which technology reinforces global relationships at the same time that local and national and local cultural identities remain remarkably strong.

In dramatic transformations of society and politics, societies have distinctive resources and liabilities. The position of Islamic societies must be viewed within the global framework of experiences if its special resources and liabilities are to be understood.

The demand and desire for democracy is widespread in contemporary global affairs. Few major political leaders or movements describe themselves as "antidemocratic." Even when a restoration of monarchy was advocated recently by some in Brazil, there was virtually no support among the monarchists for a restoration of a divine-right, absolutist monarchy. Instead, the monarchists proposed a "presidential monarchy system" and spoke of needing a system similar to the current Spanish monarchy.[1] Many people agree that perhaps "the most important global political development of the late twentieth century" is the emergence of prodemocracy movements throughout the world and their success in many countries.[2]

People who formally and publicly oppose democracy or who are willing to describe their programs as nondemocratic usually represent a marginal sect or group on the extreme of the religio-political spectrum, such as the Branch Davidians in Waco, Texas, or some of the ultra-orthodox Jewish groups in Israel. There are other, more mainstream groups that reject the term "democracy" as a foreign term that is not applicable within their tradition or society because there are other more appropriate, indigenous conceptualizations for describing the rights of popular participation and freedom. However, most politically conscious people around

11

the globe express their aspirations for political participation, freedom, and equality in terms of "democracy."

Recent democratization occurs in the context of globalization of most significant aspects of human life. Everything from the food consumed by common people to grand issues of policy decided by the leaders of the great powers reflects the cosmopolitan nature of both affairs of state and daily life in the contemporary world. Corporations large and small consider the international scene before making investment and development decisions. Communications networks, fax machines, and television satellite disks make all kinds of interactions possible on an almost instantaneous basis. Even the world of radical extremists committed to distinctive and parochial causes is cosmopolitan in its connections and interactions. Militant separatists cooperate with other militant separatists and revolutionary causes overlap with increasing frequency. The complex cosmopolitanism of terrorism is clearly reflected in the backgrounds of the people involved in the bombing of the World Trade Center in New York in February, 1993. Some participated in the anti-Soviet revolution in Afghanistan, some worked with Palestinian movements, and others were allegedly associated with an Egyptian Islamic teacher who led a mosque in New Jersey.

In the current world, the actors operating on global scales are not simply the governments and states. International affairs have clearly transcended being "*international*" in their dynamics. In the area of global economics, the old situation dominated by a few great "multinational" corporations has been transformed into a highly interactive network of transactions in which "national" boundaries have rapidly diminishing significance, even for small local companies. Cultural and educational institutions increasingly see global activities as an essential part of their mission. A small state university in New England, the University of Maine, can, for example, contract with the Bulgarian government to establish an "American University of Bulgaria," and this attracts no more attention than the expansion of the McDonald's fast-food chain into yet another country. Through electronic communications and other global media, individuals as well can establish their own private ties across the world in ways that were virtually inconceivable even in the 1970s.

MOVEMENTS OF EMPOWERMENT AND IDENTITY

The transformation of human experience on a global scale is accompanied by greater demands for participation and for recognition of special identities. These two sets of demands are related. They represent the efforts of individuals and groups to gain some control over developments and institutions that appear to be so large that they are uncontrollable. In the early 1970s, some analysts had already noted that, parallel to the globalization of human life, there were strong currents for asserting the validity of small-scale, communal ties. Zbigniew Brzezinski viewed this specifically in terms of its impact on the viability of the nation-state as an operating unit and noted the assertion of new-style communal identities in countries in which "their particular nation-state no longer corresponds to historical need. On a higher plane it has been rendered superfluous by Europe, or some other regional (Common Market) arrangement, while on a lower plane a more intimate linguistic and religious community is required to overcome the impact of the implosion-explosion characteristic of the global metropolis."[3] Written more than twenty years ago, this analysis points the way to the complex interactions and tensions between the global and local dimensions of human societies as they developed in the final quarter of the twentieth century. The processes of democratization and of global religious resurgence are both parts of this complex, developing set of human experiences which characterizes the world of the 1990s.

Democratization is the demand for empowerment in government and politics made by a growing portion of populations around the world. As the technologies of government and rule became more sophisticated, there was a growing sense of marginalization among most people, even in those states universally thought of as "democratic." High-tech administration and growing bureaucracies accompanied the increasing size and scope of governmental operations in the twentieth century. Such technologies could transform more traditional autocracies into relatively effective authoritarian dictatorships of both the right and the left, and transform leaders of old-fashioned democratic republics into elites capable of manipulating the masses and creating a sense of departure from participatory politics. The modernization and technicalization of societies in all parts of the globe led to increasing access on the part of growing numbers of people to information that was uncensorable because of the technology. In industrialized as well as Third World societies, there was a growing awareness of and antagonism toward large-scale governing institutions that seemed "out of touch with the people" or repressive. In the authoritarian regimes of the left and the right and in recognized democracies, more and more people began to demand increased empowerment and participation. Movements for democratization and transformation of governing structures of all kinds arose out of this ferment.

In theory, there may be a number of methods for increasing participation of the people in government and for providing a sense of viable popular empowerment. However, at the end of the twentieth century, the most widely accepted way of expressing these desires is the demand for democracy. It is the broad heritage of concepts and images associated with democracy that provides the foundations for democratic revolutions and movements around the globe. The discourse of democracy has become, in most societies, the dominant discourse of politics. It is for this reason that even the most authoritarian of dictators now must speak the language of democracy. This discourse is controversial because the heritage of democracy is complex.

"Democracy" is what W. B. Gallie called, some years ago, an "essentially contested concept." He noted that "there are disputes, centred on [such concepts] . . . which are perfectly genuine: which, although not resolvable by argument of any kind, are nevertheless sustained by perfectly respectable arguments and evidence. This is what I mean by saying that there are concepts which are essentially contested, concepts the proper use of which inevitably involves endless disputes about their proper use on the part of their users."[4] Gallie made the consequent point that it is important to recognize when one is dealing with essentially contested concepts. "Recognition of a given concept as essentially contested implies recognition of rival uses of it (such as oneself repudiates) as not only logically possible and humanly 'likely', but as of permanent potential critical value to one's own use or interpretation of the concept in question; whereas to regard any rival use as anathema, perverse, bestial or lunatic means, in many cases, to submit oneself to the chronic human peril of underestimating, or of completely ignoring, the value of one's opponent's positions."[5] In the current global context, most who advocate democratization still do not recognize it as an essentially contested concept. As a result, they view people with different interpretations of democracy as "perverse and lunatic," and thus are open to the perils of underestimating the strength of the alternatives. This is especially true of advocates of the styles of democracy found in Western Europe and the United States, who believe themselves to be the true heirs to the only legitimate democratic tradition and thus view any other efforts to create democracies as false and undemocratic.

For many in the West, for example, the concept of "Islamic democracy" is anathema. However, this view makes it impossible to understand the appeal and strength of many movements within the Islamic world. Because democracy is in many profound ways an essentially contested concept, it is important to understand the perception of democracy within the movements of the current Islamic resurgence. This understanding is important even for those who view the Islamic resurgence as a threat, because it is important to understand the competing definitions of democracy. It may be even more important for this group because, as Gallie suggested three decades ago, advocates of democracy in the West might also be able to learn something about democracy from others. In the global environment of the present, narrow and parochial understandings of concepts as important as democracy are dangerous and limiting, even for long-established democratic systems.

The demand for increased popular political participation and empowerment takes place alongside another demand, that for recognition of special identities or authentic communities. The assertion of the authenticity and legitimacy of communal identities takes a number of different forms. In some areas, it is the product of the assertion of a special cultural, linguistic, or ethnic heritage. In other cases, it is the affirmation of the validity of a religious message or tradition and is manifested as part of the current global resurgence of religion. In the broadest sense, these movements all represent the refutation of the old assumptions that the processes of modernization would eventually create a homogeneous and modern world of basically similar groups within a single universal society. Much of this perspective, especially in the United States, was shaped by the experience of integrating large numbers of immigrants in the late nineteenth century and by the vision of America as the great "melting pot" in which peoples from all different societies and cultures could be "melted" and turned into a homogeneous American citizenry. Already by the 1960s, it was discovered that there were some "unmeltable" ethnic groups within the United States.[6]

By the 1990s, it is clear that the assertions of basic communal identities are a major factor in global affairs. For many, this appears to be a perverse reversion to irrational and "barbarian" times, and to some extent, in the excesses of "ethnic cleansing" in the former Yugoslavia, for example, this is true. However, it is also a distinctively postmodern rejection of the enforced homogeneity of mass institutions and the nonmoral rationalism of modern secularism suggested by the agenda of modernity and feared in the old classics such as *1984*, by George Orwell. This rejection goes beyond small-scale ethnic movements and also appears in the worldwide phenomena of religious resurgence.

Along with the demand for democratization, one of the most important developments in the history of the late twentieth century has been the "virtually worldwide eruption of religious and quasi-religious concerns and themes"[7] in the context of the globalization of human action. Frequently, this has resulted in the active assertion of what are sometimes called "fundamentalist" movements of religious revival. It is important to recognize that the "resurgence of 'fundamentalistic' promotion of particularistic ideologies and doctrines (local, ethnic, national, civilizational and regional) does not by any means constitute counter-evidence [for the processes of globalization]. . . . The recent globe-wide assertion of particularistic ideas is heavily contextualized by the phenomenon of increasing *globality*."[8] Although some such fundamentalist movements may simply be reactionary and anachronistic, "other fundamentalist movements may be viewed as merely offering—if often very militantly—new modes of particularistic societal identity relative to global universalism in more-or-less 'concultural,' relatively pluralistic mode."[9]

The two great trends of democratization and identity assertion are concurrent and vital parts of the contemporary history of the world. Each represents a special demand for empowerment and identity recognition in an increasingly globalized context of human activity and experience. In each region of the world, special conditions shape the way the two trends express themselves, and they are sometimes complementary and sometimes contradictory. Although regional developments are distinctive, they also affect and are affected by global developments and cannot be viewed in isolation.

In the Muslim world, there has been an important and highly visible resurgence of Islam. This affirmation of faith and identity is a powerful force in all aspects of human life and is reflected in clothing, changing social lifestyles, and the arts, as well as the more visible arena of politics and political power. Concurrent with this resurgence is a growing demand for greater popular participation in the political system.

Most governments in the Muslim world are relatively authoritarian while also being committed to programs of modernization using Western-secular models. Token opposition parties have been allowed in some countries, but there are few places where it is realistic to assume that an opposition party could win an election and take control of the government. The experience of Turkey in its 1950 general election, when an opposition party *did* win an election and take control of a government, has not been repeated in other Muslim countries. This is true in both traditional regimes and more liberal, secular regimes like that of Habib Bourguiba in Tunisia. As a result, the authoritarian political establishments have become identified with secularist approaches to politics and modernization.

Inevitably, in this situation, the processes of democratization and Islamic resurgence have become complementary forces in many countries. The most effective opposition to authoritarian regimes is expressed through a reaffirmation of the Islamic identity and heritage. Other ideologies of opposition have much weaker appeal. As growing portions of the population gain at least minimum education and access to global media, there is increasing pressure for opening the political processes to greater popular participation. However, the new participants are unlikely to have the same perspectives and worldviews as the Western-educated secular elite.

Democratization is subject to the same social dynamics as nationalism was earlier. Almost fifty years ago, H. A. R. Gibb noted that nationalism "in its Western manifestations is confined to the intellectuals who are in direct and close touch with Western thought. As the nationalist idea penetrated into the popular mind, it was transformed, and could not avoid being transformed, by the pressure of the age-long instincts and impulses of the Muslim masses."[10] Just as the more popular nationalism's base of support, the more Islamic its orientation, democratization loses its secular dimensions as it becomes a popular, and more truly democratic movement. In this way, the pressures for democratization in the Islamic world reinforce and give added strength to the Islamic resurgence.

DEMOCRATIZATION AND POLICY

The relationship between democratization and the Islamic resurgence is complex and is a very important element in the political dynamics of the contemporary Muslim world. In more general terms, these two processes involve popular empowerment and communal identity affirmation. The definition and articulation of these aspirations in their specifics show the diversity within the Muslim world. Many different ways of advocating both the reaffirmation of Islam and the democratization of the polities can be seen throughout the Islamic world. From West Africa to Southeast Asia, Muslims undertake these efforts working within existing republics, monarchies, and authoritarian dictatorships, in pluralistic and in relatively homogeneous societies, in both wealthy and poor states.

Each of the many different Muslim experiences of democratization and religious resurgence takes place within the broader contemporary global context and within the broad heritage of Islamic history and tradition.

In global terms, the definition of "democracy" is closely identified with major elements of the political traditions of Western Europe and the United States. For many social scientists, the Western experience provides the basis for definitions of democracy. In that context, it is possible for a major scholar, Giovanni Sartori, to raise the question, "When we speak of Western experience, is the key term 'Western' or 'experience'? In other words, can there be a non-Western path to democracy?"[11] This scholar's answer comes quite clearly in his discussion of democracy in the Third World and the possibility of "exporting" democracy: "But no sooner do we apply the word democracy to most of the Third World, and in particular to the so-called developing countries, than the standard becomes so low that one may wonder whether the word democracy is still appropriate. . . . Democracy, as Woodrow Wilson said, is the most difficult form of government. We cannot hope, therefore, to export the 'complete' Western type. On the other hand, it is equally obvious that the new states and developing nations cannot pretend to start from the level of achievement at which the Western democracies have arrived."[12] This example provides a clear case of the identification of "democracy" with the Western experience that remains common among contemporary analysts and of the acceptance of the Western pattern as the appropriate model for all societies to emulate. In this context, scholars continue to examine the prospects for "exporting democracy" from the West to the rest of the world,[13] and ask questions such as, "Why has the Westminster Model failed in Africa?"[14]

Even within the Western tradition, democracy is an essentially contested term. The system of multiparty elections and parliaments that developed in Great Britain and France was not universally accepted as the sole model for democracy. During the French Revolution, for example, the Babouvists developed an important "antiparliamentary, plebiscitary" democratic style that had a long-lasting impact on European politics.[15] The major alternative tradition in the West was provided by Marxism. "Marx believed that democratic government was essentially unviable in a capitalist society. . . . The post-capitalist state would not . . . bear any resemblance to a parliamentary regime. Parliaments create unacceptable barriers between the ruled and their representatives."[16] Ultimately, Marxist political alternatives took a variety of forms in practice, but most represent, even in principle, a very different Western model of democracy from the one implied in the analysis of Sartori and advocated by U.S. policy makers.

In the broader context of the globalization of politics and political discourse, the arena for contestation becomes even larger. To the extent that democracy is identified as a Western construct, the processes of democratization conflict with the assertions of special communal identities. An effort to restrict the conceptualization of increasing popular participation in the political realm to distinctively Western approaches and institutions opens the Western advocate of democracy to the charge of cultural imperialism. In this way, democratization can be viewed by advocates of the new communal identities as a process that introduces foreign and inauthentic institutions and norms into societies. The contestation over the definition of democracy thus expands into the areas of conflict between "foreign" and "authentic."

In the Muslim world, this contestation raises the challenge of defining "Islamic democracy" in a way that is appropriate both to the demands of increasing popular political participation and to the desire to establish a clearly and authentically Islamic polity. Two of the areas of complexity in this task of definition are the changing and multiple perspectives on the meaning of democracy in the West and the dynamic diversity of approaches existing in the contemporary Islamic world. Muslims throughout the world are aware of and, to some extent, influenced by the debates about democracy taking place in the West. Thus, to understand the relationship between the Islamic resurgence and democracy, both of these factors must be at least briefly examined.

WESTERN DEFINITIONS OF DEMOCRACY

When many Western scholars and leaders talk about "democracy" outside of the United States and Western Europe, they give the impression that there is a consensus on what the term means and what institutions are necessary for establishing "democracy" in place of an authoritarian regime. When global democratization became a highly visible and important force, political leaders in the United States spoke frequently of American support for developing democracies. However, in much of this discussion, it was clear that the American leaders had a distinctive model in mind when they defined what America was supporting. As the Soviet Union began to disintegrate, Secretary of State James Baker spoke, in his address to a meeting of the Conference on Security and Cooperation in Europe (CSCE) in Moscow in September of 1991, of "democracy's season," and presented to "all Soviet citizens and their leaders" five fundamental principles that he urged them to follow, including multiparty, free elections and a Jeffersonian understanding of the rights of minorities.[17]

Similarly, in discussing American support for democracy in Africa, certain basic features were emphasized as being essential for democracy. Again, multiparty elections were a key part of the description of democracy. There was also a promise that the United States would provide direct financial aid for the "promotion of this [necessary] democratic infrastructure," described by then-Assistant Secretary for

African Affairs Herman J. Cohen as involving the creation of a "civil society" with "democratic labor unions, literary and cultural groups, bar associations, women's associations, and traditional human rights 'watchdog' groups" as well as a Western-style free press.[18] Cohen pledged two kinds of assistance from the United States:

> One is that assistance that is needed to start a democratic process: That is the assistance in the development of free and fair elections and multi-party systems. . . . But . . . we are going to do more than that . . . [and will provide] growing amounts of assistance for what we call "governance." Governance, in effect, is the entire process that will enable people to participate and to fulfill their responsibilities to make democracy work. It is the civic associations; it is the independent [judiciary]; it is the free press that will make democracy work and put a check on government.[19]

Vice-president J. Danforth Quayle affirmed, "we believe that there is no single model of democracy in Africa," but he went on to say, "Presidential systems, parliamentary systems, proportional representation, and single member districts—we can respect all of these."[20] This list tends to name conventional Western models for democratic systems and does not note the wider spectrum of democratic styles existing even in the West, including more consensual, or "unitary," as opposed to "adversary," democracies,[21] some of which might be more closely in tune with African traditions.

The Clinton Administration also proclaimed that "promoting democracy abroad" was one of the three main pillars of American foreign policy. In Secretary of State Warren Christopher's words, this involved "encouraging the global revolution for democracy that is transforming our world. By helping promote democracy, we do more than honor our deepest values. We are also making a strategic investment in our nation's security."[22] The identification of global democratization with the American model was made explicit in Christopher's discussion of American proposals to aid democracy in Russia when he noted that "through exchange programs, young Russians can be brought to the West and exposed to the workings of democracy and the market."[23] The new Undersecretary of State responsible for the democracy-support initiatives, former senator Timothy Wirth, stated, "We want a lot of small programs that can be exported to the grassroots level."[24] Democratic institutions were, in other words, things that would and could be "exported" from the United States to strengthen global democratization.

In these discussions, there is a strong sense that there is a working and effective American model of democracy and that there is a consensus on the main features of this model. In the experiences of democratization around the world, this sense of an established Western model that is supported by American policy makers is important. It sets specific and concrete standards, which themselves become elements in the contestation over definition, and shifts the debate from the content of the particular standard to whether or not it is appropriate to adopt a "foreign model." The impact of this in terms of democratization debates in the Islamic world can be seen in one analysis of President Clinton's possible foreign policy perspectives. Recalling that Clinton had been a Rhodes Scholar, the analyst noted that the

> scholarship program aside, Rhodes as a man calls to mind bitter colonial memories. He advocated democracy for the "higher races" and peonage for the "lower races." When democracy is advocated for the Middle East, many Western analysts suddenly become modern versions of Rhodes. They raise the red flag of Islamic fundamentalism and assert the entirely untested hypothesis that Islam and democracy are incompatible.[25]

These "foreign policy" discussions tend to take place in isolation from the profound debates taking place within the West in general and the United States in particular. These debates make it clear that there is no clear consensus on the specifics of the desired Western or American models of democracy. At the same time, the substance of these debates opens the way to consideration of many possibilities for defining democracy that are closer to long-standing conceptualizations within the Islamic world.

One such issue is the contrast between consensus and majority rule. In the standard conceptualization of the Western model, there is emphasis on elections and majority rule, However, "globally, consensual democracy is still at least as common as majority-rule democracy. . . . Even in Western societies, consensual decision making is far more common than we usually realize, partly because it is often disguised behind formal majoritarian procedures."[26] A similar contrast to the standard Western model can be seen in discussions of political parties. During the presidential elections in the United States in 1992, there was considerable recognition of the ineffectiveness of the political parties. Many people seriously proposed a wide variety of alternatives to the multiparty system. Ross Perot, who proposed a variety of very different changes in the national decision-making process, including national electronic referenda, received almost 20 percent of the votes cast. This represents a significant diversity of opinion about the role of political parties in a democratic system that is not reflected in the official American insistence on multiparty elections along the American pattern as the standard for judging whether or not a political system elsewhere in the world is "democratic."

Virtually every prescription for establishment of a democratic regime involves the holding of freely contested and fair elections. Such elections are widely held to be the single most important part of an authentically democratic system. However, historically, formal elections were not always an essential part of a democratic system. In Athens, for example, representatives of the people were selected by lot, thus avoiding control by the powerful and persuasive. In the debates concerning reforms necessary in Western democratic systems, many different proposals have been made. One Australian scholar, for example, states, "In order to

have democracy we must abandon elections . . . and revert to the ancient principle of choosing by lot those who are to hold various offices. . . . [Elections] inherently breed oligarchies."[27]

It is important to keep in mind the very broad scope of the debate over the definition of democracy within the West, if one is to understand the impact of the
Western experience upon global experiences of democratization. Official insistence
on a single, relatively specific model of democracy in the context of a worldwide
discussion of a wide range of democratic options makes Western governments
appear to be engaging in the effort to impose a particular model. The range of
debate emphasizes the character of democracy as an essentially contested term, and
Western governments weaken their influence when they ignore that fact and
attempt to impose their particular definition as an absolute truth. The Western
democratic heritage is a broad and rich one, and this resource for polity creators
around the globe is weakened if only a small part of the heritage is presented.

Both the officially presented Western model and the vigorous diversity of concepts within the West regarding democracy have an impact on the processes of
democratization in the Muslim world. The globalization of communications means
that Muslim intellectuals participate in the broader debates. The differences between
the "official model" and the current critiques of Western democratic systems also
play a part in Muslim responses to both Western policies and local changes.

The Islamic Heritage

Many Muslims are actively engaged in defining Islamic democracy. They believe
that the global processes of religious resurgence and democratization can be, and,
in the case of the Muslim world, are, complementary. The two processes are contradictory and competitive only if "democracy" is defined in a highly restricted way
and is viewed as possible only if specific Western European or American institutions are adopted, or if important Islamic principles are defined in a rigid and traditional manner. Then the debate about democratization shifts from discussing the
most effective means for increased popular participation to arguments over the
legitimacy of importing "foreign" political institutions.

The discussions within the Islamic world are similar to discussions in the other
major traditions of society: politics and culture. The widespread acceptance of
democracy as a legitimate basis for political order is a phenomenon of the modern
era around the world. As late as the end of the eighteenth century, most major
political systems were based on principles other than democracy. "Divine right"
of monarchs was a contested issue in European politics during the early modern
and Enlightenment periods. The relationship between the views of the founders of
the United States and democracy is at best ambiguous. "The absence of entrenched
aristocratic and ecclesiastical power gave the United States a propitious basis from
which to move towards modern democracy. This, however, was certainly not a path

the founders intended to explore."[28] At the much broader level of the history of Western philosophy and political theory,

> from the perspective of twenty-five hundred years of Western political thinking, almost no one, until very recently, thought democracy to be a very good way of structuring political life. . . . [T]he great preponderance of political thinkers for two-and-a-half millennia have insisted upon the perversity of democratic constitutions, the disorderliness of democratic politics and the moral depravity of the democratic character.[29]

The emergence of democratic theories, institutions, and practices in the West involved, and continues to involve, a combination of nondemocratic and antidemocratic traditions with existing democratic-style traditions and new perceptions of human social, religious, and political needs and rights. The fact that the "idea of popular sovereignty was simply incompatible with the theocentric concept of princely power and the increasingly rigid imperial structure of the Roman Church"[30] did not prevent people who still believed themselves to be Christian from creating democratic systems in Western Europe and North America.

The ruling elites in most major traditions of civilization had significant reservations about democracy. Yet, from a world historical perspective, it is also possible to note that "most people in the world can call on some local tradition on which to build a modern democracy. . . . The evidence is clear that both the idea and the practice of democracy are foreign to no part of the world."[31] These local democratic traditions are often consensual rather than majoritarian and frequently identified with relatively small social units.

Reconceptualization of premodern institutions played an important role in the development of democratic attitudes in Europe. As the British parliamentary system became more democratic during the nineteenth century, for example, historians sought and found the bases for parliament and democracy in early institutions. Hugh Chisholm, a prominent scholar of English history, wrote in the classic eleventh edition of the *Encyclopaedia Britannica* that "we find in the Anglo-Saxon polity, as developed during their rule in England, all the constituent parts of parliament."[32] The assemblies of yeoman peasants in the *things* of Scandinavia were reenvisioned as precursors of modern parliaments, as reflected in the very names of the parliaments in Norway (*Storting*) and Iceland (*Althing*).

The modern democratization process involves a complex process of reconceptualizing what may have been antidemocratic themes and combining these revisioned concepts with the protodemocratic and democratic elements in every societal tradition. These indigenous dimensions interact with the transformations of the modern era to create the potentialities (and obstacles) for modern democratization in the contemporary societies. This is the process, in general terms, that was experienced in Western societies and is experienced in other societies as well. Because of its very nature, each experience will be different, since indigenous foundations are different. It is in this context that the special conditions of democratization in the Muslim world need to be viewed. It is especially important to identify crucial elements in the Islamic tradition that have been redefined and reenvisioned in ways that can strengthen (or possibly weaken) the dynamics of democratization in Muslim societies.

In Islamic history, there are a number of very important concepts and images that shape the contemporary visions of what a just human society should be. These are the foundations for the Islamic perceptions of democracy. Despite the great dynamism and diversity among contemporary Muslims in terms of political views, there are core concepts that are central to the political positions of virtually all Muslims. What varies is the definition of the concepts—not recognition of the concepts themselves. Abu al-Ala al-Mawdudi, a significant Sunni Muslim thinker who lived in British India and then independent Pakistan, and who established the major South Asian Islamic revivalist organization, the Jamaat-i-Islami, stated that the "political system of Islam has been based in three principles, *viz*: *Tawheed* (Unity of God), *Risalat* (Prophethood) and *Khilafat* (Caliphate). It is difficult to appreciate different aspects of the Islamic polity without fully understanding these three principles."[33]

Other Muslim leaders might express the issues within a different format, but these three core concepts provide a foundation for understanding Islamic political perspectives. Viewing their reconceptualization in the contemporary context provides an important basis for understanding the conceptual foundations for democratization in the Muslim world.

Muslims of all traditions agree that acceptance of *tawhid* is the core concept of Islamic faith, tradition, and practice. Although it may be expressed in many different ways, *tawhid*, simply defined, is "the conviction and witnessing that 'there is no God but God,'" and the consequence of this is that at "the core of the Islamic religious experience, therefore, stands God Who is unique and Whose will is the imperative and guide for all men's lives."[34] Building on this base, in terms of political philosophy, Muslims affirm that there can be only one sovereign and that is God.

Both non-Muslim observers and some conservative Muslims have argued that *tawhid* means that it is impossible to have an "Islamic democracy," because the concept of the sovereignty of the people conflicts with the sovereignty of God. In Mawdudi's analysis, the main lines of an Islamic democratic theory that remains closely tied to *tawhid* become clear. Because there is a profound tie between God and political legitimacy, "Islam, speaking from the view-point of political philosophy, is the very antithesis of secular Western democracy. . . . [Islam] altogether repudiates the philosophy of popular sovereignty and rears its polity on the foundations of the sovereignty of God and vicegerency (*Khilafah*) of man."[35]

This position does not mean that Mawdudi and other modern Muslims reject the idea of a democratic political system. They only insist that it be framed within the worldview of *tawhid*. Mawdudi explained what these structures would be:

A more apt name for the Islamic polity would be the 'kingdom of God' which is described in English as a 'theocracy'. But Islamic theocracy is something altogether different from the theocracy of which Europe has had bitter experience. . . . The theocracy built up by Islam is not ruled by any particular religious class but by the whole community of Muslims including the rank and file. The entire Muslim population runs the state in accordance with the Book of God and the practice of His Prophet. If I were permitted to coin a new term, I would describe this system of government as 'theo-democracy', that is to say a divine democratic government, because under it the Muslims have been given a limited popular sovereignty under the suzerainty of God. The executive under this system of government is constituted by the general will of the Muslims who have also the right to depose it.[36]

Mawdudi observes that in this system, "Every Muslim who is capable and qualified to give a sound opinion on matters of Islamic law, is entitled to interpret that law of God when such interpretation becomes necessary. In this sense the Islamic polity is a democracy," but it is a theocracy in the sense that no one, not even the whole Muslim community united, has the right to change an explicit command of God.[37] It is important to note that there is recognition that decisions have to be made regarding interpretation and when to interpret.

The one existing government organized along these general lines is the Republic of Iran, which is Shii in its specifics but similar to the Sunni perspective of Mawdudi with regard to these *tawhid*-related issues. As described by one of the major Shii political theorists at the time of the Iranian revolution, Ayatollah Baqir al-Sadr (who was executed by the Iraqi government in 1980), in this structure there is a jurist who holds the position of final religious authority and formally is the "Deputy General of the Imam" (the divinely selected messianic leader in Shii theology), the position held by the Ayatollah Khomeini following the Iranian revolution in 1979. This jurist, in this system, "should have the support of the majority of the members of the consultative council of the religious authority. . . . In case there are more than one person eligible for holding the position of religious authority, people have a right to choose one of them through a referendum."[38]

Ayatollah Khomeini himself also emphasized the necessity of popular participation in selecting leaders. In his *Last Will and Testament*, he stated that it was the "heavy responsibility of the people" to select "experts and representatives for the selection of the leader or the Leadership Council." He advised the people of Iran that

In all elections, those of the president, Majlis representatives, or selection of experts for the choice of the Islamic Leadership Council, you must take part. . . . All of you, from the Maraje' [religious authorities] and great ulama to the bazaaris, farmers, workers and government employees, are responsible for the destiny of the country and Islam.[39]

In the view of Ayatollah Baqir al-Sadr, this represents a new and important era in Islamic history.

> The theory that the influential persons could represent the general public was operative in Islamic society in a particular period of history. But in view of the changed circumstances and in consideration of the principles of consultation and juristic supervision, it is essential that this theory should give place to the formation of an assembly whose members are the real representatives of the people.[40]

This is because "the people are the rightful bearers of this trust (government)."[41]

Within this framework, it is also argued that the absolute sovereignty of God makes any human hierarchy impossible, since before God all humans are equal. Thus, *tawhid* provides the conceptual and theological foundation for an active emphasis on equality within the political system. A hierarchical, dictatorial system has historically been condemned as non-Islamic. As early as Muawiya, the fifth leader of the Muslim community after the death of the Prophet Muhammad (in the historical reckoning of Sunni Muslims), the label "king" (*malik*) was a negative term for arbitrary personal domination.[42] A dictator or king who claimed sovereignty was not a legitimate ruler.

In a number of contemporary states, *tawhid* has become the basis for going beyond the affirmation of equality to the call for the revolutionary overthrow of oppressive dictators. In Iran, Ali Shariati wrote that in "the world-view of *tauhid*, man fears only one power, and is answerable before only one judge. . . . *Tauhid* bestows upon man independence and dignity. Submission to Him alone—the supreme norm of all being—impels man to revolt against all lying powers."[43] In this context, the Iranian revolution could be called by Ayatollah Mahmud Taleghani "the revolution of *tauhid*."[44] Thus, although *tawhid* might be used as a basis for a nondemocratic state, it also provides the foundation for ideologies of equality and revolution against arbitrary rule.

A second important concept related to contemporary Muslim understanding of democracy is *khilafah*. In the study of Islamic political thought, this concept has been primarily related to the issue of defining political leadership for the community. The title of the leader of the Muslim community following the death of the Prophet Muhammad was "caliph," or *khalifah*, and the general political system is called the "caliphate," or *khilafah*, with the term "caliph" having the literal meaning of "successor" to the Prophet. As a result, political thought in medieval Islam "at first centres round the caliphate and is, in fact, a theory of the caliphate, its origin and purpose."[45] The theories of the caliphate are an important part of the intellectual history of the Islamic world. In concrete terms, the political system ruled by a "caliph" lasted through two great dynasties, the Umayyads (661–750) and Abbasids (750–1258), but disappeared as an actual imperial system with the Mongol conquest of Baghdad in 1258.

The title of "caliph" remained a concept of religio-political leadership, and in the nineteenth century the sultans (the title of the imperial leadership that emerged when usage of the title "caliph" declined) of the Ottoman Empire began to revive the idea that the leader of the most important Muslim state was the "caliph" as well as the sultan. At the end of World War I, the Ottoman Empire disappeared and was replaced by the new Turkish nationalist state lead by Mustafa Kemal. The Turks abolished the offices of both the Ottoman sultanate and caliphate, and proclaimed Turkey to be a republic led by a "president."[46] The issue of restoring the caliphate in some form was an important topic for debate among Muslims during the first half of the twentieth century,[47] but gradually lost its importance.

In the traditional and modern debates over the nature of the caliphate, the institution was viewed in essentially monarchical terms. However, there is a profoundly different meaning of the term that has received increasing attention in the second half of the twentieth century. In addition to the connotations of "successor" that the Arabic term *khalifah* involves, there is also a sense in which a *khalifah* is a deputy, representative, or agent. It is possible to interpret some sections of the Quran as identifying human beings in general as God's agents (*khalifahs*) on earth, and human stewardship over God's creation as the broader cosmic meaning of *khilafah*. Mawdudi utilized the concept of *khilafah* defined in this way as a basis for his interpretation of democracy in Islam: "Let us now consider 'Khilafat', which according to the Arabic lexicon, means 'representation'. The real position and place of man, according to Islam, is that of the representative of God on this earth, His vicegerent; that is to say, . . . he is required to exercise Divine authority in this world within the limits prescribed by God."[48] The specific implications of this for the political system are that "the authority of the caliphate is bestowed on the entire group of people, the community as a whole, which is ready to fulfil the conditions of representation after subscribing to the principles of *Tawheed*. . . . Such a society carries the responsibility of the caliphate as a whole and each one of its individual[s] shares the Divine Caliphate. This is the point where democracy begins in Islam. Every person in an Islamic society enjoys the rights and powers of the caliphate of God and in this respect all individuals are equal."[49]

The identification of "caliph" with humanity as a whole, rather than with a single ruler or political institution, is affirmed in the Universal Islamic Declaration of Human Rights, a document drawn up by the Islamic Council of Europe.[50] In this framework, the first phase of the "fulfillment of social-political *Khilafah*" is "the creation of the community of believers," while the second phase "is to reach the level of self-governance."[51] This perception of "caliph" becomes a foundation for concepts of human responsibility and of opposition to systems of domination. It also provides a basis for distinguishing between democracy in Western and in Islamic terms. The Pakistani Islamist leader, Khurshid Ahmad, for example, noted that "secular democracy, as it has evolved in the post-Enlightenment era, is based upon the principle of the sovereignty of man, conceptually speaking. Islam, on the other hand, believes in the sovereignty of God and viceregency of man, the difference being that man is God's *Khalifah*, or viceregent on the earth."[52]

The absolute sovereignty and oneness of God as expressed in the concept of *tawhid* and the role of human beings as defined in the concept of *khilafah* thus provide a framework within which both Sunni and Shi'i scholars have in recent years developed distinctive political theories that are self-described and conceived as being democratic. They involve special definitions and recognitions of popular sovereignty, and an important emphasis on the equality of human beings and the obligations of the people in being the bearers of the trust of government. Although these perspectives may not fit into the limits of a Western-based definition of democracy, they represent important perspectives in the contemporary global context of democratization.

In presentations of democracy within a broad Islamic conceptual framework, much attention is given to some specific aspects of social and political operation. In particular, Islamic democracy is seen as affirming longstanding Islamic concepts of consultation (*shurah*), consensus (*ijma*), and independent interpretive judgement (*ijtihad*). Like many concepts in Western political tradition, these terms have not always been identified with democratic institutions and have a variety of usages in contemporary Muslim discourse. However, regardless of other contexts and usages, these terms are central to the debates and discussions regarding democratizations in Muslim societies.

The necessity of consultation is a political consequence of the principle of the caliphate of human beings. "Popular vicegerency in an Islamic state is reflected especially in the doctrine of mutual consultation (*shura*). Because all sane adult Muslims, male and female, are vicegerents (agents of God), it is they who delegate their authority to the ruler and whose opinion must also be sought in the conduct of state."[53] The importance of consultation as a part of Islamic systems of rule is widely recognized. Muhammad Hamidullah, in a standard introduction to Islam, places consultation in a framework that is widely accepted:

> The importance and utility of consultation cannot be too greatly emphasized. The Quran commands the Muslims again and again to take their decisions after consultation, whether in a public matter or a private one. . . . [T]he Quran does not prescribe hard and fast methods. The number, the form of election, the duration of representation, etc., are left to the discretion of the leaders of every age and every country. What is important is that one should be surrounded by representative personalities, enjoying the confidence of those whom they represent and possessing integrity of character.[54]

Some contemporary Muslim thinkers have taken this analysis further, arguing that although "the Quran envisages the Muslim community as a perfectly egalitarian, open society based on good will and cooperation" and the "Quran laid down the principle of shura to guide the community's decision-making process," the classical doctrine of *shurah*, as it developed, was in error. It viewed consultation as the process of one person, the ruler, asking other people for advice, whereas the Quranic understanding of *shurah* "does not mean that one person asks others for advice but, rather, *mutual advice* through mutual discussions on an equal footing."[55] During the nineteenth and twentieth centuries, there have been significant efforts to broaden the conceptualization of consultation, and this is associated with advocates of Islamic democracy. Fazlur Rahman emphasizes the importance of this democratizing task: "[T]he participatory association of the ummah [the Muslim community] through directly ascertaining the will of the ummah in the political and legislative decisions affecting the life of the community can neither be rejected nor postponed. Those who advocate such a course of action are wittingly or unwittingly guilty of rendering Islam null and void."[56] Ayatullah Baqir al-Sadr relates consultation to the rights of the people: "The people, being the vicegerents of Allah, have a general right to dispose of their affairs on the basis of the principle of consultation," and this should now involve "the formation of an assembly whose members are the real representatives of the people."[57] *Shurah* thus becomes a key operational element in the relationship between Islam and democracy.

A similarly important operational concept is consensus or *ijma.* Consensus has long been accepted as a formal validating concept in Islamic law, especially among Sunni Muslims. "Sunni Islam came to place final religious authority for interpreting Islam in the consensus (*ijma*) or collective judgment of the community," and subsequently "[c]onsensus played a pivotal role in the development of Islamic law and contributed significantly to the corpus of law or legal interpretation."[58] The foundation for the validity of consensus is an often-cited tradition that the Prophet Muhammad stated that "My Community will not agree upon an error." However, for most of Islamic history, consensus as a source of Islamic law tended to be limited to the consensus of the learned scholars, and general popular consensus had less significance in specific and operational aspects of Muslim community life. This also tended to be a conservative force, because a consensus on a subject tended to lead to an end of speculation in that area.

In modern Muslim thought, however, the potential flexibility involved in the concept of consensus came to receive greater emphasis. One scholar, for example, citing the tradition from the Prophet about the community not agreeing upon an error, stated, "Such a consensus has great possibilities of developing the Islamic law and adapting it to changing circumstances."[59] In broader discussions, consensus and consultation were frequently seen as the effective basis for Islamic democracy operating in modern terms. The concept of consensus provided the basis for acceptance of systems recognizing majority rule. It is noted by some contemporary scholars that, in Islamic history, because there are no explicit formulations of state structure in the Quran, the "legitimacy of the state . . . depends upon the extent to which state organization and power reflect the will of the ummah, for as classical jurists have insisted, the legitimacy of state institutions is not derived from textual sources but is based primarily on the principle of *ijma*."[60] On this basis, consensus can become both the legitimation and the procedure of an Islamic democracy.

A third operational concept of major importance is *ijtihad*, or the exercise of informed, independent judgment. In the minds of many Muslim thinkers, this is the key to the implementation of God's will in any given time or place. The Pakistani Islamist leader Khurshid Ahmad presents this position clearly: "God has revealed only broad principles and has endowed man with the freedom to apply them in every age in the way suited to the spirit and conditions of that age. It is through the *Ijtihad* that people of every age try to implement and apply divine guidance to the problems of their times."[61] In the context of the modern world, the advocacy of *ijtihad* can be a call for radical reform, as is reflected in the words of Altaf Gauhar:

> The present represents a great opportunity to reconstruct our society. The forces of Imperialism and Colonialism are on the retreat. . . . We have to break out of our present state of intellectual stagnation. . . . It is possible for a secular leader to suggest that power flows out of the barrel of a gun. In Islam power flows out of the framework of the Qur'an and from no other source. It is for Muslim scholars to initiate universal *Ijtihad* at all levels. The faith is fresh, it is the Muslim mind which is befogged. The principles of Islam are dynamic, it is our approach which has become static. Let there be fundamental rethinking to open avenues of exploration, innovation and creativity.[62]

This reflects the enthusiasm for *ijtihad* found among virtually all Muslim reformers in the twentieth century. In specifically political terms, the great South Asian Muslim intellectual reformer Muhammad Iqbal had already noted in the 1930s the relationships between consensus, democratization, and *ijtihad*:

> The growth of republican spirit, and the gradual formation of legislative assemblies in Muslim lands constitutes a great step in advance. The transfer of the power of Ijtihad from individual representatives of schools to a Muslim legislative assembly which, in view of the growth of opposing sects, is the only form Ijma can take in modern times, will secure contributions to legal discussion from laymen who happen to possess a keen insight into affairs. In this way alone can we stir into activity the dormant spirit of life in our legal system.[63]

In terms of the implications of this for representative government, Iqbal is very clear: "The republican form of government is not only thoroughly consistent with the spirit of Islam, but has also become a necessity in view of the new forces that are set free in the world of Islam."[64]

Ijtihad has always been a controversial concept because of the danger of its misuse. It is possible that the course of action for Muslims will be "the option advocated by the secularists and non-religious Muslims, which is to fling open the door of ijtihad as wide as possible, and interpret ijtihad in such a way that it can be used to justify the results, regardless of whether the rulings were based on traditional *fiqhi* [Islamic jurisprudential] criteria or not."[65] However, the importance of *ijtihad* is emphasized by this same author, who expresses the hope that appropriate *ijtihad* will make it possible for

> Muslim social scientists to study social phenomenon . . . with an Islamic framework and epistemological paradigm and then begin the process of rebuilding Islamic civilization on the basis of its own understanding of the social sciences. This deconstruction and subsequent reconstruction is what is needed if the Muslim ummah is ever to assume its divinely ordained position as a witness to other nations.[66]

Consultation, consensus, and *ijtihad* are crucial concepts for the articulation of Islamic democracy within the framework of the oneness of God and the representational obligations of human beings. These are terms whose meanings are contested and whose definitions shape Muslim perceptions of what represents legitimate and authentic democracy in an Islamic framework. However, despite the fact that within the Islamic world these terms are contested, they provide an effective foundation for understanding the relationship between Islam and democracy in the contemporary world. The contested articulations also reflect the broader global contestation over the significance and nature of democracy in the multicultural context.

In these debates, it is clear that Muslims are not willing simply to adopt Western democratic models. The period of unquestioningly borrowing techniques and concepts from Western experience has passed (if it ever took place), and now the effort is to establish authentically Islamic democratic systems. This effort is not inherently anti-Western, but it contains a recognition that there are significant problems with Western-style democracy. Muhammad Iqbal's positions in the first half of the twentieth century already show these dynamics. Iqbal is recognized as one of the major figures in modern and modernist Islam and is not thought of as a chauvinist nationalist or religious fundamentalist. Yet he presented a very strong critique of Western democracy.

> Iqbal was undoubtedly a democrat . . . yet he bitterly denounced Western democratic systems. Now, the essence of his criticism is that Western democratic societies aim only at accomplishing materialistic ends. . . . Iqbal rejected Western democratic systems because of their lack of ethical and spiritual concerns. It is not their democratic forms and processes which are in error but their orientations and value systems.[67]

The contrast between the morally concerned Muslim world and the materialist West is an important aspect of the current discussions. However, in structural and institutional terms, the Western experience continues to have great influence in the Islamic debates. Much of the discussion by Muslims in the past century has been to show that major concepts in Western democracy have their analogs someplace in the Islamic tradition. In this way, simple correlations like identifying *ijma* with public opinion are the core of the analysis of some of the famous earlier discussions of democracy and Islam, as presented by the Eqyptian authors Abbas Mahmud al-Aqqad and Ahmad Shawqi al-Fanjari.[68]

The older modernist approach to Islamic democracy is thus open to strong criticism presented by Hamid Enayat:

> What is blatantly missing from contemporary Muslim writings on democracy, in spite of all the claims to the contrary, is an adaptation of either the ethical and legal precepts of Islam, or the attitudes and institutions of traditional society, to democracy. This is obviously a much more complex and challenging task than the mere reformulation of democratic principles in Islamic idioms. It is because of this neglect that the hopes of evolving a coherent theory of democracy appropriate to an Islamic context have remained largely unfulfilled.[69]

This critique was written in the late 1970s, before the effective emergence of the newer generation of Islamist movements such as Nahdah in Tunisia, the Islamic Salvation Front (FIS) in Algeria, and the National Islamic Front (NIF) in Sudan, as well as a variety of major movements outside the Middle East. The current study has as a major goal answering the question of whether or not the current movements have succeeded in developing a "coherent theory of democracy appropriate to an Islamic context."

In the field of political theory, especially as it relates to democracy, Muslim scholars and activists are in a time of major transition. This transition is simlar to that visible in economics. A major Muslim economist Khurshid Ahmad describes that change: "Initially, the emphasis was on explaining the economic teachings of Islam and offering Islamic critique of the Western contemporary theory and policy. . . . Gradually the Muslim economists and other professionals became involved in this challenging enterprise . . . [and set in motion] the transition from 'economic teachings of Islam' to the emergence of 'Islamic economics.'"[70] A major issue in democratization in Muslim societies is whether or not scholars and leaders have successfully made the transition from listing "democratic doctrines of Islam" to creating coherent theories and structures of Islamic democracy that are not simply reformulations of Western perceptions in some Muslim idiom.

The global dynamics of democratization reflect the dramatic changes of the current time. Throughout the world, scholars, leaders, and "common people" are actively involved in the effort to create more effective democratic structures. At a time when the national political leaders in the United States are actively attempting to "reinvent government,"[71] Italians have voted to restructure their parliamentary system, and significant changes are taking place elsewhere, it is clear that there is no universally accepted or clearly defined model of democracy, even of Western democracy, that can simply be adopted by people engaging in democratization. The difficulties of the new democratic regimes in Eastern Europe reflect the problems and complexities of the global experiences of democratization.

From a global perspective, the efforts of Muslims to develop an authentic and viable Islamic democracy have great significance. The efforts to utilize long-standing traditions and conceptualizations of consultation and consensus reflect concerns prominent in Western efforts to create more effective forms of "participatory democracy."[72] The increasing density of intercommunication and networks of relationships among democratic, democratizing, and nondemocratic societies around the globe make efforts anywhere important for actions and developments everywhere. Muslims have important contributions to make in the reconceptualizations of the present. Some scholars view the major world societies as separate and distinct civilizations "whose values and interests differ significantly," and in this context predict that "governments and groups will increasingly attempt to mobilize support by appealing to common religion and civilization identity"[73] in a world of growing intercivilizational warfare. Such an apocalyptic perspective ultimately concludes that global developments such as democratization must inevitably involve the concepts and forms of one civilization dominating those of the other civilizations. However, given the general history of the development of democratic institutions and practices across significant cultural boundaries over the millennia, it seems at least possible that the new forces of globalization will not eliminate wars but will make it possible for different experiences of democratization to assist and influence each other.

In either the apocalyptic or the interactive scenario, it is important to understand the dynamics of contemporary democratization experiences in the Muslim world.

Two

State and Opposition in Islamic History

Islamic activist movements challenge some regimes and support others. The political interests of Islamic revivalist groups may lead them into revolutionary opposition to existing governments, or such movements may participate in the existing political system as opposition movements. In some cases, Islamist movements are part of the government or are themselves the ruling force in the political system. This broad spectrum provides four different general situations within which Islamic revivalism and democratization interact. These are Islamic activism as (1) revolutionary opposition to the existing political system; (2) legal or cooperating opposition operating within the existing political system; (3) active participation in government in alliance or coalition with other political forces; and (4) the controlling force in the existing political system. The current experience in each of these situations shapes both the nature of emerging democratic ideals in the Islamic world and the developing Islamically influenced new political orders.

Democratization in Muslim societies involves all of the broader issues, present in all societies, of defining and creating democratic political systems. In specific experiences, the basic issues of popular political participation and majority and minority rights should be examined. In the interaction between the processes of democratization and the development of the Islamic resurgence, Islamic activist movements both challenge and support existing regimes. This interaction raises the significant issues of the nature of opposition in democratic societies. Is it possible to suspend democratic processes, as happened in Algeria, in the name of preserving or protecting democracy? What are the limits on opposition in the current experiences of democratization? And, in terms of the Islamic context, are there special aspects of the Islamic heritage that can provide support for the developing definition of opposition within a democratizing society?

CONCEPTS OF OPPOSITION

The relationship between rulers and people who might disagree with them is a standard part of the political experience of every society. No government is "completely supported in all that it does by all the people whom it claims to govern,"[1] and one of the major tasks of a political system is to find ways of balancing government and opposition. At the same time, the "idea of organized political opposition as a normal and beneficial component of a polity is . . . a surprising one, and seems quite out of accord with the traditional concern of political speculation: the search for the good state based on universal allegiance to correct principles and practices."[2] Even in established parliamentary systems such as the British one, there continued to be reservations in the minds of at least some prominent nineteenth- and early twentieth-century intellectuals about the idea of a formally accepted and legitimate opposition.[3] The effort in traditional political theory and practice was to create the best possible political system, and opposition was frequently seen as a disruptive rather than constructive force in that creative process.

Democracy protects the rights and liberties of the people and recognizes the freedom of people to express their views. However, the "will of the people" is very frequently plural, and democratic traditions provide many different ways of defining and managing opposition. The principles of democracy clearly involve the right of individuals and groups to disagree with the government. Yet, there is always a sense of reservation about such disagreement. Although many definitions of democracy, for example, recognize the right, and in some definitions even the necessity, of opposition parties to exist, the phrase "partisan politics" carries negative implications even in the conversations of those most convinced of the need for multiparty political competition. Even more broadly, there is the basic tension in political societies between the desire for harmony and stability and the need for providing some vehicle for expression of disagreement. In classical Western theory, for example, Plato's ideal state could stress a division of labor but "Plato had no desire to institutionalize methods by which political opposition might thrive."[4] In the modern United States Pledge of Allegiance to the Flag, there is a possible tension between the concept of "one nation under God, indivisible" and some definitions of "liberty . . . for all." The boundary between permitted levels of freedom of speech and forbidden incitement to violence or revolution is a constantly contested one. The history in Egypt of the arrests and trials—and acquittals—of Shaykh Umar Abd al-Rahman, the Muslim preacher who came to New Jersey and was accused of association with terrorist activities in 1993, is an important case in this continuing debate.

Opposition can take many forms, which range from revolutionary advocacy of the destruction of the existing system to varying levels of disagreement with the people in power in a political system. It is clear that no government will allow open activity that is aimed at its destruction by violent means. In recent years, as a part of some of the efforts of democratization, there have, however, been governments who have organized, or at least cooperated with, efforts to bring about the end of the existing political system and its replacement by a system based on different principles. Most of the authoritarian, one-party regimes of Eastern Europe and the former Soviet Union engaged in this cooperative self-destruction under the pressure of massive popular (and illegal) movements of opposition. Military governments in Africa repeatedly announce the initiation of efforts to restore civilian democracy, with varying degrees of commitment and success. However, the basic minimum requirement that governments impose on oppositions is that they do not actively engage in violent acts to overthrow the government.

Most governments place additional restrictions on opposition groups. In the 1950s and 1960s, in many states in the United States, for example, one of the conditions of employment by a state institution was taking an oath in which prospective employees swore that they were "not now nor ever had been" members of a group advocating the violent overthrow of the United States government, even if the individual had never personally engaged in such activities. In this context, the basic standard of judgment is acceptance of the fundamental rules of the political system by the opposition. In the early 1960s, when military regimes were common in many parts of the world, an observation of Thomas Hobbes was often quoted, which stated that politics was "like a game of cards: the players must agree which card is to be trump. With this difference, he adds, that in politics, whenever no other card is agreed upon, clubs are trumps."[5] The "rules of the game" had to be accepted by the opposition; otherwise "clubs" would provide the basis for power.

Although the acceptance of democracy as a good political system is relatively recent and there have long been reservations (at least on the part of the rulers) about opposition to existing regimes, there have been many different structural and informal limitations on the power of rulers throughout history. No ruler has had absolute control over all things all of the time. Societies and civilizations developed important conceptualizations for limiting the power of tyrants, and these concepts reflect the distinctive heritages of different societies. Although the concept of the Mandate of Heaven, for example, may have been defined as a way of legitimizing the ancient Chou dynasty's claim to power and was an important part of Chinese concepts of imperial legitimacy, it also provided in subsequent centuries a rationale for revolution against an imperial dynasty in times of instability and trouble.

Revolutionary opposition to an existing political system is not what is meant in most discussions of "political opposition." In his characteristic manner, G. K. Chesterton put the matter clearly: "It is absurd to ask a Government to *provide* an opposition. You cannot go to the Sultan and say reproachfully: 'You have made no arrangements for your brother dethroning you and seizing the Caliphate.' You cannot go to a medieval king and say: 'Kindly lend me two thousand spears and one thousand bowmen, as I wish to raise a rebellion against you.'"[6] In most standard Western political thought, legitimate "opposition" in a democratic context is understood in a special way. "Most authors stress that opposition presupposes consent on fundamentals, that is, consent at the community and regime level. What the opposition opposes is a government, not the political system as such."[7]

This concept of opposition depends upon an underlying concept of a "constitution," or set of fundamental precepts that all people within the political system, including the opposition, accept as legitimate. The emergence of the idea of constitutional government is an important element in the development of the modern state, but it is a relatively recent development in the West. The concept of "an impersonal and privileged legal or constitutional order" is frequently tied to the idea of the state in modern Western political thought, but "it did not become a major object of concern until the late sixteenth century . . . and the idea of . . . a legally circumscribed power structure of power separate from ruler and ruled with supreme jurisdiction over a territory" is a modern phenomenon.[8]

In standard modern Western political thought, acceptible opposition in a democratic system is closely tied to the concept of constitutional government, in which there is an underlying, fundamental consensus on the "rules of the game" of politics. Opposition is the legitimate disagreement with particular policies of specific leaders within the mutually accepted framework of the principles of an underlying constitution that is either written or based on long-established practice. However, in modern Western political experiences, there is also a traditional of radical opposition that is expressed in many different revolutionary forms.

In modern Western European political history, there is a long-standing tension between two different understandings of democracy, and each of these understandings represents a revolutionary opposition to the other. J. L. Talmon (who favors "liberal democracy") identifies these two conflicting alternatives: "Concurrently with the liberal type of democracy there emerged from the same premises in the eighteenth century a trend towards what we propose to call the totalitarian type of democracy. These two currents have existed side by side ever since the eighteenth century. The tension between them has constituted an important chapter in modern history, and has now [1960] become the most vital issue of our time."[9] The two competing visions were one that emphasized individual rights and limitation on government ("liberal democracy") and another that stressed the popular will and collective structures of community. This is the continuing debate in the Western political tradition and is at the heart of any discussion of democracy.

The debate is long-standing, but in the 1990s it takes many new forms that go beyond the stark contrasts of the old liberal-socialist debates of the past two centuries. With the failure of what Talmon called "totalitarian democracy" of the socialist-communist left, the alternative to the liberal-libertarian vision is a new left (or "post-left") radical democratic perspective. In the view of advocates of one form of this radical democracy,

> a radical democratic perspective requires a view of the political that is different not only from the liberal but also from the communitarian one. The premodern view of the political community unified around a substantive idea of the common good which is found in some communitarians is antithetical to the pluralism that defines liberal democracy as a new political form of society. Radical democrats agree on the need to recover such ideas as 'common good,' 'civic virtue' and 'political community,' but they believe they must be

reformulated in a way that makes them compatible with the recognition of conflict, division, and antagonism.[10]

This "radical democracy" represents the major form of the conceptual alternative to the currently dominant "liberal democracy," in both its neoconservative form, which emphasizes the market economy, and its "postmodern" form, which emphasizes multicultural pluralism.

Historically, this radical tradition has been articulated in terms of a utopian critique of the developing industrial society that combined the capitalist economic system with liberal democracy and was the core of the radical revolutionary tradition of Western European societies. In this form, it was a violent revolutionary opposition, rather than the "constitutional opposition" envisioned in most presentations of democratic theory. Even the traditional radical vision of democratic society did not recognize the right of revolutionary opposition in a society ruled by radical democrats, and the "radical" phases of the French Revolution and their political descendants were rightly described by Talmon as constituting "totalitarian democracy."

By the end of the twentieth century, revolutions, in the old traditions of radical violence, are no longer practical or effective in the globalized context of the politics of democratization. In the conflict between liberal, capitalist democracy and new forms of radical democracy,

> revolution . . . is neither possible nor prudent—if by revolution we mean launching a campaign of violent insurrection or civil war. Revolutions of that nature are plainly pathological under contemporary conditions of interdependency. Democrats need a new conception of revolution. Its text should be John Locke, not Karl Marx, because the problem is not to show that a social class should seize power . . . but to reinvent the forms and practices that will express a democratic conception of collective life.[11]

In current world conditions, democratic revolutions of the classical nineteenth-century kind are possible only when the political regimes clearly maintain antidemocratic positions in the face of significant popular demand for democratization. In most countries in the 1990s, even the radical opposition is operating within a shared conceptual framework. Where there is an underlying difference in fundamental cosmology, as in the contrast between secular humanist political theory and political theory built on religious assumptions, there is the possibility of violent, antisystemic revolution but in most cases there is a broad acceptance of the fundamental assumptions of the need for liberty, equality, and popular political participation in some meaningful form.

The broad consensus does not, however, eliminate the possibility of opposition or even the sense of the real need for continuing opposition if democracy is to be successful. In its most sanitized version in the context of liberal democracy, there is an insistence that the "cornerstone of democratic governance is the right to conduct free and fair elections," that these elections "should be open to multiple parties," and that the "winning party should be able to form a government capable of fulfilling its mandate. It should also be willing to relinquish power if subsequent election results require it."[12] However, in this vision of an opposition party, there is a strict limitation: when such a party comes to power it "should be forbidden to alter basic constitutional provisions in an effort to seize extra-constitutional powers or stop new elections."[13] However, it is worth remembering that such limitations would have identified as illegitimate the opposition parties supporting Pierre Poujade and Charles De Gaulle in France in the 1950s, rendering the transition from the Fourth to the Fifth Republic in France unacceptable. Similarly, the opposition organization of H. Ross Perot in the 1992 elections in the United States proposed measures like national telecommunications referenda, which could also be seen as an effort to seize extraconstitutional powers.

More broadly based descriptions of the need for opposition in a democratic system assume that no governmental system, not even a functioning democracy, is ever perfect. Because "governments constantly change," the effort of "reinventing government" is not only conceivable but, in the views of many, necessary.[14] Constructive criticism and opposition become an essential part of democracy, both in terms of the need for mechanisms that will allow oppositions continued access to positions of leadership and in a more radical sense. The radical democratic perspective

> postulates the very impossibility of a final realization of democracy. It affirms the unresolvable tension between the principles of equality and liberty as the very condition for the preservation of the indeterminacy and undecidability which is constitutive of modern democracy. Moreover, it constitutes the principle guarantee against any attempt to realise a final closure that would result in the elimination of the political and the negation of democracy."[15]

The furor created by Francis Fukuyama's analysis of "the end of history" shows that many people believe that democracy, even a globally victorious liberal democracy in the late 1980s, does not represent the final stage of human sociopolitical development. In the Fukuyama debate, there were many diversions, but the core was the disagreement over Fukuyama's basic position that "what we may be witnessing is not the end of the Cold War, or the passing of a particular period of postwar history, but the end of history as such: that is, the end point of mankind's ideological evolution and the universalization of Western liberal democracy as the final form of human government."[16] In this "end of history," there is no need for further development of political principles because "the basic principles of the liberal democratic state could not be improved upon," and "at the end of history it is not necessary that all societies become successful liberal societies, merely that they end their ideological pretensions of representing different and higher forms of human society."[17]

This concept of triumphant liberal democracy as the final system that cannot be improved opens the way not only for the idea of the "end of history" but also the concept of the "end of opposition" in liberal democracy. At best, there might be contests over who would be the best leader, which would allow contested elections, but no one could advocate improving the system without falling back into the catagory of historic and therefore less-than-final positions. In this way, the concept of opposition within democracy continues to be ambiguous: both recognized as essential and mistrusted as divisive and possibly subversive.

Opposition as a simple statement of disagreement with the leaders in a political system is an ancient phenomenon. It usually was expressed through movements to overthrow or destroy the government and was, naturally, not recognized as a legitimate political option by the rulers. Opposition as an accepted option within a political system is in many ways a relatively recent phenomenon in world history. It is especially identified with the emergence of the modern ideas of democracy.

Modern democratic opposition involves a number of basic assumptions. In general terms, there is an assumption of a consensus among all in the system on the fundamental construction of that political system. If that consensus is absent, it is assumed that legitimate opposition will not lead to violent and military efforts to overthrow the existing system and that any opposition that comes to power will not so alter the system that it could not subsequently be restored by nonviolent means. Legitimate opposition may be radical, liberal, or conservative, working for long-term system transformation, system development, or system preservation, but it must do this within the framework of recognition of individual and group rights and ultimate control by the people of the political system.

The concept of opposition in a democratic society raises important questions about the relationships between democracy and Islam. In the normal understanding of "opposition" in a democratic or democratizing context, is it possible to have a legitimate "Islamic opposition"? Similarly, in the context of an Islamic state, is it possible to have "opposition" in the normal sense of that term? Are there aspects and dimensions of the Islamic heritage that could make it possible to have a democratic Islamic opposition and an Islamic democracy with opposition?

THE ISLAMIC HERITAGE

All Muslims did not always agree with their rulers and, as a result, Muslim societies have traditions of opposition similar to all other societies. Such experiences go back to the very earliest days of Islam, in the time of the Prophet Muhammad in the early seventh century. The experience of the community of believers during the lifetime of the Prophet set patterns that many later Muslims view as normative. Not only did these experiences set precedents for Muslim beliefs and practices regarding the nature of the law, the state, and the community, they also created precedents for Islamic concepts of opposition that are part of the heritage available to contemporary Muslims. Because of the specific experiences and historical development of the Islamic community (or *ummah*), Muslims have concepts and teachings that apply to many different contexts for opposition.

The ummah began as a persecuted minority in the seventh-century Arabian city of Mecca, and their message was a firm challenge to the whole political and belief system of the existing dominant elite of Mecca. Then, when Muhammad and the other Muslims moved to the city of Yathrib, which came to be called Medina, they defined a "constitution" for a pluralistic society. Finally, with the success of Muhammad's mission and the subsequent expansion of the Islamic community and state, Muslims had to define what was allowable diversity and what opposition represented sedition. This diversity of experiences provides the basis for an effective repertoire of concepts defining legitimate disagreement and opposition within the community.

In the first years after the beginning of the revelations to Muhammad in Mecca, the number of his followers grew slowly. As time went on, the Muslims were harrassed and those without powerful relatives to protect them were often attacked and persecuted. The Islamic message represented a major challenge to the existing social and political order. However, the Muslim group did not engage in violent warfare or conflict and, instead, utilized the methods of preaching, persuasion, and conversion in response to the hostility of the majority. When the Muslims moved as a group to the neighboring city of Medina, they represented a significant power grouping within a pluralist context. The new context was defined by an agreement that has come to be called, in Islamic history, the "constitution of Medina." It outlines the rights and procedures for conflict resolution and community action among Muslims (both from Mecca and from Medina) and non-Muslims.[18] Modern Muslims argue that this document and the experience in Medina provide the precedents for a pluralistic sociopolitical system in accord with Islamic traditions and revelation.[19]

The "classical" Muslim society of the centuries following Muhammad's death provides the context within which the formal definition of Islamic law, the *Sharia*, took place. It is in the context of an Islamic majority that the basic concepts and symbols of the Islamic political heritage developed. It is in this era that the ideas of consensus (*ijma*), consultation (*shurah*), and *ijtihad* were operationally defined. Also, during these years the concepts more specifically related to the issues of political opposition developed. These provide an important heritage for contemporary Islamic thinkers and leaders as they work with the issues of dealing with oppositions in the present age of global pressures for democratization.

This broad heritage of a more formalized body of Islamic traditions and law itself provided a foundation for the development of a concept of a privileged legal order above the rulers and governments, by which those leaders could be judged. Islamic law, in this sense, represented a "constitutional" order for Muslim societies. It was a set of fundamental precepts that most people within the political society accepted as legitimate and authoritative. In the modern era, such fundamental principles have been defined in a variety of ways, with some thinkers concentrating on the basic sources, the Quran and the Sunnah, and others utilizing the whole legal corpus of the Sharia as defined by medieval scholars. However, the idea that the basic principles of Islam represent a "constitution" for Muslim societies is affirmed by a broad spectrum of thinkers.

The more conservative and traditional approach is shown in the political system of Saudi Arabia, in which the Quran is officially described as "the constitution of the Kingdom," and the Sharia is the base of the Saudi legal system. "It is the fundamental assumption of the polity of Saudi Arabia that the Holy *Quran*, correctly implemented, is more suitable for Saudi Muslims than any secular constitution."[20] However, even scholars who argue that the medieval formulations of Islamic law are no longer valid also contend that the Quran and Sunnah represent the basis for constitutionalism in modern Muslim societies. The Sudanese scholar Abdullahi An-Naim, for example, states that "an Islamic justification and support for constitutionalism is important and relevant to Muslims." Although the Quran "does not mention constitutionalism . . . constitutionalism is necessary for realizing the just and good society prescribed by the Qur'an."[21]

A broad sense of constitution is an important element in providing a basis for legal opposition. It provides the basis for challenging the actions of leaders or recommending reforms without the necessity of a revolutionary overthrow. Thus, a conservative and loyal opposition in Saudi Arabia could distinguish between the eternal truths of the constitution and the fallible human beings who attempt to implement them:

> No one, whoever he may be, can monopolize defining the will of God and the prophet as set out in the Koran and Sunnah, or can exclusively determine the Shar'iah rules and impose them on the whole nation. What is required is that we should, in a practical and decisive way, differentiate between the provisions of the divine Shari'ah, which is infallible and must be accepted and carried out, and the human views and interpretations of the ulema, which must be open to examination, assessment, and question without any restrictions or limitations.[22]

The ultimate authority of the Quran and Sunnah provide the basis for critiques of existing conditions throughout Islamic history. Movements of Islamic opposition, renewal, and reform have been able to find their justification and legitimacy in this appeal to higher authority. In the modern era, this can become the basis for an Islamic constitutionalism that aids both in state definition and in providing a framework for recognizing legitimacy of opposition.

Two important ideas help to set the conceptual limits in the Islamic heritage for disagreement and opposition. These are *fitnah*, or civil disorder, and *ikhtilaf*, or disagreement, with the former being condemned and the latter being allowed. There are also concepts defining the roles and rights of minorities, especially non-Muslim minorities, within Islamic society, and concepts of limitations on the power of rulers through special recognition of "constitutional" rules beyond the control of the rulers and a de facto separation of powers. None of these, nor all of them in combination, represents an explicitly democratic conceptualization of opposition as understood in the modern era, but they do provide some basis within the heritage on which such formulations can be based.

Fitnah sets limits on what kind of disagreement is allowable in terms of the Islamic heritage. In the Quran, the term is used to describe the harrassing of the new believers by the Meccans, and represents a kind of forced trial or temptation to give up Islam.[23] Fitnah is to be actively opposed, with violence if necessary. An important passage in this regard in the Quran states: "In the path of God, fight those who fight you, but do not initiate the attack because God does not love the aggressor. Kill them whenever you meet them, and expel them from anyplace from which they have expelled you, because [their] fitnah is a worse [evil] than the act of killing" (2:189 – 190). In this early context, fitnah was an opposition to the Islamic community that threatened the very faith of the believers, and was to be opposed by force if necessary.

The meaning of fitnah expanded in later years, but it never became a generic term for all opposition to the established rulers. Instead, it retained, at least implicitly, "a notion of *fitna* defined as disturbances, or even civil war, involving the adoption of doctrinal attitudes which endanger the purity of the Muslim faith."[24] However, the general trend of medieval Islamic political theory was in the direction of recognition that "authority is preferable to anarchy,"[25] and there was a tendency to identify anything that appeared to cause anarchy as being fitnah. However, not every revolt was fitnah, and the principle that the believers had a right, and an obligation, to revolt against unbelief and ungodly rulers continued. Such revolts might in fact be viewed as the fight *against* fitnah, since fitnah is not the act of revolt, but the attack against Muslims that might threaten their faith. Such attacks might come, as they did in the early Muslim experience in Mecca, from the rulers themselves. In that case, the struggle against fitnah would be the struggle against oppressive rulers.

Many modern Muslim scholars discuss rights of expression and issues of revolutionary action in a context of the limits set by the need to avoid "fitnah." Most recognize the legitimacy of revolution against persistently unjust and tyrannical governments. The Sudanese political scientist Muddathir Abdal-Rahim notes that the community of Muslim believers has "not only the right, but the obligation, to remove them [such rulers] by force. Revolution will, in such circumstances, be the appropriate and necessary form of *Jihad*."[26] However, Abdal-Rahim goes on to argue that, in Islamic terms, revolution should only be a last resort because "it can easily get out of hand and unleash unforeseen forces and conflicts which would destroy the entire social fabric and thus precipitate *Fitna*. . . . It was with a view to averting *Fitna* and all its consequences that many distinguished thinkers and jurists in the history of Islam . . . argued (somewhat like Hobbes) that even a usurper should be obeyed [under certain conditions]."[27] Although Abdal-Rahim and most other modern scholars reject this idea of an Islamic form of legitimacy for usurpers, Abdal-Rahim concludes by emphasizing that "enjoining the doing of what is right and forbidding what is wrong vis-à-vis deviant or incompetent rulers must, in the context of *Shura* or consultation precede resort on the part of the aggrieved *Umma* or citizenry to such drastic measures as insurrection and revolt."[28] In this way, the concept of fitnah becomes part of the definition of legitimate opposition in modern Muslim political thought.

Fitna is also an important concept in defining freedom of expression. One legal scholar, Mohammad H. Kamali, argues that although modern interpretations of seditious speech have tended to limit freedom of expression, the Sharia "tends to advocate the opposite, as it confines the scope of restrictions to measures necessary to repel an imminent danger to normal order in society," or fitnah.[29] "Seditious *fitnah* applies to words and acts that incite dissention and controversy among people to such a degree that believers can no longer be distinguished from disbelievers."[30] Kamali, like Abdal-Rahmin, sees issues involving the definition of fitnah as being related to the broader issues of the citizens' obligation to commend the good and prohibit the evil. This is directly related to the government's ability to encourage popular political participation: "The seditious *fitnah* of our time is closely related to the consultative capacity of the government and the degree to which it can involve its citizenry in the decision-making process as well as to offering inspiration and moral leadership to its people."[31]

The idea that disturbances and anarchy can threaten the faith of Muslims sets strong limits to the concept of opposition within the Muslim heritage. Disrupting the unity of the community is such a disturbance, and people who have revolted against the state in Muslim societies have from the early centuries been charged with causing fitnah. However, fitnah is a complex concept that can be used both to limit opposition and to oppose rulers. It provides a concept with a rich heritage for contemporary Muslims and lies behind much of the debate over the rights of opposition in democratizing Muslim societies.

The Islamic heritage also has a number of dimensions that define the nature and role of acceptable diversity within society. Despite the emphasis on *tawhid*, or the absolute oneness of God, as the foundation for the Islamic worldview, there have been a number of ways in which significant diversity has been recognized as legitimate within an Islamic society. Two important concepts provide an introduction to the modes of recognition of diversity among Muslims, as well as multireligious diversity, within society. These are the legal concept of *ikhtilaf* or disagreement among Muslims, and "the people of the covenant" (*ahl al-dhimmah*) or "the people of the Book" (*ahl al-kitab*) as they define the significance and place of non-Muslims in relation to Muslims in society.

Ikhtilaf is a relatively obscure technical term in the study of Islamic jurisprudence, but it reflects an important, broader attitude toward diversity of views in the Islamic heritage. Islamic law did not develop as a single, monolithic corpus. Instead, it emerged from the thinking and legal decisions of many different groups in the first centuries of Islamic history. In the rapidly expanding Islamic world of the seventh through tenth centuries, local rulers and judges were called upon to make many decisions within the general framework of the developing understanding of the fundamentals of Islam in diverse contexts. As a result, a number of different legal traditions developed and gradually became formalized into separate schools of Islamic law. In the world of Sunni Islam, four schools emerged from this complex situation, and by the end of the thirteenth century they provided the basic texts and interpretations for Islamic law. These schools "generally practiced mutual toleration," an attitude that "goes back to the time of the ancient schools of law, which had accepted the original geographic differences of doctrine as natural."[32] The differences among these schools in the specific definitions of Islamic law are ikhtilaf.

These differences reflect "the characteristic freedom of legal thought in early Islam"[33] and provide an indication that the revelation, in Islamic terms, did not mean a single and monolithic structure of canon or imperial law. By the time of the definition of the law schools, it was widely accepted that a tradition from the Prophet Muhammad states that such "disagreements in the community of Muslims were a sign of divine favor."[34] Major Muslim thinkers throughout Islamic history were aware of ikhtilaf, and sought to explain the differences and disagreements. Many even attempted to harmonize the differences among the schools, and such efforts were often a part of revivalist movements. Major figures in the movements of Islamic revival and reform in the eighteenth century, such as Shah Wali Allah, the great South Asian teacher, and Muhammad Hayah al-Sindi, a teacher of the founder of the strict Wahhabi tradition in Arabia, wrote special works on ikhtilaf that describe the historical causes of differences.[35] Although these scholars attempted to explain differences, they did not treat the fact of their existence as evil.

Modern Muslim thinkers continue this attitude of seeing legal diversity as a benefit rather than a difficulty. Two major figures in the development of the new-style Islamic movements of the twentieth century, Hasan al-Banna and Abu al-Ala Mawdudi, affirm this position. Mawdudi has noted that the "differences that appear in the four schools are but the natural outcome of the fact that truth is many-sided."[36] Al-Banna has been described by Yusuf al-Qaradawi, a leading contemporary Islamist thinker, as a major figure in understanding "the essence and ethics of disagreement. . . . Despite his unflinching commitment to the cause of Muslim solidarity . . . he was convinced of the inevitability of disagreement."[37] Al-Banna stated, "We believe that disagreements on subsidiary religious issues are inevitable for various reasons. . . . [Groups in different regions have different views.] If you were to force them to follow one opinion, you would create *fitnah*."[38]

Scholars later in the twentieth century continued to maintain this position regarding differences of interpretation, although all agree with al-Banna on the necessity of unity on fundamental principles while accepting disagreements on subsidiary issues. Saeed Hawwa, an important scholar in the Muslim Brotherhood tradition, commented on al-Banna's position and then stated,

> According to the learned men of the True Faith, only the holy Quran and the Prophet's traditions are free from error, and for this reason errors and mistakes are found in the ideas and thoughts of other people. . . . During the different periods of the Islamic history various and different viewpoints were held by different groups, and the *ulema* have rejected the opinions of one another freely. . . . If there is a possibility of holding a certain viewpoint, and the intention is above board, then we should be tolerant towards the personalities, and instead of condemning them and attacking them, we should show mercy on them.[39]

Yusuf al-Qaradawi reaffirms the traditional idea that the ikhtilaf are in fact a benefit to the Muslim community:

> One of the most serious problems is the failure of some religious people to observe that the *ahkam* [judgements] of *al Shariah* are not equally important or permanent, and therefore, different interpretations can be permitted. . . . Disagreement—based on authentic *ijtihad* [informed, independent judgement]—on these issues represents no harm or threat. On the contrary, it is a blessing on the *ummah*, and demonstrates flexibility in *al Shariah*.[40]

Qaradawi notes that there even were different interpretations during the lifetime of the Prophet Muhammad, and then criticizes modern extremists.

> [T]here are people these days who not only assume that they know the whole truth and all the answers, but also try to coerce other people to follow them. . . .They tend to forget that their own understanding and interpretation of the texts are not more than hypotheses which may be right or wrong. Moreover, no human, i.e., no *alim*, is infallible, even though he satisfies all the conditions and requisites of *ijtihad*.[41]

In terms of contemporary experience, Hasan al-Turabi, a Sudanese Islamist leader, describes this more flexible approach as a goal of the system in Sudan. "Intellectual attitudes are not going to be regulated, not going to be codified at all. The presumption is that people are free. . . . I don't think it poses such a problem that people will have dissenting views to the prevailing majority understanding of Islam, because this is commonplace in Islamic history; people are entitled to all the *madhhabs* [schools of law]."[42] Turabi added that the extreme case is that of apostasy, which, he said, in Sudan, "to become punishable [as a capital offence] . . . has to be more than just intellectual apostasy. It would have to translate into not only sedition but actually insurrection against society."[43] In the notorious case of Mahmud Muhammad Taha, who was executed in 1985 by the regime of Jafar Numayri, Turabi said that the judge changed the charge from sedition to apostasy and that, in his judgment, "this was definitely a bad decision."[44]

The legitimacy of legal pluralism is also recognized formally in the Islamic Republic of Iran. The Iranian constitution names the Shii Twelver Jafari school as the official school of Iran, but adds:

> Other Islamic schools, including the Hanafi, Shafi'i, Maliki, Hanbali, and Zaydi, are to be accorded full respect, and their followers are free to act in accordance with their own jurisprudence in performing their religious rites. These schools enjoy official status in matters pertaining to religious education, affairs of personal status (marriage, divorce, inheritance, and wills) and related litigation in courts of law.[45]

This openness to diversity within the framework of accepted fundamentals is not limited to details of the law. It is also visible in the broader areas of political theory as it developed in the classical era. In

> the Sunni community there was no one universally accepted doctrine of the caliphate. . . . The very basis of Sunni thought, in fact, excludes the acceptance of any one theory as definitive and final. What it does lay down is a principle: that the caliphate is that form of government which safeguards the ordinances of the Sharia and sees that they are put into practice. So long as that principle is applied, there may be an infinite diversity in the manner of its application.[46]

Viewed more broadly, the human mission of khilafah can be viewed within this framework, which accepts differences of implementation as legitimate. Such a structure is at least broadly analogous to the concept of a "constitutional opposition," especially in the context of the expanded vision of human beings as "caliphs" in the implementation of God's will.

The more widely known aspect of Islamic acceptance of diversity is in its treatment of non-Muslims in the premodern era. The Quranic message itself recognizes the recorded revelations to Jews and Christians as revelations from God. Islam contains a formal recognition of the special rights of the "people of the Book," who are those people to whom the divine message has also been revealed by prophets. As the Muslim political system developed and Islamic law became more precisely defined, the rights and place of non-Muslims became more clearly defined in law but showed great diversity in different areas in terms of practice. The fundamental concept was that there was a *dhimmah*, or "indefinitely renewed contract through which the Muslim community accords hospitality and protection to members of other revealed religions, on condition of their acknowledging the domination of Islam."[47] From this, non-Muslim participants in Muslim society were frequently called *dhimmis*.

It is clear that dhimmi status involved important restrictions on activities and a "second-class" standing in terms of political structures. However, it is also clear that such minorities were formally recognized as legitimate participants in Muslim societies with real rights and protections from persecution. Many have noted that this was in contrast to practice in most Western societies in premodern times. Although the concept of the "people of the dhimmah" is clearly not the same as the modern democratic concept of minority rights, it does have many analogous features, and provides a clearer foundation for such democratic concepts than are found in most other premodern societies. It also shows some recognition of the legitimacy of diversity of opinion and custom and, to the extent that recognition of minority rights is important for the existence of democratic opposition, the concept of the dhimmah provides some foundation for concepts of constitutional opposition.

In the history of Western political systems, another foundation for constitutional opposition is seen in the development of separate organizations that could restrain the functioning of the rulers: "in the time of the Republic of Rome the creation of the tribunes of the *plebs* provided with the right of *intercessio* would correspond exactly to the notion, in the beginning at least; later the Church played this kind of role towards the feudal monarchs of the Middle Ages."[48] In later times, a concept of the separation of powers developed that played an important role in the conceptual foundations of modern democratic political systems. Although the competition between the legislative, executive, and judicial institutions of government is not what is usually meant by political opposition in a democratic system, it also is an important element in the concept of democratic government, and is the kind of "organized opposition" that Maurice Duverger called "an essential feature of 'Western' democracy, its absence a feature of 'Eastern' democracy."[49]

In the long-standing concept of "oriental despotism," there is no sense of a separation of powers or structures limiting the power of the ruler. However, such unlimited power was not available to leaders in classical Muslim societies, and this situation is visible both in the Islamic law of political structures and in actual historical practice. Although no formal "church" structure developed in Islamic societies, an Islamically identifiable class of people recognized for their knowledge of Islam, called the *ulama* (plural of *'alim*, "learned person"), emerged in the early centuries. It was the consensus of these scholars, and not the commands and rules of the caliphs, that provided the basis for formal Islamic law. No ruler was recognized as being above the law, and all rulers could be judged by that law.

In this historical context, it is possible to say that "religion" and "politics" are not separate in Islam: the realm of "politics" is defined and shaped by the "religious" worldview. It is also possible to state that an institution that could be called a "church" did not emerge in Islamic societies, and therefore, at least in that sense, there is no issue of separation of "church" and "state" in Islamic history. However, the development of state institutions and institutions of social order relating to Islam, like the development of schools of law and the emergence of the ulama, the class of learned scholars, mean that the Islamic state was not simply a religio-political monolith. In his analysis of religion-state relations in classical Islamic society, Ira Lapidus concludes:

> In the development of Islamic institutions we have come from an early iden-tification of politics and religion to a differentiation of political and religious life into organized and partly autonomous entities. . . . Though the modali-ties of "state" and "religion" in the Islamic world are quite different from those of "state" and "church" in the west, Islamic society, in fact, if not in its own theory, is one of those societies in which religious and political institu-tions are separate.[50]

This general separation could lead to a formal concept of a religio-political con-tract between rulers and the community of Muslims. This concept was articulated clearly by Ibn Taymiyyah, a fourteenth-century revivalist scholar whose ideas have been important in the late twentieth century resurgence. After the fall of the Abbasid caliphate, he argued that the caliphs after the first four successors to the Prophet were temporal rulers whose "authority as imams is acquired by a mutual contract with the Community in general, whereby the temporal princes, in close collaboration with the ulama, carry out their religious and political functions as the sharia directs and receive in return loyal obedience from the people."[51] Some analysts of the contemporary Islamic resurgence emphasize that Muslim radicals in the 1960s and 1970s used the ideas of Ibn Taymiyyah as a justification for holy war.[52] However, these analysts do not always note the elements of the "social con-tract" that are involved in both Ibn Taymiyyah and the modern revolutionaries who use his ideas; even in the authorization of holy war, Ibn Taymiyyah speaks only of the right of revolt against rulers who do not implement Islamic law, which forms the basis of the contract between ruler and community.

In later centuries, in the Ottoman Empire, this sense of contract was formalized in the legal structure. The empire was an Islamic empire and its head, the sultan, was subject to Islamic law but had the recognized power to issue executive decrees that served as law. However, the ulama of the imperial system had the accepted right—which was not often exercised, because of political reasons—to invalidate any regulation issued by the sultan if they judged it not to be in accord with Islamic law.[53] Even more, the head of the hierarchy of official ulama in the empire, the shaykh al-Islam, could issue judgments deposing the sultan for violating the basic Islamic law. Although this power was exercised infrequently, it actually was exer-cised in the depositions of sultans Ibrahim (1648), Mehmed IV (1687), Ahmed III (1730), and Selim III (1807). In these formal actions, the historic check on the power of the ruler formed by the fact that the ulama were the representatives of the "constitution," that is, the Islamic law, is fully reflected. It shows the potential dimension of the separation of powers in the Islamic heritage.

The tradition of separation of powers in this special manner is a formal part of the political system of the two contemporary states in which Islamists have come to power, Iran and Sudan. The basic political theory of the Islamic republic in Iran is "governance by the scholars of Islamic jurisprudence," or *vilayat-i faqih*. This broad concept was presented in some detail by the Ayatollah Khomeini in a series of lectures in 1970, which were published as a book entitled *Islamic Government* (*Hukumat-i Islami*).[54] Khomeini notes that "[i]t is an established principle that 'the *faqih* [scholar of Islamic jurisprudence] has authority over the ruler.' If the ruler adheres to Islam, he must necessarily submit to the *faqih*, asking him about the laws and ordinances of Islam in order to implement them. This being the case, the true rulers are the *fuqaha* themselves, and rulership ought officially to be theirs."[55] In the Shii thought of Khomeini's "Twelve-Imam" tradition, the true ruler is the divinely designated and infallible Imam, but, in the current age, this Imam is in occultation, or divinely arranged seclusion, and therefore not present to rule directly. In this context, governance by the scholar "exists only as a type of appointment, like the appointment of a guardian of a minor. With respect to duty and position, there is indeed no difference between the guardian of a nation and the guardian of a minor. It is as if the Imam were to appoint someone to the guardianship of a minor, to the governorship of a province, or to some other post."[56] This is officially established in the Iranian constitution, which states that during the occultation, authority and leadership of the community "devolve upon the just and pious *faqih*, who is fully aware of the circumstances of his age; courageous, resourceful, and possessed of administrative ability."[57]

In the Islamic Republic of Iran, however, the faqih/leader is the authoritative guide, not the executive leader; the latter's duties are performed by the president of the republic. The constitution provides for a very carefully structured set of checks and balances and even provides mechanisms, in Article 111, for the dismissal of the faqih/leader himself. The Islamic Consultative Assembly, which is the elected national assembly, must give a vote of confidence for the formation of the Council of Ministers (Article 87), and the assembly can issue a vote of no confidence in individual ministers or the president himself. The actions of the assembly are reviewed by a Guardian Council to ensure the compatibility of legislation with Islam.

In operation, the system has provided for a remarkable degree of flexibility and power balancing. Debates and disagreements in the assembly have resulted in the forced resignation of cabinet members following votes of no confidence (e.g., in August 1983), and votes of confidence for presidents (and, before the constitutional revisions of 1989, prime ministers) have sometimes been far from unanimous. In some cases, the Council of Guardians rejected legislation, but its judgments are not absolute. In the case of a law passed by the assembly allowing women to claim wages in cash from husbands who file for divorce, for example, the Council of Guardians rejected the law, but the Council of Expediency, led by the president, secured its final approval in 1992.[58] In this constitutional context, a variety of kinds of "opposition" are possible within the framework of a complex structure of checks and balances, in which the ultimate authority rests in the leader-guide who is outside the system of the actual operation of government structures.

The Sudanese structure has been gradually evolving since the coup of 1989. There has been a major effort to create a system of participatory government that is different from the old multiparty parliamentary system. As articulated by a Sudanese official, "the question is not whether to revert to a western style multiparty democracy again since it failed to deliver the goods three times since Sudan's independence . . . the question is which other form of democracy to have."[59]

The developing political system has been directed by the group of military officers led by Umar al-Bashir and has involved the gradual civilianization of the structures, leading to the creation of a pyramid of popular committees and congresses from the local to the national level. The worldview underlying the effort is clearly Islamic, and the leadership provides the self-identification that this is a process of Islamization. However, an important part of this development is the fact that much of the intellectual content for the new politics comes from people in the National Islamic Front (NIF), led by Hasan al-Turabi. Although he has been described by foreign journalists as the "mastermind" of the National Salvation Revolution, or the "de facto ruler" of Sudan,[60] Turabi emphasizes that he is not part of the government. However, Turabi provides much of the intellectual framework and inspiration for the Islamization efforts. Although the position is not as clearly defined or as formally instituted as the Guide's position in Iran, Turabi's position in the Sudanese system has many parallels to the role of the Scholar/Guide in Iran.

Although the relationship between executive leader and leader/guide is clearly not one of opposition, it does mean that power is not centralized. In the view of Ghazi Salah al-Din Atabani, a prominent Islamist in Sudan who has served as minister of state with a number of different portfolios in the current political system, multiple centers of power helps to distinguish the current Sudanese government from "autocratic government where absolute power lies in the hands of a single ruler. . . . What we are doing is to institutionalise power structures by creating and integrating various power centres within the state and society altogether."[61] In this structure, legitimate power can be outside the formal state structures. In the view of Turabi and others in the NIF, the Sharia provides the basis for a moral civil society and acts as a restraint on autocratic rulers.[62]

This format of a scholar/guide who is outside the formal administrative structure of government is not unique to contemporary Iran and Sudan. In different forms, it may have been part of the structure of a number of movements of renewal in Islamic history. Perhaps the most similar is the establishment of the Saudi state and the Wahhabi movement in the eighteenth century in the Arabian Peninsula. At that time, a revivalist teacher, Muhammad ibn Abd a-Wahhab, joined together with a local chieftain, Muhammad ibn Saud, to form a state dedicated to the propagation of Ibn Abd al-Wahhab's message of Islamic renewal. Although the two men made a formal agreement covering some matters, the division of leadership between the two, with one assuming the political and military leadership and the other acting as teacher and religious guide, was a natural result of the historic conditions of the time.[63]

The Islamic heritage contains both broad concepts of potential positive significance for democratization—such as consensus and consultation—and also many concepts and traditions that could provide the foundation for concepts of "constitutional opposition" and limits on arbitrary government power. As is true in any society, there are limits set on opposition, and, in the Islamic heritage, the idea of fitnah provides an important example of these limits. However, within those limits, concepts like ikhtilaf and the covenant with non-Muslim minorities have the potential for providing foundations for diversity and opposition within an Islamic democracy. The broader sense of limited sovereignty of the ruler, a idea of social contract within an broader constitutional consensus, and an effective separation of powers within the state are all already part of the Islamic repertoire of political concepts available to those participating in the processes of democratization in contemporary Islamic societies.

Within this framework, it becomes possible in the contemporary context to provide the intellectual and ideological foundations for Islamic oppositions. The concept of fitnah provides a conceptual basis for opposition in revolutionary terms, and other concepts provide a foundation for becoming a "constitutional" opposition. In recent years, Islamic opposition has been most frequently articulated in democratic terms and in the context of cooperation within existing political systems. However, such opposition can become revolutionary in tone if they are declared to be revolutionary by existing regimes. In this context, it is useful to examine six cases, two (in Algeria and Egypt) in which the Islamic movements are illegal and suppressed movements of opposition, two (in Malaysia and Pakistan) in which they maintain the status of legal opposition and participate within a multiparty parliamentary system and (in Iran and Sudan) two in which the movements have become the foundation for the political system.

THREE

Iran

Revolutionary Islam in Power

The Iranian revolution has been described as "one of the greatest populist explosions in human history."[1] In the minds of many, Iran's Islamic revolution of 1978–79 represents the quintessential example of political Islam, "Islamic fundamentalism." The revolution encompassed many of the issues associated with contemporary Islamic revivalism—issues of faith, culture, power, and politics. Emphasis on identity, cultural authenticity, political participation, and social justice was accompanied by a rejection of Westernization, government authoritarianism, corruption, and maldistribution of wealth. Khomeini's Iran became the paradigm and source of fears of revolutionary or radical Islam, its export and threat to governments in the Muslim world and in the West. Cries of *Marg bar Amrika,* "Death to America," are not soon forgotten, nor have they ceased to be heard from time to time. Iran continues to be a primary reference point or exemplar for many when discussing the nature and threat of "Islamic fundamentalism" in relation to issues ranging from Islam and revolution to Islam and democracy.[2] Nothing symbolized Iran's Islamic revolution more than the juxtaposition of the two symbols of Iran's identity and of the revolution: the Shah of Iran and the turbaned Ayatollah Ruhollah Khomeini. The self-proclaimed Shahanshah, or king of kings, whose predecessors had taken the title "Shadow of God on Earth," fled before the triumphant return of the bearded mullah named Ruhollah, "the breath of God."[3] The Pahlavi dynasty had crumbled before an "Islamic revolution" that promised greater political participation, the preservation of national identity and independence, and a more socially just society. The Islamic Republic of Iran was to be a modern state that gave proper recognition and place to Iran's religio-cultural heritage and identity.

Iran's Islamic republic remained an important symbol of revolutionary Islam, but by the mid-1990s, after more than a decade and a half in existence, its experience and example provide an important case study of modern political Islam in practice. It is clear that the Iranian model represents an important experiment in trying to create a modern-religious state. Its emerging structures do not fit patterns of democratic practices as they developed in Western societies. The resulting polit-

ical system combines authoritarian rule and popular, contentious political participation in ways that reflect very important issues in the relationships between Islam
and democracy.

SHII ISLAM AND IRANIAN NATIONALISM (IDENTITY)

Shiism has been integral to Iranian identity and a source of political legitimacy
since the sixteenth century, when it was first declared the state religion of Iran. Shii
Islam has been embroiled in politics from its origins, and as such provides a history and system of belief that can be interpreted and used in political crises. In
Iranian history, Twelver Shiism (Ithna Ashari) has often been apolitical, finding a
tolerable accommodation with the state. However, at critical points throughout
history, Shii belief, leadership, and institutions have played an important role in
Iranian politics and society. Shiism has been interpreted and utilized to safeguard
national identity and independence and to mobilize popular support. During the
nineteenth and twentieth centuries, the ulama, regarding themselves as protectors
of the nation vis-à-vis the government, participated in popular protest movements.
They opposed a government that was "not only tyrannical but was also engaged
in selling the country to foreign imperialists."[4] In the Tobacco Protest of 1891–92,
the ulama were members of an opposition movement that effectively led a nationwide embargo of tobacco: "A handful of intellectual activists, with the strong support of the important merchants, were able to uncover their tremendous potential of the use of clerical domination over the masses for the purpose of mass
mobilization."[5] As with the Reuter Concession of 1872, in which the shah had
granted a monopoly on railway construction, banking, and mining to a British subject, the opposition in 1891–92 forced the shah to withdraw his sale of a monopo-
listic concession on tobacco to a British firm.

During the Constitutional Revolution of 1905–11, the ulama again joined
bazaaris (merchants and artisans) and modern reformers (intellectuals and secular nationalists) in demanding constitutional reforms to limit royal absolutism.
However, despite these stirrings of an early nationalist movement and opposition
to foreign penetration, Iran, like most of the Muslim world, experienced the impact
of European imperialism:

> The country had become a semicolony in which 'Belgians administer[ed] the
> customs service ... Swedish officers command[ed] the state police ... Rus-
> sian officers staff[ed] the [gendarmerie] ... Hungarians administer[ed] the
> Treasury .... The Dutch own[ed] and operate[d] the only telegraph line ...
> and large industrial operations [textiles].[6]

The legacy and impact of foreign presence and influence in Iran created several
interlinked crises of sovereignty, legitimacy, and participation that would resurface
during the Pahlavi period.[7] It also established a strong precedent for Shii Islam to

be reinterpreted to provide an ideology of protest and opposition and for the ulama, who historically were both apolitical and political, to assert their role as protectors of Islam and of the Shii community/nation vis-à-vis the absolutism and tyranny of the government/state.[8]

MODERN IRAN

The history of modern Iran is dominated by the Pahlavi dynasty (1925–79). Under Reza (Khan) Shah (1925–1941) and his son Mohammad Reza Shah (1941–1979), modern Iran took shape and form. During the late 1920s and 1930s, Reza Shah, a military officer, seized power and created the Pahlavi dynasty. Influenced by the example of his Turkish contemporary Mustafa Kemal (Ataturk), he focused on modernization and the creation of a strong centralized government based upon a modern army and bureaucracy. Unlike Ataturk, he did not pursue a policy of total secularization of society. Rather than eliminating religious institutions, he limited and controlled them. Politically, the Iran of Reza Shah was a dynastic monarchy rather than a republic, a modernizing state whose policies (containment of rebellious tribes, establishment of a strong central government and military) and goal were national integration not political participation.

Reza Shah paid lip service to Islam in the early years of his reign and enjoyed the support of Shii leaders. However, several policies that struck at Islamic faith and identity as well as the ulama's power and status progressively alienated many of the ulama and traditional classes. Zoroastrianism was established alongside Islam as the state religion. The government chose a pre-Islamic name (Pahlavi) and symbols (the lion and the sun), and adopted Western-based legal and educational reforms. Dress codes restricted the wearing of clerical garb, mandated Western attire for men (1928), and outlawed the veil (1935). The government assumed control of religious endowments (1934). As in Egypt and other modernizing Muslim states, the ulama were deprived of a major source of their power and wealth as they were replaced by modern secular courts, lawyers, judges, notaries, and teachers. Pahlavi reforms suited and benefited the upper and new middle classes and widened the socioeconomic and cultural gap between these Westernized classes and the majority of Iranians, in particular the traditional elites.

Mohammad Reza Shah's reign began in 1941, when the British deposed Reza Khan and placed his son on the Peacock Throne. However, it was not until after his U.S.-orchestrated and British-backed return from exile in Italy in 1953 that the shah began to effectively consolidate his power with significant assistance from Western governments (in particular the United States and Britain) and Western multinational corporations.

Increasingly dependent upon the West, the shah relied on the protection of his Western- and Israeli-trained military and police as he pursued an ambitious Western-oriented socioeconomic modernization program, the White Revolution

(1963–77). However, its implementation did not include significant political participation, but instead was accompanied by reliance upon cooptation and repression to control any opposition. As he became more autocratic during the 1970s, the shah turned to SAVAK (State Security and Information Agency), his CIA- and Mossad (Israeli)-trained secret police, to repress the opposition: liberal secular and religious nationalists as well as Marxists. As James Bill has noted, the shah "abandoned his past policy of balancing coercion with cooptation, repression with reform. . . . [H]e would no longer tolerate internal dissent or political opposition. . . . The new policy resulted in a reign of terror."9

Mohammad Reza Shah enjoyed the support of the ulama during the early years of his rule. Many regarded the monarchy as a protector against unmitigated secularism and the threat of communism. Although an effective opposition did not form until the 1970s, there were early critics of the regime's excesses, as religious institutions in the 1960s began to come under government attack. Pahlavi policies had progressively extended state control over many areas previously the domain of the ulama. Government reforms of education, law, and religious endowments under the Shah's father in the 1930s were now accompanied by land reforms in the 1960s that further limited the property, revenue, and power of the ulama. Moreover, as a class whose status and power had long been reinforced through intermarriage with the political elite, the bifurcation of Iranian education and society resulted in a significant difference of identity and outlook between modern secular elites and intelligentsia and the religious-minded clergy. As power became more concentrated in the hands of the shah and secular, Westernized elites, ulama-state relations began a long, slow process of deterioration. The religious class gravitated toward a more natural alliance with the traditional merchant (bazaari) class and identified with more populist political, economic, and social issues vis-à-vis the state bureaucracy.

By 1962–63, the Ayatollah Khomeini had emerged as an antigovernment voice among a growing vocal minority of ulama who saw Islam and Iran endangered and their power in decline, and who advocated the political involvement of the ulama. The Shah's Westernizing modernization program (in particular, land reform and the vote for women) and Iran's close ties to the United States, Israel, and multinational companies were perceived as a threat to Islam, to Iranian Muslim life, and to national independence. From his pulpit in Qom, Khomeini became an uncompromising voice of opposition to absolutism and foreign "rule" or influence.

> The government has sold our independence, reduced us to the level of a colony, and made the Muslim nation of Iran seem more backward than savages in the eyes of the world! . . . If the religious leaders have influence they will not permit this nation to be the slaves of Britain one day, and America the next . . . they will not permit Israel to take over the Iranian economy; they will not permit Israeli goods to be sold in Iran—in fact, to be sold duty free!

... Are we to be trampled underfoot by the boots of America simply because we are a weak nation and have no dollars? America is worse than Britain; Britain is worse than America. The Soviet Union is worse than both of them. ... But today it is America that we are concerned with.[10]

Clashes in Qom (March 22, 1963), and Mashhad (June 3, 1963), led to Khomeini's arrest on June 4, and ulama-led popular demonstrations in major cities were brutally suppressed.

Khomeini was sent to Turkey in exile in 1964; he moved to Iraq in 1965 and then to France in 1978. From his exile, he continued to teach, write (e.g., *Islamic Government*), and speak out against the Shah and condemn his "un-Islamic" policies. Tapes and pamphlets of Khomeini's speeches were smuggled into Iran and distributed widely through the mosques. His Islamic ideology was holistic, regarding Islam as a total and complete way of life that provided guidance for social and political life:

> Islam has a system and a program for all the different affairs of society: the form of government and administration, the regulation of people's dealings with each other, the relations of state and people, relations with foreign states and all other political and economic matters. . . . The mosque has always been a center of leadership and command, of examination and analysis of social problems.[11]

The safety of exile enabled Khomeini to remain an outspoken, uncompromising critic who initially called for reform, not revolution. By the end of the 1960s, already it was possible to argue that "there is a persistent current of religiously inspired and led opposition to the [Shah's] regime which is sustained by continued allegiance to the figure of Ayatullah Khumayni. . . . Despite all the inroads of the modern age, the Iranian national consciousness still remains wedded to Shi'i Islam."[12] The alternative to the Shah's political regime was, increasingly, articulated in Islamic terms.

MONARCHY, NATIONALISM, RELIGION

As previously noted, historically, Iran's rulers and the ulama had reached an accommodation. Technically, Shiism recognized the Imam as the only legitimate (religio-political) leader of the community; temporal rule was thus illegitimate. In practice, during the absence of the Imam, the shahs as temporal rulers were acknowledged as quasi legitimate rulers or caretakers of the state. This was formally acknowledged in the constitution of 1906. In exchange for this legitimacy, the shah was to protect the interests of the ulama, the guardians of Islam and of Islamic law.

Like much of the Muslim world, Iran had experienced both the impact of European colonialism and the rise of nationalism. Faced with Muslim decline, Iranian

Muslims, like the worldwide Muslim community, both Sunni and Shii, were divided in their perceptions and responses. A minority of new elites, modern-educated and influenced by the example of Europe, had concluded that Islam in the hands of a backward clergy was responsible for the intellectual and cultural decline of Muslims and that secularization (the separation of religion and public life and the restriction of religion to personal life) and modernization (based upon European models) were the only ways to revitalize the community and reclaim its independence. For other Muslims, Islam was the solution, not the source, of the problem, which was laid at the doorstep of authoritarian regimes, Western secular elites, and Western governments and multinational companies. Although secular nationalists prevailed, when necessary, secular and religious factions had formed coalitions in the national interest, as in the Tobacco Protest and the Constitutional Revolutions.

The Iran of Mohammad Reza Shah was a nominal constitutional monarchy. In theory, modern Iran was governed by an amended version of the constitution of 1906, whose provisions provided both for constitutional limitations on the monarchy and for the Islamic character of the state. Although it had a modern constitution, Iran was not a secular state in the sense of separation of church and state. The monarch was to be a follower of the Jafari law school of Twelver (Ithna Ashari) Shi'ism and the defender of the faith; the parliament was to include five eminent clerics to ensure that no legislation would be contrary to Islamic law. Constitutional provisions were to limit the power of the monarch and make him accountable to a representative assembly.[13]

Despite the constitution, the Pahlavis, Reza Khan and Mohammad Reza Shah after his return from exile in 1953, ignored the constitution, building instead a state based upon their personal authority, identifying Iranian nationalism with the Pahlavi dynasty, and coopting and coercing the ulama rather than working with them.

The relationship of the Pahlavi shahs and their governments to political participation veered from cooptation and cooperation to opposition and repression. Reza Khan, like his contemporary Ataturk, brooked little opposition. However, the Allies' reoccupation of Iran in 1941 and the forced abdication of Reza Shah ushered in a period of "incomplete democracy."[14] During the first decade of Mohammad Reza Shah's rule, the young monarch was less a ruler than a survivor.

A more open political arena created a context in which a number of political forces struggled to gain dominance. Politically activist Islamic groups emerged at this time. One was led by Ayatollah Khashani, who called for the repeal of Reza Shah's secular laws and the implementation of Islamic law. The other was a smaller terrorist group, Fedaiyan-i Islam. "Kashani was politically pragmatic [and] the Fedaiyan was dogmatically committed to fundamentalist Islam."[15] However, the strongest political force to emerge in opposition to the Shah's regime was the National Front of Mohammad Mossadeq, which reflected the importance and power at that time of modern, more secular nationalism. The Islamic groups became a part of the opposition that was basically led by Mossadeq.

As in the Tobacco Protest, Mosaddeq organized a coalition that opposed the shah's having given an oil concession to the British, as well as Iran's economic dependence, and called for the nationalization of the British-owned Anglo-Iranian Oil Company.[16] The dispute resulted in the shah's flight into exile in Rome in 1953. However, he returned in six days with the assistance of Britain and, in particular, the United States. The following decades were marked by growing dependence on the West, consolidation of the shah's personal power through restricted political participation and a heavy reliance on security forces, and the identification of Iranian nationalism with the cult of the shah and the Pahlavi dynasty. Brief periods of liberalization were followed by a reassertion of royal absolutism. Thus, the reformist administration of Prime Minister Ali Amini during the early 1960s, which was a response to pressure from the Kennedy Administration to introduce political reforms, ended in January 1963 with the imprisonment of the leadership of the Nationalist Movement. The lifespan of political parties was short, and political leaders were often caught in a revolving door between freedom and prison. Although Iran had a two-party system until 1975, it existed more in name than in substance. The relationship of Mardom (the People's Party or opposition party) to Novin Iran (the New Iran or government party) was more that of a pseudo opposition.[17]

By the mid-1970s, it was clear that the modernizing and secularizing policies of the Shah were not creating a democratic political system. The mounting discontent and dissent created by the Shah's policies affected the ulama, traditional classes, and religiously minded intellectuals as well as Marxists, leftists, and liberals. However, the structures of government control and repression left little opportunity for legitimate expression of the growing opposition.

RELIGION AND POLITICAL OPPOSITION

Throughout the 1970s opposition to the Shah grew. Lack of political participation, the erosion of national autonomy as the state became more dependent upon the West, and the loss of religio-cultural identity in a Westernizing society provided common grievances that transcended political and religious differences. Issues of faith and identity, political participation, and social justice became rallying points for a growing opposition movement. The clergy were joined by both secular and Islamically oriented intelligentsia, whose message was particularly influential among intellectuals and students. In particular, in light of history, their message of the dangers of cultural alienation and dependence on the West as a threat to Iranian identity and nationalism struck a responsive chord among many: secular and religious, traditionalist and modernist, lay and clergy.

Jalal-e-Ahmad, a former member of the Tudeh (Communist) party, warned of the dangers of Iran's fixation on the West, the cultural danger of Westernization or what he called "Weststruckness":

> I say that [Weststruckness] is like cholera. . . . It is at least as bad as sawflies in the wheat fields. Have you ever seen how they infest wheat? From within. There's a healthy skin in place, but it's only a skin, just like the shell of a cicada on a tree. . . . We're like a nation alienated from itself, in our clothing and our homes, our food and our literature, our publications and, most dangerously of all, our education. We effect Western training, we effect Western thinking, and we follow Western procedures to solve every problem.[18]

Dr. Ali Shariati, a Sorbonne-educated intellectual, represented a new breed of religiously minded lay intelligentsia whose reformist interpretation of Shii Islam combined Third World anti-imperialism, Western social scientific language, and Iranian Shiism to produce a revolutionary Islamic ideology for sociopolitical reform. Thus, he denounced "Weststruckness":

> Come friends let us abandon Europe; let us cease this nauseating, apish imitation of Europe. Let us leave behind this Europe that always speaks of humanity, but destroys human beings wherever it finds them.[19]

Shariati's reinterpretation of Islam, like Catholic liberation theology in Latin America, combined religion with the Third World socialist outlook of Che Guevara and Frantz Fanon. He insisted that the defeat of Western imperialism in Iran required the reclaiming of Iran's national, Islamic religio-cultural identity. The twin foci of his revolutionary vision were national unity/identity and social justice to break the grip of "world imperialism, including multinational corporations and cultural imperialism, racism, class exploitation, class oppression, class inequality, and *gharbzadegi* [Weststruckness]."[20]

The ideas and outlook of Jalal-e-Ahmad, Ali Shariati, and Mehdi Bazargan (an engineer, politician, and Islamic modernist thinker) influenced a generation of students and intellectuals. They were drawn from the traditional and modern middle class; many were graduates of secular universities in science and engineering. Most were from urban areas; many had migrated from village and rural areas to the cities for their higher education and employment as a result of the shah's modernization program. These lay Islamically oriented students and young professionals joined with the clergy, seminarians, and bazaaris. The result was a broad spectrum of people with diverse ideological orientations: writers, poets, journalists, university professors and students; liberal nationalists and Marxists; secularists, traditionalists, and Islamic modernists.

Cultural alienation was exacerbated by military, economic, and political dependence. From 1972 through 1977, Iran became even more heavily dependent on the West. Enormous oil revenues enabled the shah to purchase $6 billion in arms from the United States with another $12 billion on order:

The shah dreamed of making Iran one of the five conventional military powers of the world, and Washington fueled his ambitions to some extent by anointing his regime the policeman of the Persian Gulf. Many Iranians saw this surrogacy of the shah's regime as a sign of Iran's complete subservience to the United States and its loss of independence. This popular perception developed into a profound source of alienation.[21]

At the same time, the initial economic oil boom and its rising expectations went from boom to bust by 1977, contributing to growing dissatisfaction. Politically, the shah further consolidated his political power by restricting political participation. He abolished political parties, including the government-backed Novin and created a single party, the Rastakhiz (Resurgence) Party in 1975 which all were expected to join: "Those who did not wish to be part of the political order, he remarked, could take their passports and leave the country."[22]

The Shah's repressive policies and increased reliance on Savak during the mid to late 1970s provided a common cause for a broad-based opposition movement, as reformers were transformed into revolutionaries. Shii Islam increasingly emerged as the most viable, indigenously rooted vehicle to mobilize an effective mass movement. It offered a common sense of history and identity, symbols and values. Shiism offered an ideological framework that gave meaning and legitimation to an opposition movement of the disinherited and oppressed, with which a variety of factions could identify and within which they could function. The ulama-mosque system provided religio-political leadership and organization, a nationwide network of centers for communication and political action, as well as a vast reservoir of grass roots leadership. Clergy such as the ayatollahs Khomeini, Mutahhari, Taleqani, and Beheshti, along with lay intellectuals such as Mehdi Bazargan and Ali Shariati had developed Islamic reformist and revolutionary ideologies. Although influenced by the writings of Sunni Islamic activists such as Hasan al-Banna and Sayyid Qutb of the Egyptian Muslim Brotherhood, Mawlana Abul Ala Mawdudi of the Jamaat-i Islami and Muhammad Iqbal of Pakistan, they had reinterpreted Shii history and belief to respond to their local conditions. As a result, Iran's revolutionary ideology was distinctively Iranian and Shii.

The religio-political paradigm for the Iranian revolution became the martyrdom of Husayn, by the Sunni "usurper" caliph Yazid, at Karbala in the year 680. Husayn was the son of Ali, Muhammad's son-in-law and, Shii believe, rightful heir as religio-political leader of the Islamic community. This metahistorical event offered the central sacred story—a symbol of oppression and revolt, of suffering and martyrdom, a righteous struggle (jihad) against the forces of absolutism and social injustice. This was a battle of oppressor and oppressed; the disinherited rising up to fight against political (royal absolutism and tyranny) and social injustice. The paradigm of the martyrdom of Husayn was joined to Shiism's messianic expectation for the return of the Imam. Twelver Shiism (Ithna Ashari, or "twelve";

the dominant community in Shii Islam and in Iran) acknowledged a line of twelve Imams or religio-political leaders of the community. The twelfth Imam, who disappeared in 874, was believed to have gone into seclusion; his future return as a Mahdi, or messianic guide, was awaited. Shii believe that the return of the Hidden Imam would bring an end to tyranny and corruption and the restoration of just rule and a society in which oppression and injustice were replaced by equity and social justice.

The pattern of religious-lay alliance, in particular, of mosque and bazaar, under the banner of Islam was resurrected during the late 1970s. The combination provided religious legitimacy and authenticity (a religio-national-cultural identity), as well as independent economic resources. Issues of foreign domination, preservation of national identity and autonomy, constitutionalism, and the place of Islamic law in the state resurfaced. However, in contrast to the Tobacco Protest and the Constitutional Revolt, clergy did not assist but led the revolution of 1979 and dominated the future government.

THE ISLAMIC REPUBLIC OF IRAN

Although the Arab oil embargo of 1973 had symbolized in the eyes of many a return of Muslim economic power and success, Iran gave the modern Muslim world its first successful "Islamic" political revolution—one that was fought in the name of Islam, with its battle cry ("Allahu Akbar"), Shii revolutionary ideology and symbolism, and clerical and Islamically oriented lay leadership. Sunnis and Shia could revel in a decade that saw a greater emphasis on Islamic identity and practice, accompanied by apparent signs of the restoration of Muslim pride and power in a world long dominated by foreign superpowers. Moreover, the Ayatollah Khomeini offered the Iranian experience and agenda as a guide to the political and ideological transformation of the worldwide Muslim community (*ummah*), which was to unite all Muslims in a political and cultural struggle of East and West. Iran alone had won its struggle, and, now victorious, seemed poised to implement its principles at home and promote them abroad under "The Ayatollah Khomeini—the man who brought down the shah, ended a 2,500-year tradition of monarchy in Iran, turned three decades of U.S.-Iranian amity into bitter enmity, and for 10 years was the uncontestable leader."[23]

The years 1979 through 1981 witnessed the creation and institutionalization of Iran's Islamic Republic. Khomeini and the revolution had appeared to embody major components of the Islamic Republic's legitimacy: antiimperialism and nationalism, religion and national/cultural identity, political participation and constitutionalism (in this case, the limitation of royal power). All had been sources of the historical development of Iranian nationalism.[24] From the late nineteenth century, Iranian nationalists had struggled against the encroachment of Britain and Russia, and later America, challenged the right of rulers to sell concessions and contribute to foreign penetration and dependence, and attempted to limit the powers of the monarchy. Shii Islam had been the state religion, and the clergy had on occasion joined with other sectors of society in nationalist causes such as the Tobacco Protest. Khomeini had for decades been a symbol of resistance to the excesses of Pahlavi rule; he and his clerical supporters had provided the backbone and infrastructure of the revolution.

The shah had been condemned on religious, nationalist (dependence and subservience to the West, in particular America), and constitutional (repression and lack of political participation) grounds. Religion, nationalism, constitutionalism, and legitimacy continued to be intertwined realities in the new postrevolutionary period. Religion's relationship to the state, and its identity, institutions, and leadership became critical and contentious issues in the process of state formation. Initially, two streams of leadership seemed to work side-by-side: lay (often Western-educated technocrats) and clergy. The Pahlavi top-down, elite-dominated model seemed to have been replaced by a more populist model of participation. Khomeini returned to Qom, while lay leaders like Bazargan, Abol Hasan Bani-Sadr, Sadiq Gotbzadeh, and Ibrahim Yazdi held prominent government positions.

Substantive constitutional and institutional changes were undertaken electorally. A referendum in March, 1979, transformed Iran's government from a monarchy to an Islamic republic. A clerically dominated Assembly of Experts was elected to draft a new constitution, which was ratified by a popular referendum (November–December, 1979). However, Iran's identity crisis was reflected in constitutional debates over the nature and leadership of the state. Debates occurred not only between those who wished a secular rather than an Islamic government but also among those who wished an Islamic government but rejected Khomeini's doctrine of the *faqih* (the supreme legal expert/authority).

Khomeini had developed his doctrine or interpretation of rule by jurist(s) many years earlier in his seminary lectures and writings. In the absence of the just ruler, the Imam, Shii doctrine taught that Muslim society should be guided by Islamic law—the shariah—and jurists (*faqih*)—the interpreters, or *mujtahids*, of shariah. Khomeini's writing on Islamic government and the role of jurists was little known and seemingly ambivalent. Khomeini was critical of religious leaders who remained aloof from politics or cooperated with Iran's rulers. While recognizing the importance of prayer and ritual, he emphasized an activist sociopolitical interpretation of Islam: "It is of course important for you . . . to teach ritual manners. But what is important are the political, economic, and legal problems of Islam. This has always been, and still ought to be, the pivot of [our] activity."[25] Khomeini had written, "We do not say that government must be in the hands of the *faqih*; rather we say that government must be run in accordance with God's law, for the welfare of the country and the people demands this, and it is not feasible except with the supervision of the religious leaders."[26] However, Khomeini also argued that "[i]t is an established fact that 'the *faqih* has authority over the ruler'

. . . This being the case, the true rulers are the fuqaha themselves, and rulership ought to be theirs, to apply to them, not to those who are obliged to follow the guidance of the fuqaha on account of their own ignorance of the law."[27] As experts on the shariah, Khomeini argued, the fuqaha were best equipped to assure governance according to Islamic law. He maintained that guardianship or governance by the jurist is similar to that exercised by the Prophet Muhammad. The jurist has the same authority to govern and administer the affairs of state, although not the same status, as the Prophet. Such governance could be exercised by a group of jurists or even a single individual. Although during the constitutional debate secular and Islamic reformers (lay and clerical) rejected Khomeini's interpretation, he insisted, "The *veleyat-e-faqih* is not something created by the Assembly of Experts. It is something that God has ordained."[28]

Modernist lay leaders such as Mehdi Bazargan and Bani-Sadr, as well as senior ayatollahs such as Shariatmadari and Taleqani, regarded Khomeini's interpretation of direct clerical rule as an unwarranted innovation of Shii doctrine and opposed its adoption. They believed that the ulama should retire to their seminaries and mosques and that ulama involvement in government should be restricted to an advisory committee on the legislation and its compatibility with Islam.

The clerical majority in the Assembly of Experts, who supported Khomeini's ideological interpretation, differed and prevailed over the minority who warned of its authoritarian and dictatorial dangers. The final version of the constitution, ratified by the nation in November 1979, was based upon Khomeini's concept of Islamic government (*vilayat-i-faqih*, rule by the jurisconsult). Thus, it established the ultimate authority of clerics in the management and guidance of the state.

The constitutional debate and the eclectic nature of the constitution itself reflected the complexity of the attempt to blend elements of theocracy with those of a republic. It revealed the tensions between notions of divine sovereignty and popular sovereignty, clerical and lay leadership. Twelver Shiism (not simply Islam or Shii Islam) was declared the official religion of the state. Although technically the constitution accepted the doctrine of popular sovereignty, God's law and its representative, the faqih, enjoyed paramount status. Although the president, who is directly elected, represents the voice of popular sovereignty, the faqih represents the divine sovereignty of God's law. Although not directly elected by the people, the faqih is elected by the Assembly of Experts, which is in turn directly elected by the people.

The principle of government of the jurist (vilayat-i-faqih) and the primacy of Islamic law (and thus of divine sovereignty) were enshrined in Iran's constitution. The faqih was to be assisted by a twelve-member Council of Guardians composed of Islamic jurists, six appointed by Khomeini and six by the parliament. The council was to supervise the election of the president and the parliament (National Consultative Assembly, or *majlis-i-shura*), interpret the constitution, and ensure that all legislation complied with Islamic law and the constitution. Its scope was reflected in the Iranian constitution's article 96, which declared that the Council of Guardians had veto power over all laws passed by parliament that it judged un-Islamic. A Supreme Judicial Council dominated by *mujtahids* (Islamic jurists) was created as well.

Although its theocratic characteristics—in particular, the rule of the shariah and governance of the faqih—make clear that Iran is not an absolute, popular democracy, it is clearly identified in its constitution as a "republic." The faqih and the Council of Guardians have veto power over the parliament and are invested with wide-ranging powers, as seen particularly in the term and power of the faqih. During the constitutional debates of 1979, Ayatollah Khomeini issued a directive that the new system not be called the "Democratic Islamic Republic." For Khomeini, as for some other Islamists, the term "democracy" is often associated with the West and thus Western penetration, as well as with a society governed by human rather than divine law.

At the same time, the constitution of the Islamic Republic includes democratic institutions. It provides for a parliamentary system of government with executive, legislative, and judicial branches; separation of powers and a system of checks and balances; and a president elected by absolute majority vote. (In 1989, the constitution was amended, and a strong presidency replaced the office of prime minister.) The constitution affirms in its preamble that it "guarantees the rejection of all forms of intellectual and social tyranny and economic monopoly, and aims at entrusting the destinies of the people to the people themselves."[29] In specific articles, it emphasizes the importance of public opinion and electoral politics: "In the Islamic Republic of Iran, the affairs of the country must be administered on the basis of public opinion expressed by means of elections, including the election of the president, the representatives of the National Consultative Assembly, and the members of councils, or by means of referenda" (article 6).

The constitution also presents a complicated structure of checks and balances that makes even the veto power of the Council of Guardians conditional. In 1988, Khomeini created a "Committee to Determine the Expediency of the Islamic Order," a council for arbitrating legal issues in those cases in which the parliament and the Council of Guardians are unable to agree. The powers of this "expediency council" were confirmed in article 112 of the constitution (as amended in 1989), and its effectiveness could be seen in 1992, when the Council of Expediency affirmed a bill passed by parliament but rejected by the Guardians that allows women to claim wages in cash from husbands who divorce them.[30]

The constitution named Khomeini the faqih for life. After his death, the office was to pass to a qualified successor or to a council of from three to five jurists. Under the constitution, the faqih is invested with final authority as the supreme religiopolitical leader of the state. He is the final interpreter of Islamic law; appoints the Council of Guardians and the heads of the judiciary, military, and Revolutionary Guards; and serves as a check on the president, prime minister, and parliament.

The supremacy of Islamic law and, thus, of jurists (the faqih, the Council of Guardians, the judiciary) provided in Iran the basis and legitimacy for a clerically run state. A populist revolution that in the first year of its existence enjoyed mass support increasingly saw its social base grow narrower. What appeared to be a popular reconstruction of the state, with a lay-led and clerically supported representative electoral system of government, began to disintegrate. The militant clergy consolidated its power and emerged in full control of the government during the early 1980s. The secular, authoritarian Pahlavi state gave way to the religious authoritarianism of the Islamic Republic, in which royal absolutism and a top-down approach to government were accompanied by a carefully limited participatory government. In absolute terms, the new system lacked many of the attributes of a fully democratic state. However, in its regional context, "Iran, when compared to its Arab neighbors, does appear to have some political characteristics typical of democratic governments."31

The structure involves a complex balance of authority and popular participation. At the apex of power were the faqih, the Supreme Judicial Council, and the Council of Guardians of the Revolution. They controlled the executive, legislative, and judicial branches of government; the press and other news media; and the Islamic Republican Party, which by 1980 had won a majority of seats in parliamentary elections. Although in the first days after the revolution many parties had cropped up, now only Bazargan's Freedom Party was permitted to exist alongside the IRP, and the Freedom Party's offices were often raided and ransacked and its leadership harassed. All other parties were suppressed. Candidates for election had to be approved by the Council of Guardians. Support for the Islamic Republic was the sine qua non for candidacy, as it was for key positions in government, education, and other sectors of society. Genuine and lively debate and differences were permitted in parliament. Parliamentary members representing differing factions not only debated but also fought over varying policy agendas, and felt free to criticize and reject the recommendations of senior government officials. However, parliamentary debate was circumscribed. Neither criticism of the Ayatollah Khomeini nor of the government's ideological foundation was tolerated.

The Revolutionary Guards (*Pasdaran*) provided internal security and an alternative check to the power of the regular military. Revolutionary committees (*komiteh*) and organizations (the Revolutionary Guards, the Foundation for the Disinherited, the Jihad for Reconstruction, the Commission for Reconstruction and Renovation of the War Zones) covered a host of activities, from security to development and social services. Opposition newspapers were banned, and the government used media censorship and its own "Islamic programming" to promote its beliefs and values.

OPPOSITION AND DISSENT

From its inception, the government of the new Islamic Republic of Iran contained the seeds of dissension and polarization. The revolution had brought together a diverse cross section of religious and secular elites, social classes, parties, and guerilla movements who represented a variety of political and religious orientations. Although the opposition had a common enemy (Pahlavi despotism and foreign control) and a common purpose (a more just and egalitarian society), there had been no prior agreement on the form or leadership of the new government. Many were not prepared for what was to transpire in the early years after the establishment of Iran's Islamic Republic. Most were unaware of Khomeini's writings and views on the nature of government and politics. His criticisms of the Shah and call for a new sociopolitical order had sounded not unlike that of many other critics of Pahlavi rule. Moreover, his advisors in Paris and in the early days after his return had included the French-educated Abol Hasan Bani-Sadr, and the American-educated Sadiq Gotbzadeh, Mansur Farhang, and Ibrahim Yazdi— modern laymen influenced by the outlook of Ali Shariati. Even as Khomeini emerged as the principal symbol and leader of the revolution, many had expected that the clergy would return to their mosques and madrasas (seminaries) after the revolution.

Khomeini and the militant clergy who supported him proved to have little tolerance for substantive dissent or dissenting parties. The broad-based coalition that had brought about the revolution crumbled as religious authoritarianism replaced the shah's secular authoritarianism. As with the shah, national cohesion was not based on power sharing, pluralism, and the tolerance of opposition, but repression, the concentration of power, and the imposition a new "Islamic" order. Officials and members of the old regime's institutions (the military, police, ministries, universities, and schools) were purged. Secular, Islamic, and leftist dissidents or rivals alike were silenced through execution, imprisonment, and exile. Most opponents of the government fled to Western Europe and America. Appointments were based on revolutionary/Islamic credentials and ideological rectitude, as determined more by the ruling clergy than by professional expertise. Prominent lay leaders such as Bazargan, the first prime minister (February–November, 1979), and Bani-Sadr, Iran's first president, fell from power. Although Bazargan stayed on to lead his opposition Freedom Party, Bani-Sadr fled, fearing for his life, to Paris. Sadiq Gotbzadeh, who had held a number of posts including Foreign Minister, was executed for his participation in a plot to assassinate Khomeini. Ayatollahs who disagreed with Khomeini's "Rule of the Jurist" or who were critical of the excesses of the Islamic Republic were harassed and sometimes silenced.[32] The merchants of the bazaar, long allies of the ulama, became disenchanted with proposed economic reforms and threatened to withdraw support for the regime.

LEADERSHIP IN THE ISLAMIC REPUBLIC

Dissident clerical and lay voices were offset by a critical mass of committed clergy and laity, and a set of policies were initiated to impose and defend ideological purity. The Society of Militant (Combatant) Clergy, clergy committed to the revolution, became a major arm of the ulama, identifying and confirming true, as distinct from dissident, clergy, and transforming the traditional Shii religious structure and its institutions into a political arm of the ulama. A network of Friday mosque preachers (*imam-jumah*) was created to serve as Khomeini's representatives and promote the ideology and policies of the revolution in the cities, towns, and villages of Iran. The Friday congregational prayer, with its religio-political sermon, was an important way to ideologically Islamize (that is, to preach and educate concerning the regime's brand of Islam) the public and to mobilize public opinion. The militant clergy were supported by the "lay second stratum of the Islamic Republic which served in government and filled many of the key positions in the bureaucracy."[33] Most shared a common social and educational background. They were from lower middle class and bazaari families, and were often the first generation to obtain university education at home and abroad. Most were under forty, and had been trained in the sciences and medicine; they were men like Prime Minister Hussein Musavi, Foreign Minister Ali Akbar Velayati, and a host of ministry officials, civil servants, and members of parliament.[34] Thus, the Islamic Republic was based upon a clerical-lay alliance and committed to the Imam Khomeini and to the revolution despite differences of vision and policy. Its social base increasingly became narrowed as bazaaris joined with secular and Islamically oriented reformers, disaffected clergy, and women. As a result, "the Islamic state became clearly petit bourgeois in nature with extensive support from the migrant poor in the cities."[35]

Islamization of Iranian society included the eradication of un-Islamic elements and the implementation and imposition of an Islamic order. The extensive changes in personnel and revolutionary committees were accompanied by new laws and policies to educate and foster an Islamic society. The Office for the Propagation of Virtue and Prevention of Sin was to address the moral ills of society. Music and dancing in public were banned; nightclubs and bars were closed down. Alcohol, gambling, drugs, prostitution, homosexuality, and pornography were banned. Quick justice and severe penalties were meted out by revolutionary courts; prostitution, drug trafficking, and other forms of "corruption" were subject to capital punishment. The mosques and the media were employed to propagate the state's Islamic guidance and ideology. Thousands of teachers were purged, textbooks reviewed and revised, and coeducational institutions transformed into single-sex schools. Islamic Associations were created in schools; its members often monitored un-Islamic behavior and reported teachers and dissident students.[36]

Women in particular felt the impact of the new Islamic order. Many, secularly as well as Islamically oriented, had been part of the revolution, and donned the chador as a symbol of protest and because it provided anonymity. Although the Preamble to the Constitution of the Iranian Islamic Republic speaks of the equality of men and women before the law, after the revolution, the regime's attempt to "liberate" women and implement norms of Islamic modesty included an initial attempt to require that all women government employees wear the chador at work. Mass demonstrations brought a clarification from Khomeini, and the regulation was rescinded. The Family Protection Law of 1967–75, which had restricted polygamy, was repealed. The government implemented strict enforcement of a dress code that required that all women wear the hijab (headscarf) and clothing that concealed everything but their hands and faces. The dress code affected Muslim and non-Muslim women as well as Western visitors. Revolutionary committees often sought out and punished women who wore makeup, or did not dress modestly (or Islamically). The government placed primary emphasis on women's roles as wives and mothers and certain forms of employment (as judges and lawyers) were deemed inappropriate. As a result, a relatively united women's movement became polarized, as women supportive of the clergy-dominated regime broke with their more secular, as well as more Islamically oriented, sisters who opposed the new restrictions.[37]

Over time, the Islamist women assumed more active and visible roles in the Islamic Republic, utilizing the ideological emphasis of equality within recognition of difference. By the 1990s, growing numbers of women stood for election to parliament and were able to win contested seats, creating a core of people actively sensitive to women's issues. These women, and their colleagues in a growing number of nongovernmental women's organizations (by 1995, more than fifty), have succeeded in bringing about significant change while remaining clearly within the framework of the Republic. By the mid-1990s, such changes included changes in the divorce laws that entitle divorced women to compensation for the domestic work if divorced and in lifting restrictions on female enrollments in university programs such as law and engineering. In 1994, 30 percent of government employees and 40 percent of the students in universities were women.[38] Women within the Islamic Republic's power structure, such as Khomeini's daughter, Zahra Mostafavi, and Hashemi Rafsanjani's daughter, Faezah Hashemi, have gained for Iranian women "a greater political voice" and "more equal job opportunities" through active advocacy of principles of Islamic equality, with the result, in the words of one recent observer, that "to Muslim women elsewhere in the strictest parts of the Islamic world, the Iranian woman riding to work on her motorbike, even with her billowing chador gripped in her teeth, looks like a figure to envy."[39]

Initially, many in the nonelite sectors welcomed the more populist nature of the government and society. The Islamic Republic did seem to possess a more socially inclusive base of support and political participation (for those who acquiesced to the rule of the mullahs) and did deliver services to the less fortunate in urban areas and in the villages. Substantial disaffection was delayed until even after the euphoria and promise of the revolution had begun to fade by the force of Khomeini's charismatic personality, as well the decimation and the fragmentation of the opposition. It was also substantially sidetracked by the Iraq-Iran war (1980–88), in which governments played upon centuries-long Arab-Persian, Sunni-Shii rivalries. Iranian nationalist sentiments and support for the regime were rekindled as Khomeini led a "righteous" war against Saddam Hussein, and Iranians pulled together to defend their homeland. However, the shock of the cease-fire (perceived by many Iranians as a "defeat"), the war's heavy human toll, and Iran's shattered economy contributed to significant disaffection and opposition, as many now experienced life as significantly worse than that under the shah. The shock of the cease-fire was followed by the death of Khomeini in 1989. Many observers had thought that his death would be the end of the Islamic Republic, since it had been created by the rule of the mullahs in the 1980s. However, power passed quickly and in an orderly and constitutional manner to people who had been the crucial leaders in Khomeini's final years. Ali Khamenei, who had been president, was selected as the spiritual guide (faqih), and Hashemi Rafsanjani, who had been the influential speaker of parliament, became president, with additional powers as a result of constitutional amendments in 1989.

The post-Khomeini political system had a greater number of visible and active centers of power, but these were all formed from the old core of committed clerics and other supporters. The majority of the population continued to accommodate itself to the political reality of a state controlled by a minority, who had a monopoly on the power of the state, and its security forces. However, elections held within the guidelines of the leadership were often hotly contested, and the parliament did not automatically approve measures brought before it. Within this framework, strong criticism of corruption among government officials was voiced, and voices of opposition could be heard by the mid-1990s in an active but careful press. Members of organized opposition to the Islamic Republic itself were virtually all in exile, with little impact on the developments within the country.

PLURALISM AND DISSENT

The revolution held out a promise. The political authoritarianism and social corruption of the Pahlavi monarchy would give way to an independent, Islamic republic, which would implement a more democratic and socially just society. The revolution promised freedom, freedom from the tyranny of the shah's autocratic rule, symbolized by SAVAK and Teheran's Evin Prison. The shah's government had been denounced by its critics for repression and massive violation of human rights: censorship; the banning of political parties; the arrest, imprisonment, torture, execution, and assassination of opposition members; and the creation of a society in which the fate of individuals personally and professionally was dependent on royal favor. Critics demanded political participation; basic freedoms of speech, assembly, and association; and a free press.

The purges and repression in the early 1980s and again in the late 1980s disabused many of its supporters and well-wishers of the advantages of Iran's version of "Islamic justice." A "royal reign of terror" was replaced by a "clerical reign of terror"; only the political actors or players changed, not the practices. Imprisonment, arbitrary trial, torture, censorship, and monitoring by security forces continued. If the notorious and dreaded Evin prison was emptied of its Pahlavi prisoners, it was filled again by those of the Islamic Republic. SAVAK was renamed SAVAMA; although the shah had departed the political scene, his legacy of repression endured, now legitimated in the name of Islam: "Street gangs of Hizbollah [Party of God] strong-arm opponents, breakup opposition rallies, and harass women. The prisons are full, torture is still used, executions are far more frequent than in the prerevolutionary era."[40] The fervor of Hizbollahi is revealed in a Ministry of Guidance document:

> The Hizbullahi is a wild torrent surpassing the imagination . . . . He is a maktabi [one who follows Islam comprehensively], disgusted with any leaning to the East or West . . . . He is simply sincere and angry. Stay away from his anger, which destroys all in its path. Khomeini is his heart and soul . . . . The Hizbullahi does not wear eau de cologne, wear a tie or smoke American cigarettes. . . . You might wonder where he gets his information. He is everywhere, serving your food, selling you ice-cream.[41]

Hizbollahi were just one of many groups of religious zealots, often uncontrolled and uncontrollable, who functioned as "religious enforcers." Even then-president and the subsequent successor of Ayatollah Khomeini as faqih, Ali Khamenei, chided zealots: "Do not be more revolutionary than Imam Khomeini."[42]

Postrevolutionary Iran witnessed the replacement of the Shah and his secular elites by the Imam and his "clerical autocracy." Not just Pahlavi officials, but all who differed with the new order, Islamic and Marxist dissidents alike, were silenced. Women and religious minorities, as well as a wide variety of political and intellectual dissidents, felt the swift arm of Islamic justice as meted out by revolutionary guards and courts. Trials and executions often occurred in such summary fashion that the Ayatollah Khomeini himself felt constrained to intervene and warn against such excesses. The Islamic Republic's first prime minister, Mehdi Bazargan, resigned in disgust; Abol Hasan Bani Sadr, its first elected president, fled to exile in France; and Sadiq Gotbzadeh, foreign affairs minister, was executed for his participation in an alleged plot to assassinate Khomeini. All had been protégés of Khomeini and brought into office with his blessings. Religious leaders who did not accept Khomeini's doctrine of "rule by the jurist" were silenced or put under house arrest by fellow clerics. The widespread repression of dissent in the early 1980s occurred again in the late 1980s, with a new wave of arrests and executions. Not only were these documented and criticized by international human rights organizations but also by prominent clergy such as the Ayatollah Ali Montazeri, who at the time had been designated by Khomeini to succeed him as faqih. Montazeri wrote an open letter to Khomeini: "For what valid reasons . . . has our judiciary approved these executions, which can result in nothing but damaging the face of our revolution and the system?"[43]

Amnesty International reported that, in 1993, "Political arrests, torture, unfair trials, and summary executions were reported throughout the country."[44] Those arrested included suspected government opponents; journalists; followers of Ali Shariati; dissident Sunni and Shii clergy, including followers of Ayatollah Montazeri; former and current members of the military and security forces; and representatives of ethnic minorities, such as Baluchis and Arabs.[45] In addition, Iran continued to be accused of abducting and killing opponents outside Iran.

Perhaps the most notorious and publicized case of Iranian extrajudicial justice is the Salman Rushdie affair. As most analysts of Iran were speaking of its moving toward normalization with the West and even the possibility of improved relations with America, the tide abruptly turned on February 14, 1989, with the storm created by Salman Rushdie's *The Satanic Verses*. Riots and deaths in Pakistan and India over the publication of *The Satanic Verses* occurred in the midst of Iran's official celebration of the revolution's tenth anniversary. The Rushdie affair provided radicals with an issue that would shift Khomeini away from the influence of the more flexible, pragmatic camp, and offered Khomeini an occasion to reassert his Islamic leadership internationally and rekindle and mobilize militant fervor for the defense of Islam, and thus distract attention from Iran's pressing socioeconomic problems and growing social discontent. Khomeini's condemnation of the book, its publishers, Britain, and the United States, and his call for the execution of the author, precipitated an international crisis.

No significant element of the previous opposition-in-exile gave support to the new leaders after Khomeini's death. Within Iran, there were many different forms of resistance to government economic policies, repression, and corruption. However, these

> different forms of resistance to the Islamic Republic do not have as their main goal a regime change, but seek to end abuses of official power, violations of fundamental individual rights, and the creation of space within which people can pursue their own lives and work without official encroachments. They strive to bring about change by working within the framework of the existing laws and through persuasion, public education and creation of informal networks.[46]

In some ways, at least, this can be conceived of as the emergence of a "loyal opposition," because there is little indication that the majority of people in Iran desire an end to a system that could be called an Islamic Republic.

The potential effectiveness of this kind of opposition is illustrated in the development of population policy under the republic.

> The development of population policy in Iran indicates that, contrary to its image in the West, the Islamic republic has demonstrated much resilience and adaptability in the face of rather harsh socioeconomic reality. It has shown a keen awareness that creating an informed public and building a broad consensus is one of the most important elements of success in any development plan, particularly as it touches upon the most intimate and day-to-day aspects of people's lives. Unlike the monarchy, the Islamic regime has popularized the fundamental relevance of the population question to human society.[47]

While this does not represent what liberal perceptions would describe as democratic openness, it does show both the general popular acceptance of the basic principles of the regime and regime's concern for the general principle of creating consensus.

The record of the Islamic Republic in its treatment of ethnic and religious minorities has been mixed. Constitutionally, the rights of recognized religious minorities are protected. Article 13 of the constitution states: "Iranian Zoroastrians, Jews and Christians are the only recognized religious minorities that, within the limits of the law, are free to practice their religious rites and to conduct their personal affairs and education according to their own beliefs." Article 14 invokes the authority of the Quran regarding the obligation of Muslims to treat non-Muslims justly and to respect their rights. Iran's main minorities include 3.5 million Sunni Muslims, many of whom are Kurds, 350,000 Bahai; 80,000 Christians; and 30,000 Jews. Jews, Christians, and Zoroastrians hold seats in the parliament based on proportional representation (Zoroastrians, 1; Jews, 1; Armenian Christians, 2; and Assyrian Christians, 1).

Despite constitutional guarantees and a general ability to live and function in society, religious and ethnic minorities have at times found their existence difficult if not precarious. The regime's record of religious tolerance fluctuates often, reflecting domestic politics and the struggle between pragmatists and militant ideologues. Religious minorities have been required to observe the prohibition of alcohol and the segregation of the sexes at public functions. Proselytizing among Muslims is forbidden and apostasy is a capital offense. There have been instances of religious persecution, although the extent and causes have been disputed.

Although the Jewish community had shrunk to half its size prior to the revolution owing to emigration and weathered some difficult times in the early years after the revolution, in general, Jews have been able to practice their religion "discreetly" and function in society.[48] Under Rafsanjani, Jews were again given multiple-exit visas and Teheran television for the first time since the revolution broadcast a Seder during Passover.[49]

In general, Christians and Christian churches have been able to practice their faith and function in society, although not to proselytize. However, instances of persecution have occurred. Protestant leaders have been arrested and imprisoned from time to time. During the first week of July, 1994, two Protestant leaders were killed in apparently religiously motivated murders. Rev. Tateos Michaelian, chairman of the Council of Protestant Ministers in Iran, was apparently assassinated. Rev. Mehdi Dibaj, a pastor of the Assemblies of God church, had been imprisoned for ten years on charges of apostasy (conversion from Islam to Christianity). In January, 1994, he was sentenced to be executed but released from prison in response to international pressure. Several days after his release, Bishop Haik Hovsaepian Mehr, who had organized the campaign for Dibaj's release, was murdered. On July 3, Dibaj himself was murdered. While some charged that radical elements within the government were determined to cripple the Christian community, the government blamed the Mojahideen-e-Khalq, and arrested several members of the mojahedeen, who allegedly confessed to the crimes.[50]

In January, 1994, Sunni Muslims clashed with authorities after reports that their places of worship were to be closed.[51] Ethnic minorities', such as the Kurds', demands to use their national languages and enjoy some degree of self-government have been rejected.

The Bahai, Iran's largest religious minority, who throughout modern Iranian history have been subjected to sporadic anti-Bahai policies and riots, were again subjected to execution and persecution in the 1980s, with more than 200 executed and thousands imprisoned. Bahai have their origins in Babism, an offshoot of Islam, whose founder in 1844 declared himself the door (bab) to the Hidden (Twelfth) Imam. As a result, Babism was crushed in Iran. Mirza Hussein Ali, the founder of the Bahai, declared himself the "Glory of God" (Bahaullah) in 1863. The ulama condemned the Bahai as apostates, the equivalent of traitors in Islam. Throughout the twentieth century, Iran's clergy called upon the state to suppress the Bahai. Bahai were socially rejected, their loyalty suspect on religious and political grounds. Religiously, they were regarded as apostates and heretics. Politically, they were seen as collaborationists, tools of British imperialism charged with spying for the British during World War I and holding important positions under the Pahlavi shahs. The clergy often incited anti-Bahai riots and pressured the government to suppress the Bahai. Bahai were politically disenfranchised, denied the vote as apostates. From time to time, their schools and centers were seized or closed down. Bahai were attacked and their property destroyed. Muhammad Reza Shah's government had accommodated the clergy during an ulema-led anti-Bahai campaign in 1955. The Army chief of staff and the governor of Teheran had participated in the destruction of the main Bahai center in Teheran. However, fearful of international reaction, the Shah resisted the clergy's attempt to pass a bill in parliament that outlawed the Bahai and would imprison its members and seize and distribute its property for use in Islamic religious schools and activities.

During the early years after the revolution, the Bahai again were persecuted.

They were declared illegal and forbidden to hold government positions; many were arrested and imprisoned; hundreds were executed.[52] However, the government insisted that any action taken against Bahai was not on religious grounds but for political crimes stemming from their cooperation with the Shah or anti-revolutionary forces. Others charged that the government had attempted nothing less than "the total destruction of the country's Bahai community."[53] The initial period of persecution abated for some years after an international outcry. However, in the 1990s, a new wave of persecution began. In September, 1993, an Islamic judge in Teheran who had found two Muslim brothers guilty of the abduction of one man and the burning of another refused to jail them or award blood money to the family of the murdered man because the victim was an "unbeliever," a Bahai. In December, three Bahai were condemned to death for celebrating religious feasts, owning books, "as unprivileged infidels at war with the Muslim nation," and for communicating news of their trial for their lives to the United Nations and Bahai organizations outside Iran.[54] The rationale for this persecution was contained in a confidential document, a code prepared by the Supreme Revolutionary Cultural Council in February 25, 1991, and approved by Iran's spiritual leader, Ayatollah Khamenei. The code called for the denial of employment and admission to schools to Bahai, the expulsion of Bahai from universities, and punishment for "their political [espionage] activities."[55]

CONCLUSION

"In many ways, the Islamic republic is the closest thing to democracy Iran has ever had. Khomeini created an Islamic state by popular consensus; the majority of Iranians may still support the regime. But for those who object to the strictures of Islamic law, the consequences are horrible."[56] Many might dispute talk of majority support for the regime. However, its quasi democratic nature is clear. On the one hand, Iran has functioning executive, legislative, and judicial branches. It has survived the death of the Ayatollah Khomeini, and has an elected president and a parliament that engages in lively debate and, within limits, feels free to disagree with its leadership. On the other hand, Iran enjoys at best a limited pluralism. Freedom of expression is circumscribed by Iran's Islamic ideology and the belief that Islamic laws and values are to guide society. Individuals, organizations, political parties, private associations, and institutions must operate within the often fluid and shifting parameters of Iran's revolutionary Islamic identity and commitment. Thus, the Islamic ideology and guidance of the state has meant state control of the press and media as well as enforcement of regulations that govern drink, dress (for women and men), and worship. Yet, even here, the press, like the Iranian parliament, is diverse and, within limits, critical on issues from leadership and land reform to education, trade with the West, and women's status.

From the beginning of the Islamic republic, however charismatic and authoritative the Ayatollah Khomeini, factions have vied for power and the government's tolerance of pluralism and dissent has been tested. Although the leadership in Iran remained committed to the revolution, significant differences of opinion and policy existed between rival factions over domestic and foreign policy issues such as land reform, nationalization, promotion of the revolution abroad, and relations with the West. Even the clerically dominated Islamic Republican Party was dissolved in 1987 as a result of factional disputes.

Postrevolutionary attempts to articulate and implement an Islamic alternative to the Shah's modernization program have brought to the surface deep divisions between those who favored private-sector freedom and those who advocated radical socioeconomic reforms through state control of the economy. Competing interpretations resulted from differing interpretations of Islamic law, as well as conflicting class interests. A majority in parliament managed to pass laws that would bring about substantive social reform through land reform, the expansion of state control over the economy, and the consequent restriction of free enterprise. Merchants, who had been the financial backbone of the ulama and the revolution, along with landowners (among whom are many clerical leaders) strongly opposed such measures. They effectively lobbied the Council of Guardians so that body fairly consistently vetoed reform legislation as contrary to Islamic law. While these traditionalists have been content to cite centuries-old norms, more radical reformers have argued that new circumstances require fresh legal interpretations.

Differences over economic policies were equally matched by deep political divisions between pragmatists and more radical hard-liners. The former were represented in the 1980s by Hashemi Rafsanjani, the speaker of the parliament, Ali Akbar Velayati, the foreign minister, and Ali Khamenei, the president. The latter were led by Mir Hussein Musavi, the prime minister, and Ali Akbar Mohtasheimi, the minister of the interior. Differences between these factions were made evident in a series of events. In October, 1986, Mehdi Hashemi, head of the bureau in charge of the export of the revolution, was arrested and executed. Hard-liners had leaked to the press information about meetings between Robert McFarlane, former U.S. national security advisor, and Rafsanjani, and about the sale of U.S. arms to Iran for the release of American hostages in Lebanon.

Islamic government has also proven far from monolithic in its social policy, particularly that of population control. After an initial period in which birth control was condemned as un-Islamic, and the population exploded to among the world's highest at an annual rate of 3.9 percent, the Rafsanjani government reinstituted a birth control program and announced that some 70,000 women had been voluntarily sterilized.[57]

Evaluations of the Iranian experience as an Islamic Republic vary greatly, but few doubt that major changes have taken place. In assessing these changes after a decade of Khomeini's leadership, Fouad Ajami, a critical analyst of state structures in the Middle East, states: "A transformed Iran has emerged after the appropriation of political power by the theocrats and their flock. . . . Judging by its record over a decade, it is a revolutionary state with cunning to match its ferocity, a state capable of organizing great campaigns and retreats and adjusting to things that can and cannot be."[58] The state created by the revolution has a special populist strength: "For all the swagger and arrogance of the shah, his turbaned successor has been presiding over a far sturdier state. The theocratic republic has closed the paralyzing gap between state and society that previously had been the hallmark of Persian political life."[59] Whether or not this bridging of the gap between state and society marks a move in the direction of a more democratic political system can be debated. However, it has provided the basis for greater public debate and for a consensus allowing for the successful transition to the post-Khomeini era. "The broad consensus that allowed the smooth transition of power in Iran was reached by the spring of 1989 after a remarkably open debate of nearly a year," and it was correctly predicted at the time that in the new era, "Iranian politics will involve much ongoing intra-regime bargaining, national debate and forming and reforming of a consensus acceptable to most of the important actors and their constituencies."[60]

By the time of the sixteenth anniversary (in 1995) of the revolution, the Islamic Republic had also successfully survived more than a half-decade of existence after Khomeini, and was moving beyond simply being viewed as the "post-Khomeini" regime. In terms of some of the basic issues of democracy and the Islamic Republic, there was a continuing affirmation of the importance of popular participation, consensus, and freedom. In his speech marking the sixteenth anniversary, Rafsanjani claimed as one of the great achievements of the revolution that the people "understand freedom. . . . Of course Iran confronts vice and unjust issues and no one denies that. But there is complete freedom for any kind of ideology and constructive move."[61] In the sixteenth anniversary statement issued by the Teheran Militant Clergy Association, there was an affirmation that the Islamic Republic "presented a new definition of democracy," that "our people are the base of the sacred system of the Islamic Republic of Iran," and that "the Islamic Republic of Iran's government has been the most outstanding example of government by the people."[62] Even the more hard-line Ali Akbar Mohtashami stated, "The imam [Khomeini] respected public opinion. He was not ready to jeopardize it. He involved people in their own future. This was the secret of the imam's success, the victory of the Islamic revolution, and the establishment of the Islamic Republic of Iran."[63] In other words, although the actual practice of the Islamic Republic is open to strong criticism for human rights abuses, suppression, and authoritarian rule, its leaders continue to affirm in the definition of the republic itself the importance of popular participation and maintaining the republic as a government of the people.

In Iran's developing political structure, there is no multiparty system or effective opposition that is allowed a voice. Even those opposition groups who advocate peaceful and evolutionary change rather than violent overthrow called, on the occasion of the sixteenth anniversary, for all groups to "unite in a bid to pressure Islamic leaders in Iran to end their bullying, conduct free elections and revive the rule of the people."[64] However, regular elections have been held, and they continue to be actively contested by people holding significantly different views, even if those views are all within the Islamic Republican perspective. At minimum, the elections have served as a major arena for the debates between the major factions. This was clearly reflected in 1992 in the first parliamentary elections after the death of Khomeini. At that time, it could be observed that the "holding of regular elections is gradually developing into a process of regulating factional rivalry between Iran's religious power blocs."[65]

The active participatory dimensions of the politics of the Islamic Republic do not represent what could be called "liberal democracy." The practice of the regime in a number of areas is not in accord with its own affirmations of freedom and constitutional rights. However, in the context of the political systems and practices of the region, the high level of allowed popular participation is noteworthy. In the Persian Gulf region, some have observed, many people "believe that the Iranian experience demonstrates the compatibility of representative government with cherished traditional values. Ironically, the Western preoccupation with *hijab* tends to ignore the fact that Iranian society generally is more open and more liberal than its counterparts across the Gulf. . . . Disenfranchised Arabs see in the Islamic government of Iran what appears to be a good example of democracy within an Islamic context."[66]

The Iranian experience does not provide definitive answers to questions about the relationships between Islam and democracy. Iran does demonstrate the extent to which issues of popular political participation and consensus have become part of the political horizon in the Islamic Republic of Iran and are employed by government and opposition, and thus the diverse ways in which "democracy" is being defined. For some, the Iranian experience affirms the possibility of creating an Islamic democracy. For others, it only emphasizes the authoritarian nature of Muslim political institutions and practice.

FOUR

Sudan

The Mahdi and the Military

Current efforts to establish an Islamic state in Sudan are identified with Hasan al-Turabi and the Sudanese Muslim Brotherhood. However, these efforts are part of a history of more than a century of conscious activities aimed at the development of Islamic social and political structures in Sudan. In the late nineteenth century, the Sudanese Mahdi movement, like its successor at the end of the twentieth century, attracted international attention as it successfully raised the banner of Islamic revolution. The followers of the Mahdi created both an Islamically identified political system and the first independent Sudanese "national" state.

During the twentieth century, movements affirming national identity and independence and efforts to establish political systems that would reflect popular aspirations were closely tied to the Islamic experiences of Sudanese peoples. The affirmation of local identity and the desire for popular political participation are not, in other words, new phenomena in Sudan in the late twentieth century. They are developments with deep historical roots in modern Sudanese history, although the specific forms of Islamic resurgence and democratization also manifest the conditions of the final quarter of the twentieth century.

HISTORICAL FOUNDATIONS OF THE CENTRAL STATE

The emergence of a centralized state controlling the territories of what is now Sudan is part of the modern history of that country. Before the nineteenth century, the area was a collection of different communities ranging from relatively small and distinctive ethnic groups to larger state structures in the Nile valley and Darfur. The creation of a single state ruling most of the area was the result of the conquest of the region by the armies of the Ottoman governor of Egypt, Muhammad Ali, in the 1820s. This "Turco-Egyptian" regime lasted until it was defeated by the Mahdist revolution in the 1880s. Many of the basic issues of the definition of the nature and role of the central state had already emerged in this nineteenth-century experience.

Because of the great human diversity in the area controlled by the Sudanese state, even when the rulers are "Sudanese" in origin, they do not represent a homogeneous majority population. For example, although 51 percent of the population of Sudan was reported in the 1955–56 census as speaking Arabic, only 39 percent were identified as "people of Arab stock."[1] More than one hundred different languages are spoken in the country, and there is an even larger number of distinctive ethnic and communal groups. It is religion that provides the basis for the most common shared identification among Sudanese. About 75 percent of the population is Muslim, and although there are many different Muslim groups, they recognize Islam as a common bond. The Muslims are concentrated in the northern two-thirds of the country. This means that in the southern part of the country, the majority of the people are non-Muslim, but they do not share a common linguistic, ethnic, or religious identity.

In this pluralistic society, central governments faced the problems of creating an identity that could provide legitimacy and of establishing mechanisms for determining and responding to popular sentiments. Issues of consensus/identity and consultation/participation are of major importance for any central government in Sudan. To the degree that governments failed to establish these foundations of legitimacy, they have had to rely on military means to stay in power. However, even foreign rulers such as the British made significant efforts to go beyond simple rule by force, utilizing a variety of mechanisms of consultation to provide for a sense of popular participation.

From the time of the establishment of the central government by the Turco-Egyptian conquerors in the 1820s, rulers in Sudan have utilized Islamic themes as a way of appealing to the largest single group within the population. The armies of Muhammad Ali included Muslim teachers from the great Islamic university of al-Azhar in Cairo, who urged local peoples to accept the new rulers as representatives of the great sultan-caliphs of Islam. Later, the whole justification for the Mahdist state was clearly based on an appeal to Islamic principles. Even the British sought to present themselves as the protectors of Islam and worked closely with local Muslim notables. However, because Islamic experience in Sudan is complex and not monolithic, Islamic themes could always be used for both rule and opposition to rulers. Just as the Mahdi's opposition to the Turco-Egyptian rulers was based on Islamic principles, the arguments made by opponents of the Mahdi were equally couched in Islamic terms. In the twentieth century, the two great themes of the Sudanese nationalists—unity of the Nile Valley and Sudan for the Sudanese—both appealed to Muslim sensibilities. Following independence in 1956, both military and parliamentary regimes appealed in various ways to Islamic themes and symbols for at least part of the basis for their legitimacy.

This history is an important reminder that the regime created by the military coup in 1989 was not the first to make a direct appeal for legitimacy in Islamic terms. All central governments since the early nineteenth century had made similar appeals. However, each political system presented its Islamic dimension in very different ways. It is the new style of Islamic renewal advocated by the National Islamic Front (NIF) that makes the political system established in 1989 distinctive, not the fact that it appealed to Islamic themes.

Before the twentieth century, the central governments made little effort to consult public opinion or to provide ways for the Sudanese to gain a sense of popular participation in the government. There was little sense of a need for recognizing democratic principles or the rights of popular self-rule. In the Turco-Egyptian era, when local people were brought into governmental activities, it was as a matter of convenience, efficiency, or securing local support for the government. In this way, leaders of large Sufi brotherhoods, especially the Khatmiyyah, cooperated with the Egyptian governors and helped to secure popular acceptance of the Turco-Egyptian regime. One Khatmiyyah leader, for example, played an important role in the negotiations that brought an end to a major mutiny of local troops in Kasala in 1865.[2] When the Mahdist revolution broke out, the Khatmiyyah represented one of the major sources of opposition to the movement and support for the government. Similarly, some Sudanese tribal notables were appointed provincial governors, but this basically involved the "political desirability of advancing the leading Sudanese"[3] rather than a recognition of the rights of Sudanese to rule themselves or the need for popular participation.

There was a high level of popular participation in the Mahdist movement, which began in the early 1880s as an Islamic revolution aiming at overthrowing the Turco-Egyptian rulers and ultimately at establishing an authentically Islamic state and society throughout the Muslim world. In the Mahdiyyah, popular participation and mass mobilization involved the recognition of the messianic authority of the Mahdi. There was no thought of democratic participation in government. The structure of the state was hierarchical, although there was consultation and mediation in matters of practical policy that did not directly involve subjects explicitly covered in the proclamations of the Mahdi. Prominent local teachers and commanders played an important role in mobilizing and directing the activities of the general population.

The experiences of the central state in the Turco-Egyptian and Mahdist periods created traditions and foundations for political operation that continue to have importance in the twentieth century. One dimension of this is the importance of mediating structures between the general population and the central state. The nineteenth-century experiences created a situation suitable for what Albert Hourani has called the "politics of notables," in which local "notables" provide the critical link between the general population and the central government.[4] In this system, the

> political influence of the notables rests on two factors: on the one hand, they must possess 'access' to authority, and so be able to advise, to warn, and in general to speak for society or some part of it at the ruler's court; on the other,

they must have some social power of their own, whatever its form and origin, which is not dependent on the ruler and gives them a position of accepted and 'natural' leadership.[5]

The notables in Sudan were the leaders of large ethnic and tribal groups and of major Islamic associations. As the socioeconomic changes of the modern era undermined the autonomy of tribes in many areas, the "Islamic notables" gained increasingly important roles in this political pattern. This trend began in the nineteenth century and continued throughout the twentieth. However, whether the notables were tribal or religious, at the beginning of the twentieth century a pattern had been firmly set in which the central government usually dealt with the general population through the mediation of the "politics of notables."

The two important trends of the late twentieth century—affirmation of identity and desire for popular political participation—find some beginnings in these nineteenth-century experiences that have a specific character. When rulers in the central government affirmed an identity more than that of military victor, it was articulated in Islamic terms, and when rulers recognized the need to provide some sense of recognition of the desires of the people, it was done through the mediating structures of a politics of notables. This heritage was important for the heirs to rule in the twentieth century Sudan.

Beginnings of Political Participation and Parties

Sudan was ruled by the British from 1898, when the last Mahdist forces were defeated by an Anglo-Egyptian army, until 1956. In international law, the governing structure was an Anglo-Egyptian Condominium, but, in practice, Great Britain controlled Sudan. The early government was essentially a military government, but gradually the governmental structures developed until the independent Sudan emerged in 1956 with a Westminster-style parliament. This evolution involved a transformation of the politics of notables, but in many ways it also represented a continuation of that style of politics. This is an important aspect of the experience of Sudan with parliamentary political systems, which have been established and overthrown three times since independence. The failure of the Westminster-style parliamentary system in Sudan is the context within which Sudanese Muslims attempt to define the relationship between Islam and democracy in the final years of the twentieth century. The origins of that parliamentary system, with its strengths and weaknesses in Sudan, are in the period of British control.

Sudanese participation in national political affairs gradually evolved under British control. For most practical purposes, this participation was a phenomenon of the northern Sudan. Few southern Sudanese were active in "national" affairs, and increasingly the southern region was separated from the north. In this context, the mechanisms of participation were defined in the framework of a basically Muslim society, and Islamic themes were of importance in this situation. For the first three decades of British control, the imperial rulers relied consciously and explicitly on a politics of notables to maintain contact with the general population. Although a few tribal leaders were recognized as having local significance, it was the leaders of major Islamic groups who were viewed by the British as representing local opinion and being the "natural leaders" of the people. Receiving particular recognition were Sayyid Ali al-Mirghani, the head of the Khatmiyyah, and Sayyid Abd al-Rahman al-Mahdi, who reorganized the followers of the Mahdi, his father, into an effective religio-political force. It was the great Sayyids who spoke for the Sudanese on major political occasions, and, generally, both the British and the majority of the northern Sudanese accepted them in this representative role. Sayyid Ali Al-Mirghani was head of the delegation that went to London in 1919 to congratulate the British monarch on victory in World War I, and he, Sayyid Abd al-Rahman, and a third religious notable were the patrons of *Hadarah al-Sudan*, the major local newspaper of the 1920s.

As leaders of large mass organizations, the two major Sayyids, Sayyid Ali al-Mirghani and Sayyid Abd al-Rahman al-Mahdi, continued to play important roles as the political situation evolved. When the modern educated Sudanese, who were a small minority of the population, began to express nationalist sentiments, they had little impact initially. However, when nationalist movements, and then political parties, received the patronage of the Sayyids, they became mass movements. This "religionization" of nationalism and politics was confirmed during the 1940s. The Graduates' Congress had been formed in 1938 as an organization expressing the views of the modern educated Sudanese. In 1942, during World War II, the Congress presented demands that the Sudan be granted self-determination at the end of the war; the British summarily rejected the Congress memorandum because they said that the Congress did not speak for the Sudanese people but simply represented a small minority. As a result, most of the politically active, educated Sudanese divided along sectarian lines, and the largest political parties to emerge by the end of World War II were those that received the patronage of the two major Sayyids and their sectarian organizations.

The Ansar, the followers of Sayyid Abd al-Rahman al-Mahdi, provided the mass support for the Ummah Party which advocated an independent Sudan. The followers of Sayyid Ali al-Mirghani provided the mass support for the advocates of the "Unity of the Nile Valley," which would mean independence in union with Egypt. In the excitement of the emergence of party politics in the 1940, many different political parties were formed. By the early 1950s, it was estimated that at least twenty-four different political groups had been organized.[6] However, as the arrangements for electing a self-governing parliament were completed, it became clear that few of these parties had the resources or support to contest elections.

By the time of the first elections, late in 1953, virtually all political groupings advocating an independent Sudan had combined in the Mahdist-supported

Ummah Party, and the "unionists" had joined together in the Khatmiyyah-supported National Unionist Party (NUP). There was a third northern party that contested the elections, the Socialist Republican Party (SRP), organized by some prominent tribal notables and others who wanted to create a party that was not "sectarian." Many informed observers at the time thought that the SRP was going to become a major political force,[7] but it won only three of the 97 parliamentary seats (compared with 50 for the NUP and 23 for the Ummah) and soon went out of existence.[8] The experience of the SRP emphasizes the significance of Sayyid-supported political organizations in the emerging parliamentary system. The importance of the politics of notables continued, but in the context of elections and a parliament.

The habits and structures of popular political participation that had been established under British rule provided the foundations for the basic institutions of the independent Sudan. A Westminster-style parliamentary system had been created with an actively competitive multiparty structure. However, the key to the actual operation of this multiparty parliamentary system was the active involvement of the major Islamic associations. The most effective means for securing mass political participation in democratic political processes was the "religionization" of party politics.

In the development of the sectarian parliamentary parties under the patronage of the major Sayyids, there was virtually no debate about whether or not Islam and democracy were compatible. It was an accepted, usually unspoken assumption that there was no contradiction. The speeches of Sayyid Abd al-Rahman and his son, Sayyid Saddiq, who was the head of the Ummah Party, reflect the transformation of Mahdism from authoritarianism to providing the ideological foundations for participation in a Western-style parliamentary system. In the discussions in the Ummah Party early in the 1950s, for example, about whether an independent Sudan should be a republic or a monarchy, Sayyid Abd al-Rahman firmly supported a republican system in a major proclamation in 1953, "since the democratic republican system is a system deeply-rooted in Islam, our pure, tolerant, and democratic religion."[9]

For most Muslims in Sudan, there was no contradiction between Islam and democracy as their country achieved independence. It seemed natural that the major political parties would be associated with major Islamic associations. Prominent Muslim leaders like Sayyid Abd al-Rahman spoke of a democratic Islamic republic, and the phrase was not controversial among northern Sudanese. Without the active political participation of the major Muslim organizations, effective popular participation in the parliamentary system would have been limited, and political parties would have been organizations simply of the small educated urban elite. For all practical purposes, the Muslim organizations made a popular parliamentary system possible in Sudan when it became independent.

ISLAM AND INDEPENDENT CENTRAL GOVERNMENTS

The new parliamentary state in the independent Sudan had many problems and some inherent weaknesses. The multiparty system was effectively tied to the political life of northern Sudanese because of its identification with Islam. Political organizations of southern Sudanese were weak and had little popular organizational basis for mobilizing support among southerners. In the north, the sectarian basis for the major parties provided mass support, but it also limited the ability of the parties to appeal effectively beyond their sectarian base. No sectarian party could become an effective "national" party and, as a result, parliamentary politics rapidly became involved in a constantly changing struggle to create coalitions and alliances in order to win or continue in the various offices of government.

The weaknesses of the parliamentary system in Sudan made the central government relatively unstable. A cycle developed in which the ineffectiveness of civilian politics would lead to a military takeover of the government. However, military regimes also had difficulties in Sudan and, after being in power for a while, faced popular opposition. When military regimes were overthrown because of this opposition, the strength of the old parliamentary parties would be reasserted, because they continued to represent large Muslim associations. As a result, the overthrow of military regimes resulted in the reestablishment of civilian parliamentary regimes basically the same as that established in 1953–1956.

The rise and fall of parliamentary politics has occurred three times since the Sudan achieved independence in 1956. The first parliamentary era came to an end with the military coup in 1958 led by Ibrahim Abboud. The October Revolution of 1964 brought an end to the Abboud era and began the second era of parliamentary politics with basically the same parties and leaders as before. The second parliamentary era came to an end with the May Revolution in 1969, which was a military coup led by Jafar al-Numayri, who ruled Sudan until 1985. At that time, popular resistance and a resulting military coup created a transition to the third parliamentary era, 1986–1989, in which the same sectarian parties ruled Sudan. The third military takeover of government in Sudan brought to power a regime that advocated the creation of an Islamic state but actively opposed the old sectarian associations under the aegis of the Islamic renewalist program of the National Islamic Front (NIF).

Major Islamic organizations advocating the establishment of a democratic and Islamic republic in Sudan were the core of multiparty and parliamentary politics in the modern Sudan. Although the Ummah and the NUP joined forces in a major attempt to exclude Sudanese Communist Party members who had been elected to parliament in 1965, the Islamic associations remained consistent supporters of multiparty politics. The Ummah Party opposition to the Abboud military regime, for example, was called the "jihad in the path of democracy."[10] The Sudan provides an important example in which Islamic parties came to power through elections and did not, once in power, establish a regime that brought an end to the multiparty system. When parliamentary periods were brought forcibly to an end, it was not by action of Islamic parties in power. The failure of multiparty, parliamentary systems was at least in part because of the inevitably sectarian nature of multiparty politics in Sudan.

ANTISECTARIAN POLITICAL OPTIONS

Some political organizations attempted to provide a nonsectarian alternative in Sudan. The largest group initially was the least effectively organized: modern-educated, secularist intellectuals. Many of the leaders of the Graduates' Congress formed in the late 1930s hoped to provide a nonsectarian basis for the developing nationalist politics. Some of the small unionist parties of the 1940s were nonsectarian. The most important of these groups was led by Ismail al-Azhari. However, in the political developments leading up to the elections of 1953, al-Azhari joined forces with the Khatmiyyah to establish the National Unionist Party. Soon after independence, a dispute within the NUP led to the creation of an explicitly Khatmiyyah party, the People's Democratic Party (PDP) and the continuation of a more nonsectarian NUP led by al-Azhari. However, the NUP continued in many ways to be led by old-style notables, and soon accommodated itself to the context of coalitions and alliances. Eventually, in the second parliamentary era, the NUP formally resumed its sectarian nature by combining with the PDP in the Democratic Unionist Party (DUP) in 1967.

Most other groups led by secularist intellectuals had limited political power. Professional associations, labor unions, and student groups could mobilize participants in demonstrations and played key roles in the revolutions of 1964 and 1985, but they did not have the organization or mass membership to compete effectively with the sectarian political parties in the parliamentary eras. The Sudanese Communist Party (SCP) was the largest and most effectively organized alternative to sectarian parties in the 1960s. In the elections of 1965, Communists and Communist "sympathizers" won eleven of the fifteen parliamentary seats especially set aside as "graduates' constituencies," but the party won no territorial constituency, and gained more than 1 percent of the vote only in Khartoum Province, where it won 11 percent.[11] The results reflected the real strength of the SCP among the educated minority and its lack of mass support. The time of greatest strength for the SCP was in the first years of the Numayri era, when Communists held many important governmental posts and articulated much of the ideology of the regime. However, a group of Communist officers failed in an attempt to overthrow Numayri in 1971, and the SCP was vigorously suppressed in the following years. It remained a small part of the opposition in exile, and in the elections in 1986 it won five of the 264 contested seats in the parliament as a minor but visible actor in the political arena.

The elite nature and gradual decline of the Communist Party and the evolution of the NUP meant that there was no civilian secular political organization to compete with the mass organization and appeal of the sectarian parties. Military rulers attempted to create alternative structures that could bypass the grassroots organizations of the Ansar and Khatmiyyah. Ibrahim Abboud attempted to create a structure of "guided democracy" that involved "a pyramid of councils from local through regional and up to central government. But it was a pyramid built from the top down, and membership at all levels would be a mixture of election and nomination in an effort to ensure an element of guidance."[12] For all practical purposes, Abboud's guided democracy was a return to the older politics of notables in which popular opinions were provided to the central government through notables chosen by and consulted by the rulers. Abboud's political structure disappeared with his overthrow in 1964. The second military ruler, Jafar Numayri, attempted to create a mass mobilization party similar to those established by Nasser in Egypt and Arab Socialists in other states. The resulting Sudan Socialist Union (SSU) maintained an administrative and bureaucratic identity until the fall of Numayri in 1985, but it had little impact on government policy and created no real sense of popular political participation. The SSU and Abboud's guided democracy did not provide effective models for secular alternatives to the mass political organizations of the sectarian parties.

A new secular alternative emerged in the early 1980s, when Numayri's policies of division of the south and Islamization led to a renewal of the civil war in the southern part of the country. The major movement organizing the resistance was the Sudan People's Liberation Movement (SPLM), organized by John Garang de Mabior. Garang affirmed that the goals of the movement were *national* liberation, not southern separatism, and he worked to create an ideological and organizational base for this national goal.[13] As the program of the SPLM was articulated in the 1980s, one of its major principles was an insistence on secularism in the political system. Even as divisions developed within the SPLM in the 1990s, all in the movement insisted upon a secularist system.

The SPLM was unable to win a significant following among northern Muslims and did not participate in the party politics of the third parliamentary era. The war in the south continued. Following the military coup in 1989, when the major civilian parties again were in exile, there were efforts to create a unified opposition to the new regime. However, even in the context of a common opposition to a regime, the SPLM made little progress in winning support among the older political organizations. The issue of secularism was a major one in discussions both with the government and among the exile opposition groups, and no unified secular alternative had emerged by the middle of the 1990s.

The third military regime, which took control of the government in 1989, is identified with the National Islamic Front (NIF), a major movement which was both Islamic rather than secular in orientation and antisectarian. The NIF is the product of the long-term development of a renewalist movement and, under the leadership of Hasan al-Turabi, is internationally visible as a part of the Islamic resurgence of the late twentieth century. In the discussions of the 1990s regarding the relationships between Islamic revival and democracy, it is the ideology and policies of the NIF, rather than the older sectarian parties, that are most frequently discussed.

ISLAMISTS AND DEMOCRACY IN SUDAN

The advocates of programs of Islamic renewal have been active in Sudanese politics since the beginning of party activities. The longer tradition of Mahdist fundamentalism had been adapted by the descendants of the Mahdi and became the foundation for the sectarian Ummah Party. However, the new style of Islamist affirmation expressed by movements like the Muslim Brotherhood, established in 1928 in Egypt, and the Jamaat-i Islami in South Asia, created in 1941, began to find advocates in Sudan by the 1940s. In each stage of the political development of Sudanese politics, the Islamists played a role that increased in importance as conditions changed over time. The experience of the Islamists in Sudan provides an important example of participation within a parliamentary political system as well as an example, in the 1990s, of an Islamist movement in power.

New-style Islamic activists have generally operated as a part of the emerging multiparty political system in Sudan since World War II. There was a general development from being a small organization among students and intellectuals into being a political association that worked to win mass popular support as a political party. In all of these phases, there was little debate about the compatability of Islam and democracy. This compatability was part of the basic assumptions of any political platform formulated by Islamists. Differences among the Islamists arose, rather, over the manner in which the Islamist movement should participate in the Sudanese political system. It was not until after the military coup of 1989 that the Islamists were in a position to define basic political ground rules, which made the developments of the 1990s an important new phase in the evolution of the Islamist movement in Sudan.

The emergence of an influential Islamic Sudanese movement began at the end of World War II. Although the British feared the development of a modern-style pan-Islamic movement in Sudan during World War I, and there were various groups advocating activist Islamic renewal in the 1920s and 1930s, it was not until the 1940s that an effective Islamic revivalist movement began to be organized.[14] At that time, Sudanese students who had come into contact with the Muslim Brotherhood while studying in Egypt, began, along with Egyptian supporters, to establish groups in Sudan. At the same time, students in the Hantoub secondary school began to form a group which, when they came to the university in Khartoum (then called Gordon Memorial College), became formally organized as the Islamic Liberation Movement (ILM).[15]

By the early 1950s, these two tendencies represented a number of overlapping and interacting groups. After tensions arose among competing leaders, a major congress was held in 1954 that brought together most of the people involved in both groupings. This congress adopted the name of the Muslim Brotherhood (al-Ikhwan al-Muslimun), in recognition of the ties to the broader Islamic movement, but it also "resolved that the movement was to be 'a Sudan-based' movement (i.e., not directly connected with the Egyptian group) and that it would maintain its independence from all other political parties."[16] The new organization defined itself as "an educational movement calling for complete Islamic reform."[17] Although a few people opposed the resolutions of the congress, they had little impact, and by 1955 the organization represented a unified movement that was ready to act in the context of the independent Sudan.

The Brotherhood did not create a new political party to contest elections but it did participate in the political arena. It did not reject the political system but worked within it, advocating some specific policies. It was actively anticommunist and also, following the suppression of the Muslim Brotherhood in Egypt by the new regime led by Nasser, opposed Nasser's influence in Sudan. The major goal of the Brotherhood was the ultimate establishment of an Islamic order in Sudan. As a result, its first major political initiative in the political era of independence was the formation of the Islamic Front for the Constitution (IFC), a "national front"-style organization with the Brotherhood at its center advocating the adoption of an Islamic constitution. The IFC's "model constitution" proposed "a parliamentary system with regional devolution in a unitary state."[18] There was also emphasis on economic and social justice. Through the IFC, the Brotherhood made a major effort to educate the public about the nature of an Islamic constitution, but it worked as a pressure group rather than a political party. The IFC "did not ignore the parties. Instead, it tried to pressure and embarrass them about Islam into accepting its call" for an Islamic constitution.[19]

The constitutional commission that had been established after independence did not accept the proposal for an explicitly Islamic constitution. However, most major political leaders proclaimed their support for some type of Islamically based political system, and the IFC played an important role in making the issue of an Islamic constitution part of the northern Sudanese political agenda. The IFC itself collapsed in 1958, when its leaders clashed with the leaders of the Brotherhood over the issue of putting candidates forward in the 1958 elections. The Ikhwan saw itself as a nonpartisan association, and when the IFC attempted to put forward candidates, it lost Ikhwan support and disappeared.

The Ikhwan itself remained a small but visible interest group acting within the political system rather than becoming either a political party or an antigovernment revolutionary group. However, by late 1958, the Ikhwan leadership had become strongly critical of the dominant sectarian parties. On the day before the Abboud military coup, the Brotherhood newspaper carried an editorial by al-Rashid al-Tahir, the leader of the Ikhwan, in which he stated, "There is no question that the democratic system is the best humanity has succeeded to devise after a long struggle. But disaster comes always at the hands of those who abuse the system and cause it to degenerate into mere vacuous forms."[20] The Brotherhood affirmed its belief in democracy but announced its approval of the new military regime in the following days.

Despite the first responses, the Abboud regime's general restrictions on civilian political groups, including censorship of newspapers and the forced suspension of the publication of Ikhwan papers, soon brought the Brotherhood into opposition, along with most of the other civilian political organizations. Public opposition was most visible among the students in Khartoum University and, since the Ikhwan was the largest group within the Khartoum University Student Union (KUSU), the Brotherhood was an important voice in the call for a return to civilian government. However, al-Rashid al-Tahir, the Ikhwan leader, joined with some discontented military officers in an unsuccessful coup attempt in 1959, and his imprisonment cost the movement its most prominent leader. More important, his involvement in the coup attempt created a significant controversy within the organization and the movement outside of the university "lapsed into a phase of inaction."[21] As a result, although most people in the movement supported the aims of the opposition organized by the old parliamentary parties, with the exception of the student activists, they were not an effective part of the opposition until the events leading up to the revolution of October, 1964.

In 1964, the Sudanese Muslim Brotherhood entered a new phase in its development. This began with the return to the Sudan of Hasan al-Turabi, who had been active in the movement in the 1950s but went to Paris in 1959 to complete work on a doctorate in law. Turabi had returned briefly to Sudan in 1962, when he was influential in convincing a Brotherhood congress to adopt a strategy of creating an Islamic united front. In the summer of 1964, Turabi returned to Sudan with his doctorate to teach in the Khartoum University Law School. He immediately involved himself in the events leading up to the October Revolution, delivering a major public speech in which he argued that the solution for the problems faced by Sudan, especially the civil war that was intensifying in the southern region, was the end of military rule. This brought the Brotherhood back to the center of the political arena and catapulted Turabi into a major leadership position in the emerging Islamic front.

The Brotherhood played an important role in the events that led to the overthrow of the Abboud regime in October, 1964. The Brotherhood's experience was similar to other nonsectarian political organizations who were active in organizing the opposition, such as the Communists, the Nasserites, and various professional groups. Although they had been important in driving Abboud from power, in the transition to the second parliamentary era, it became clear that the old political organizations remained powerful. The PDP—the explicitly Khatmiyyah party—boycotted the elections, but the Ummah and NUP won a combined total of 130 of the 173 seats in the new parliament elected in 1965.

There was considerable debate within the Islamist movement over the most effective structures for the new era. Turabi had emphasized the importance of moving beyond the elitist format of a small association of highly dedicated people. As Turabi emerged as the leading figure in the Ikhwan, his concept of creating a mass Islamic organization became the basis of Ikhwan development. At the end of 1964, the Brotherhood created the Islamic Charter Front (ICF) as a popular political organization. However, this was not a single, integrated structure. The ICF was created on the model of a national front, bringing together various Islamically oriented groups and individuals. In this structure, the Ikhwan "maintained for itself, as a precaution, independence from the Front in its own affairs while maintaining full control" of the ICF's actions.[22] This was not the unified mass organization envisioned by Turabi, and his later assessment of this era was that the dual structure led to tensions between the leaders and structures of the Ikhwan inner core and those of the larger ICF.[23] These tensions were heightened by the fact that the ICF contested the elections in 1965 and 1968 with relatively little success, winning only seven of a total of 173 parliamentary seats in 1965 (with about 5 percent of the total vote) and five of 218 seats in 1968.[24]

The Islamic movement, both the more numerous supporters of the ICF and the Ikhwan inner core, was firmly committed to a democratic form of government. The ICF promulgated its Islamic Charter early in 1965; it called "for a presidential system, regional devolution and an economic system that fostered social justice without compromising democracy."[25] The ICF actively promoted this program in the constitutional discussions of the time, and succeeded in getting important Islamic references included in the permanent constitution, which was drafted by the National Commission for the Constitution but was not approved before the second parliamentary era was brought to an end by the military coup of 1969.

In the second parliamentary era, the Islamist movement had moved from organizing a nonparty interest group (the Islamic Front for the Constitution) to creating a national front organization that participated as a political party. It identified itself with the forces promoting a multiparty parliamentary system, but was, along with the Sudanese Communist Party, one of the few effective political organizations that advocated a change from a political system dominated by sectarian-based political parties. Although the Brotherhood succeeded in ensuring that the adoption of an Islamic constitution and implementation of the Shariah would be major political issues, it was not successful in changing the essentially sectarian basis for Sudanese parliamentary politics.

Divisions within the movement and lack of electoral success brought the Brotherhood to a position of weakness by 1969. At a general congress in April, 1969, the anti-Turabi group, favoring a more restricted membership and a strategy of aloofness from society inspired by the writings of the Egyptian Islamist radical, Sayyid Qutb, almost overcame the Turabi leadership. As a result, it was a divided movement that faced the challenge of the new military regime led by Numayri that came to power the following month, in May, 1969. With the end of multiparty, parliamentary politics came the end of the ICF as well.

For almost the first decade of the Numayri era, the Brotherhood was part of the banned opposition. The Numayri regime had a pronounced leftist, anti-Ikhwan orientation at the outset, and the Brotherhood worked to organize opposition immediately after the coup. Leaders of the old major political parties attempted to deal with Numayri, but after a short time the Ummah Party, the DUP, and the Ikhwan created the National Front in exile to coordinate opposition to the new military government. A Mahdist revolt inside Sudan in March, 1970, was crushed by the new regime, leaving the National Front as the major organization of opposition. Within the Sudan, after the failure of the Mahdist revolt, the Ikhwan organization among the students was the major source of opposition. In 1973, in the Sha'ban Uprising, major Ikhwan-led student demonstrations received support from the Railway Workers Union and other professional associations, who went on strike. However, the government suppressed the uprising and the opposition shifted to activities that could be organized outside of Sudan. One result of these efforts was a major attempt to coordinate an invasion with internal popular demonstrations in 1976. The failure of this major effort brought significant divisions within the National Front and growing mistrust among the opposition of the long-term intentions of Sayyid Sadiq al-Mahdi, the leader of the Ummah.

The experience of opposition in the early Numayri years brought the Ikhwan and its leadership to an important point of transition. Three important elements helped to determine how this transition affected the position of the Brotherhood regarding the desirable political system for Sudan and organization's long-term political goals.

First, both in the Shab'an Uprising and the 1976 invasion, many in the Ikhwan felt that the old political parties had proven to be unreliable allies. These parties also began to work with the Sudan Communist Party in opposition, raising doubts about the prospects of support from the opposition groups for the Brotherhood's long-term Islamic goals. In broader terms, the Westminster-style parliamentary system seemed inevitably tied to the sectarian political parties, and calls for the return to "civilian politics" seemed tied to advocating a return to the domination of Sudan by those sectarian parties. As a result, Ikhwan definitions of democracy began to evolve, with greater emphasis on consultation and popular consensus, within the framework of a clearly defined structure of institutions for all major sectors and needs of society.

This evolution of political goals was reflected in a second element of the Ikhwan experience in the 1970s: the dramatic reorganization of the structure of the Ikhwan itself. This involved "sweeping internal reforms" that resulted in the "complete democratization of the structures of the movement," giving increased power to the students and younger members and reducing the power of the older organizational establishment.[26] In these new structures, it is possible to see the somewhat different approach to the principles of consultation and consensus involved in the Ikhwan critique of the old Sudanese political system. The democratic model envisioned by the Ikhwan was evolving, but the mistrust of sectarian-based multiparty politics did not represent a departure from the Ikhwan's established assumption that an Islamic system was a democratic one.

A third important element in the transition of the Brotherhood in the 1970s was the increasing independence of the Brotherhood's ideological formulations. In the first three decades of the Islamic movement's history in Sudan, major Islamists from outside Sudan provided the most important conceptualizations for the developing ideology. In the early years, the writings of Hasan al-Banna of the Ikhwan in Egypt and Abu Al-Ala al-Mawdudi, the South Asian Islamist, were very influential in shaping the thought of Sudanese Islamists.[27] In the 1960s, some of the Sudanese Islamists became influenced by the writings of Sayyid Qutb. However, during the 1970s, many of the members engaged in intensive study and thought, often under the conditions of forced inactivity created by detention or exile. This resulted in a changing theoretical orientation for the movement, which began articulating theoretical positions on organization, the propagation of the message, the position of women, and other critical areas so that the movement no longer relied on "the experiences of other Islamic movements."[28]

Hasan al-Turabi was becoming an internationally visible articulator of a new style of Islamist ideology, which was reflected, for example, in his small book on the role of women that first appeared in 1973[29] and his broader call for a renewal of the foundations of Islamic jurisprudence, which appeared in 1980.[30] In this emerging perspective, there was a greater emphasis on converting society than on gaining political position. Turabi told an interviewer in 1982 that the "State is only the political expression of an Islamic society and . . . an Islamic state evolves after an Islamic society."[31] The goal continued to be defined as a democratic system: "The Islamic state is based on consultation or *shura*, that means a democratic society where everybody should participate."[32]

This organizational and ideological transition paved the way for the Brotherhood's participation in Numayri's policy of national reconciliation in 1977. Major leaders of the Ummah Party and the Ikhwan returned to Sudan and began a policy of guided cooperation with the Numayri regime. Some of the restrictions on Brotherhood activities were lifted, and a variety of new educational, social, and cultural organizations were formed by people in the Islamic movement. In 1979, Turabi was named the attorney general, with responsibility for the review of laws to establish conformity with the Shariah. The Ikhwan also encouraged and participated in the establishment of financial institutions and banks run in accord with Islamic economic principles.

Cooperation with the policy of national reconciliation involved a high level of risk for Turabi and his supporters in the Ikhwan. Many of the old opposition groups condemned the action and the Brotherhood lost some ground among student activists. In addition, the regime remained clearly under the control of Numayri, and the Ikhwan could thus be identified with policies that it did not in fact favor. On the positive side, the new situation provided opportunities for active educational and social reform efforts. This was in accord with the broader ideological position that Islamization of society was the most important task of the movement and that political power was not the first priority at that stage of social development.

The most dramatic and controversial development in the era of Ikhwan involvement with the Numayri regime came when Numayri promulgated the "September Laws" in 1983. This involved a series of presidential decrees for the purpose of the instant implementation of the Shariah. Although these decrees were in accord with the general goals of the Brotherhood, no major person in the movement was involved in the process either of drawing up the decrees or of deciding upon their implementation. As a result, there were a number of aspects of the new decrees about which the leadership of the Ikhwan had reservations.[33] On the whole, however, the Brotherhood welcomed the decrees, seeing the new situation as an important breakthrough and an opportunity. Turabi later noted that "although the Shariah measures in the era of the May Revolution were nothing more than a program of legal regulations, the movement directed [this Islamization] into a deeper and more profound direction."[34]

The situation also provided the opportunity for the Brotherhood to expand its base of popular support. A huge parade on the occasion of the first anniversary of the September Laws demonstrated the substantial strength of the Ikhwan. As Numayri's power waned, he became increasingly suspicious of the Ikhwan, and eventually he arrested the leaders and actively suppressed the movement early in 1985. However, Numayri himself was overthrown in April, 1985, by a military coup, and the Transitional Military Council (TMC) pledged to hold national elections in a year. Despite objections by the leaders of sectarian and secular opposition groups, the TMC allowed the Ikhwan to participate in the politics of transition.

In the new context, the Brotherhood took a major organizational step in creating the National Islamic Front (NIF) in April, 1985. This was not a front within which the Brotherhood continued to maintain a separate identity. Instead, under Turabi's leadership, the Brotherhood was incorporated into the NIF, creating a single mass Islamist movement that would work actively for the continuing Islamization of society and could also participate directly in the party politics of the time.

The third period of multiparty parliamentary politics was similar in many ways to the two previous experiences. The major parties continued to be the old sectarian parties, the Ummah and the DUP, who together won about 70 percent of the votes in northern Sudan in the 1986 elections. (Elections were not held in most parts of the south because of the continuing civil war.) The new factor on the political scene was the power of the NIF. In contrast to the very limited success of the Islamic Charter Front in the elections of the 1960s, the NIF won almost 20 percent of the vote in northern Sudan. Not only did the NIF win twenty-three of the twenty-eight graduates' constituencies, it also won twenty-eight seats in geographical constituencies. Although most of the NIF successes were in the major urban areas, it gained more than 15 percent of the vote in the largely rural Ummah stronghold of Darfur Province.

The strength of the NIF in the 1986 elections reflected a relatively strong hope that there would not be a return to sectarian "politics as usual." The antisectarian options were basically the secularist groups and the NIF. Various professional associations and trade unions with secularist perspectives had been important in organizing antigovernment demonstrations in the last weeks of the Numayri regime. However, the National Gathering for the Salvation of the Homeland, which they formed as a national front with the old sectarian parties, was not an effective mass political organization. It broke up in the electoral campaigns of 1985–86, and no secularist party emerged as a significant electoral force. The Sudanese Communist Party had limited appeal. The only large organization advocating a secularist position was the Sudan People's Liberation Movement (SPLM), the primarily southern movement led by John Garang. The SPLM refused to accept the TMC, and continued to wage the civil war in the south. In this context, the leftist and secularist groups in the north had little political appeal or power. It was the NIF that represented the most effective option for those northerners who hoped to transcend sectarian politics.

By 1989, the older dynamics of shifting coalitions and rivalries had been reestablished. The level of violence in the civil war had increased, there were growing economic difficulties, and there was little sense of political stability or direction in the central government. For a short time the NIF had been part of a coalition government, but most of the time it was in opposition. It did not advocate the overthrow of the system, but rather maintained its pressure for the continuation of the implementation of the Shariah within the framework of the parliamentary system. Its long-term strategy continued to rely on the importance of the Islamization of society as the precursor to the establishment of an Islamic state. It remained pragmatic in terms of tactics, operating within the ground rules of multiparty parliamentary politics.

The situation was once again transformed when a military group under the leadership of Umar Hasan al-Bashir took control of the government. The new rulers were Islamically oriented but were not directly associated with the NIF and Hasan Turabi.[35] NIF leadership was arrested along with the leaders of the other political parties. However, the Bashir government rapidly began to utilize NIF people, and within a few weeks could legitimately be identified as an NIF-influenced regime. Turabi and Bashir established a complex relationship in which Turabi had no formal position in the government but was the ideological guide for the regime. NIF people were in many important positions of power, but many outside observers tended to ignore the fact that what has come to be called the National Salvation Revolution was an operating alliance between Turabi and Bashir, and not simply an NIF creation.

ISLAMISTS AND NATIONAL UNITY

The leaders of the National Salvation Revolution (NSR) affirm their adherence to the ideals of democracy but they also affirm the necessity of breaking the old cycle of civilian-military rule in Sudan. Now, more than at any time since independence, there is a growing agreement that the old style multiparty system should not simply be restored. The platforms promulgated by most of the opposition groups, even those based on the old parties, note the importance of avoiding a return to simple sectarian party politics. In the framework of the ideology of the NIF as developed by Hasan al-Turabi, the NSR government is working to create an alternative to the sectarian politics of the old-style parliamentary politics. In that framework, there is also a commitment to opposing leftist secular alternatives that would deny the necessity of an Islamic orientation for the state in Sudan.

The major challenge to all who are working to define an effective political system for Sudan is the continuing civil war. Since a military mutiny of southern Sudanese troops in 1955, there have been tensions and open fighting in the southern regions of Sudan. In 1972, Numayri succeeded in negotiating a settlement based on recognition of southern political autonomy. This agreement created the basis for almost a decade during which no major fighting occurred. However, Numayri's unilateral attempt to partition the southern region led to a resumption of fighting in the early 1980s, with the SPLA leading the militant opposition. The imposition of the September Laws added strength to the opposition from the primarily non-Muslim southern Sudanese. In this context, the demand for a *secular* democratic system became one of the most important parts of the SPLA's platform and negotiating position.

During the 1980s, the achievement of national unity and a settlement for the civil war became closely tied to the issues of the relationship between Islam and the state. The SPLA refused to participate in the politics of the third parliamentary era, and the conflict in the southern region intensified in that period. As a result, the regime of Bashir and the NIF faced the major challenges of national disunity and civil war when it came to power in 1989, and it made little real progress toward a negotiated settlement in its first six years in power. There were many attempts at negotiation but all foundered on the stark contradiction between the irreducible demand for a secular state by the SPLA and the absolute commitment to an Islamically based political system by the NIF and Bashir.

The development of Islamist ideology in Sudan since independence did not provide a significant, readily available foundation for policies of national unity in the 1990s. In the early, formative years before 1956, the issue of a religiously plural-ist country was not important in the primarily northern political arena in which the early Islamic Liberation Movement and Brotherhood operated. It was not until the second parliamentary era and the Islamic Charter Front that formal program-matic positions needed to be taken by the Islamists. The Abboud regime's mis-handling of the southern question provided the basis for the dramatic attack on military rule made by Turabi in his speech in 1964 when he returned to Sudan. However, the substance of Turabi's position was a critique of military rule, and not an analysis of the southern question from an Islamist perspective.

The ICF participated in the discussions of the 1960s, and was a participant in the Round Table Conference convened in 1965, whose declaration laid important foundations for the 1972 agreement. In these discussions, the ICF position was con-sistently and basically traditional in its interpretation of the desired state structure. The state defined in the Front's charter was democratic, but needed a clear Islamic identification. When the Round Table Conference established its terms of refer-ence, it was agreed that "any scheme which advocated separation or preserving the *status quo* should be excluded"; on this basis, the proposal presented by the South-ern Front was excluded because it implied a separate state, and that of the ICF was excluded because it "implied preserving the existing constitutional and adminis-trative set-up, namely the centralized system of government."[36]

In the subsequent discussions of the National Constitution Committee, the ICF continued its advocacy for identifying the state as Islamic, but the implications of this were relatively standard. The state was to be democratic, unitary, and central-ized, with a multiparty, representative system of government. The rights of non-Muslims were seen as fully protected by the traditional Islamic definitions of the roles of the People of the Book in society. In this, the ICF was simply reflecting the general spirit of Islamic movements of the 1960s. The politically radical implica-tions of the ideas of Mawdudi were only beginning to be explored by Sayyid Qutb in Egypt, and in Pakistan Mawdudi's movement was operating within the more standard framework. The international organization of the Egyptian Muslim Brotherhood in exile in the 1960s reflects this nonradical interpretation. A pam-phlet published in 1963 by the Islamic Centre in Geneva provides a clear statement of what might be taken as the interpretation of the "establishment" Brotherhood of the day: "the outward forms and functions of such a state [an Islamic state] need not necessarily correspond to historical precedents. All that is required of a state in order that it might with justice be described as 'Islamic' is the embodiment in its constitution and practice of those clearcut, unequivocal ordinances laid down in the Qur'an and authentic Traditions which have a direct bearing on the commu-nity's political life. . . . They are of such a nature as to leave the widest possible scope to the needs of any particular time or socio-economic situation."[37]

Such a general position did not provide a solid foundation for presenting specific plans for conflict resolution or national unity in Sudan. This remained the basic stance of the Brotherhood until the intellectual and organizational reorientation of the late 1970s. When the Numayri regime, for example, began the negotiations leading up to the 1972 agreement, the Muslim Brotherhood in opposition noted its rejection of any settlement that did not recognize the principle of an Islamic constitution for Sudan.[38] However, in the era of National Reconciliation, in Turabi's words, as the movement became more directly involved in state and society, it "established a positive strategy toward the south, calling for its inclusion in the Sudanese Islamic project rather than ignoring or or separating from it."[39] This reflected debates within the movement in the 1970s in which some argued that the separation of the south would remove an obstacle to the establishment of an Islamic order, but Turabi's view won out.[40] Instead, the Brotherhood began to organize missionary and welfare efforts in the southern region. One important part of this was providing support and recognition for southern Muslims.

The Brotherhood also began to rearticulate the Islamic positions on non-Muslims living within an Islamic society. Turabi began a broader definition of the Islamic tradition. He continued to base much discussion on the concept of the People of the Book, but he also gave substantial emphasis to the experience of the early Muslim community in Medina. In that situation immediately following the Hijrah, when Muhammad and the early Muslims moved from Mecca to Medina, the community as a whole was religiously pluralistic, with that condition defined in what came to be called the Constitution of Medina.[41]

This changing articulation of the general principles did not result in a significant change of Islamist positions specifically regarding the issue of Sudanese national unity in the third period of parliamentary politics. The primary political goal of the NIF in that era was to oppose the abrogation of the September Laws and accomplish as much implementation of Islamic law as possible. The NIF tended not to participate in attempts to negotiate a settlement to the civil war, and its advocacy of an Islamic state brought secularist groups and non-Muslim groups to see the NIF as a major enemy.

The NIF made some efforts to define an Islamic state in terms that could include a significant level of religious diversity, within a relatively decentralized political system. The Sudan Charter of the National Islamic Front, which was issued in 1987, defined a system of provincial autonomy for all parts of Sudan and did not single out a special arrangement for the south: "The National Islamic Front stands for the adoption of a federal system in the constitutional regulation of decentralization in the Sudan, with equal regard for all regions, or with special arrangements for some, and through any process of gradual transition."[42] Within this structure, regions with a non-Muslim majority could opt for the implementation of laws based on the customs or religion prevailing in the area. This charter affirmed the rights of adherents of all believers to practice their faiths, but recognized that Islam was the faith of the majority of the Sudanese, which gave it a special place. The charter also stated that "none shall be legally barred from any public office only because of his adherence to any religious affiliation."[43] This meant that, in principle, the head of state could be a non-Muslim.

The government established by the NSR in 1989 inherited this general set of formulations. In terms of the issue of national unity, there has been important continuity. The Bashir regime has insisted upon the importance of an Islamic state in Sudan, but within the framework of a federal system with the option of special regional autonomy. Like the earlier NIF, the NSR maintains that the majority of the Sudanese are Muslim and want a state that is Islamically defined. The Bashir government has consistently proposed a national referendum on having an Islamic state. Most people agree that the majority of Sudanese would vote for an Islamic state even if, in a multiparty election, that same majority would not vote for the NIF. Secularist and non-Muslim groups still clearly are a minority in the contemporary Sudanese political scene. It is this insistence on an Islamic state that clashes directly with the demands by the SPLA for a "secular democratic" state, and this direct contradiction is an important obstacle to any negotiated settlement between the government and the SPLA.

THE ISLAMIST STATE AND DEMOCRACY

The Islamist government of the National Salvation Revolution has made a major effort to transform the structures of politics in Sudan. The actions have been taken within the framework of a formal commitment to the establishment of an Islamic state and social order. These have involved some continuities with past programs and practices but have also involved new initiatives.

The new regime has attempted to create a new-style political system. The new system is federal in principle, reflecting much in the older NIF charter. However, the federal structure is directly related to the mechanisms of popular participation, and the system is not multiparty. Instead, local, regional, and provincial consultative conferences are seen as a pyramid of representative bodies with a national conference at the top. In official terms, the result is a "devolution of central government into 26 states and 70 districts," with the popular exercise of power, "much of it on tribal and geographical bases rather than in centralised patterns (central government or national parties)."[44] The formal structures of this system were established in a step-by-step process, starting with local conferences, and effective power was transferred even more slowly. This reflected the gradualism of the NIF charter, which noted that "federalism requires the setting up of adequate infrastructure—material and human, and presumes the provision of sufficient financial resources independently raised by or transferred to the regions. All this may not be possible except through a process or a period of preparation and gradual transition."[45]

In actual practice, most control over government policy and power remains in the hands of the leaders of the central government. However, there have been important structural changes moving in the direction of the increasing civilianization of the government. From the very beginning, the special relationship between Bashir and Turabi and between the government and the NIF meant that this was not a purely military regime. In 1993, the Revolutionary Command Council, which had been the core of the participation of the military in governmental affairs, was formally disbanded, and its powers were transferred to a reorganized council of ministers and the Transitional National Assembly, which represented the central government level of the system of popular conferences.

In addition to the governmental structures, other important popular organizations were created. Hasan Turabi established the Conference of Arab and Muslim Peoples, with its secretariat in Khartoum. This is an international organization that attempts to bring together people from Islamic movements throughout the Muslim world. It holds periodic congresses and has made efforts to mediate disputes among Muslim powers. It is not a mass political organization, but it does provide ways in which Sudanese Islamist groups can establish and maintain contact with groups around the world. One example of this is the assistance given by the congress in the convening of a major congress on interreligious dialogue that was held in October, 1994, in Sudan. Among the participants were Cardinal Francis Arinze of the Roman Catholic Church and Archbishop Gabriel Zubeir, secretary-general of the Sudanese Council of Churches, as well as Hasan al-Turabi and Sudanese government leaders. One result of the conference was the establishment of the Sudanese Association for Dialogue among Religions.[46]

In general terms, one characteristic of the strategy of the Islamist movement in the 1990s has been to encourage the creation of nongovernmental associations and councils. According to the perspectives developed in the late 1970s, such groups can be important mechanisms in the Islamization of society. These are not political organizations, and activities of nongovernmental organizations in general have been tightly controlled by the government. Groups that do not have ties with the NIF, such as some human rights organizations, associations of intellectuals, and trade unions, have difficulties, and their leaders are frequently detained. The repression of such groups has been regular reported by international human rights organizations such as Amnesty International and Human Rights Watch/Africa.[47]

In practice, the emerging political system has limited the opportunities for expression of political opposition. Intellectuals critical of the regime have been detained, jailed, and, at times, tortured. Expressions of opposition on university campuses have been actively suppressed, in an ironic outcome of the success of a movement which in its own early days was an important part of campus dissent.

Religious organizations that are not actively involved in supporting the Islamist program have been subjected to severe constraints and, on occasion, attacks. Not only have the old sectarian political parties been banned, but the popular religious organizations on which they are based have also been suppressed. Properties of the

Khatmiyyah and of the Mirghani family have been confiscated, for example, and events of the order, such as the commemoration in May, 1994, of the anniversary of the death of Sayyid Ali al-Mirghani, have been disrupted by government security forces. Even the previously non-politically activist group, the Ansar al-Sunnah, has had its leader arrested and meetings disrupted.[48]

Christian organizations have been restricted in their activities and subject to suppression. Even church leaders who work with the government, like Archbishop Gabriel Zubeir, criticize "the state of religious intolerance in the country."[49] Pope John Paul II, during a visit to Khartoum in 1993, took the opportunity to publicly criticize the regime's record and call for more effective recognition of religious pluralism in Sudan. Christian leaders in the opposition go further and accuse the regime of active suppression of Christians and of undertaking a program of forced conversion to Islam.

The record of the National Salvation Revolution is mixed. It has worked to create new structures that could avoid the problems of the old sectarian multiparty system. These new structures have, in concept, been imaginative adaptations to the Sudanese context of the principles of consensus and consultation. However, because of the strength of opposition forces and also the dedication of the leadership to the cause of Islamization, the new system has also used methods of repression and violent suppression to overcome challenges. The commitment to Islamization is itself a major obstacle in resolving the most important problem facing any government in Khartoum, the problem of bringing an end to the civil war and creating a real sense of national unity in which both northern and southern Sudanese can participate. On this issue, the experience of the third parliamentary era is a reminder that the multiparty parliamentary system also had major difficulties in providing a sound basis for national unity.

CONCLUSION

The Sudanese experience provides an important example of the complexities of the relationships between Islam, Islamic movements, and democracy in the modern world. Because of the continuing strength and adaptive abilities of the older Islamic associations, the issue of defining a democratic system in Sudan is not simply a choice between secular and Islamist alternatives. Instead, because of the modern experiences of Sudan, the alternative of a multiparty, Westminster-style parliamentary system has become identified with sectarian politics, creating a third option. This option remained, throughout the three periods of parliamentary politics, the one chosen by the majority of the people of Sudan in open and fair elections.

The sectarian political system was not able to resolve the basic issues facing Sudan. As a result, each of the three experiences of multiparty, parliamentary politics came to an end with popularly supported military coups. Sectarian politics could not create a viable basis for *national* unity. As a result, a variety of nonsectarian alternatives have been tried under the leadership and control of the military regimes.

Under current conditions, a fully secular political system would have to be imposed by force on Sudan. The majority of the Sudanese would, if given a choice in a referendum, opt for a political system that is in some way identified with Islam. However, a fully Islamic political system could only be established by force in the southern Sudan, unless the southern Sudanese could be persuaded that such a system would guarantee them equal rights and opportunities not provided by previous definitions of an Islamic state.

The leaders of the National Salvation Revolution and the National Islamic Front have undertaken an effort to establish a nonsectarian but clearly Islamic system. The establishment of such a system also clearly requires a degree of force. The continuing civil war and the suppression of opposition in the northern Sudan reflect this. However, the northern Sudanese people have shown themselves in the October Revolution of 1964 and the opposition to Numayri in 1985 to be capable of overthrowing military regimes. Such a revolution has not faced the NSR/NIF regime, providing it with a continuing opportunity to develop new institutions and structures for popular participation.

The conflict, in principle, is not between Islam and democracy in Sudan. The Islamists have long participated in democratic politics, and define their desired political system in democratic terms. The real conflict is between different options for defining the relationship between Islam and democracy in the Sudanese context. The established relationship is the failed system of sectarian politics. The option of a secular political system seems improbable under current conditions. The kind of option remaining is to create a nonsectarian system that is both Islamically identifiable and able to include, voluntarily, secularist and non-Muslim Sudanese. In the mid-1990s, the NSR/NIF regime seems to have made significant progress in changing the sectarian nature of participatory politics, but has failed to create an inclusive system attractive to secularists and non-Muslims.

FIVE

Pakistan

The Many Faces of an Islamic Republic

Since Pakistan's creation as a Muslim homeland in 1947 and its designation in its first constitution in 1956 as an Islamic Republic, religion, identity, and democracy have been intertwined and manipulated.[1] Military and non-military governments, religious and secular political parties, and movements with competing agendas and interests have appealed to Islam in order to enhance their legitimacy and to support a variety of political, economic, and class interests. Islam has been adopted in diverse ways to legitimate both government and opposition movements and to rationalize a range of options from democracy to political and religious authoritarianism.

Pakistan has struggled throughout its history with the meaning of its Islamic identity. A review of Islam's role in Pakistan reveals the diverse and often contending usages of Islam, its linkage to democratic claims, and, too often, its potential to divide rather than unite. At a time when many are concerned about political Islam and its compatibility with democratization, Pakistan offers an extensive test case of the role of religion in government-engineered state building, as well as of the ability of Islamic organizations to participate within the political system. The Jamaat-i Islami and other Islamic organizations and parties in Pakistan offer an instructive example of participation within a multiparty political system. Islam and democracy have often existed more in form than substance, subordinated to political and social realities rather than acting as a controlling or guiding forces. Yet, throughout Pakistan's history, governments have had to contend with "Islamic politics" in a society in which religion, identity, legitimacy, and democracy have often been intertwined.

ISLAM AND STATE FORMATION

From the late 1930s, when Mohammed Ali Jinnah (1876–1948) and the Muslim League (founded in 1906) mobilized mass support for an independent Pakistan with the cry, "Islam in Danger," religion has been a factor in Pakistan's political development: a source of national identity, legitimacy, and social protest. Muslim nationalism was supposed to unite almost two thirds of South Asia's Muslims in a country that was in fact a composite of diverse linguistic, ethnic, regional, and cultural identities/communities, and whose two wings (West and East Pakistan) were separated by more than a thousand miles of Indian territory. Although Pakistan's Muslim nationalism was rooted in an appeal to a common Muslim heritage and call for a Muslim homeland, its meaning (the relationship of Islam to the state) has been as diverse as its population. Although Mohammed Ali Jinnah and Muhammad Iqbal, fathers of the Pakistan movement, shared a common call for the creation of Pakistan, their ideological visions differed significantly. Jinnah's two-nation theory maintained that the Muslims of the subcontinent shared a common cultural identity and thus constituted a separate community from Hindus. Muslim nationalism was based on the use of religion to provide a common bond and to mold disparate ethnic/linguistic communities into a single nation. However, for Jinnah, Islam was simply the common cultural heritage and identity of the Muslim majority; Pakistan was to be a Muslim homeland or state in this sense. It was to be a secular state "without any distinction of cast, creed, or sect."[2]

In contrast, Iqbal, the renowned Islamic modernist and poet-philosopher, who had fired the imaginations of many Muslims with his call for a Muslim state in the 1930s, differed from Jinnah in regarding Islam as a religio-social order. He and many others believed that the creation of Pakistan as a Muslim homeland and its emergence as a modern state necessitated an Islamic state, one whose institutions and law should be based upon Islam.

The ulama of the Indian subcontinent were divided in their response to the Pakistan movement. Many regarded nationalism and the modern nation-state as a Western concept and part of the West's attempt to divide the Muslim world. They believed that the partition of "Muslim India" would weaken and divide the Muslim community. They also distrusted Jinnah, whom they regarded as a Westernized Muslim and secularist, inimical to Islam and Islamic principles, and whom they believed would establish a secular, not an Islamic, state. However, after independence, those who were in Pakistan accepted the political reality. As a result, a number of religio-political parties—such as the Jamiyyat i-Ulama-Islam (the Organization of Islamic Ulama), the Jamiyyat i-Ulama-i-Pakistan (the Organization of Pakistani Ulama), and the Jamaat-i Islami (the Islamic Society)— became prominent in Pakistani politics. They proved to be vocal although diffuse voices for an Islamically oriented state and constitution throughout Pakistan's subsequent history.

The definition and implementation of Muslim identity in Pakistani state and society remained ambiguous. Its early years were occupied with the reality of nation-building. The Ahmadi affair of 1953 and the constitution of 1956 reveal the interplay of religion, identity, and politics and the extent to which Islam was a source of conflict and compromise rather than an effective source of national unity.

The issue of religion and national identity emerged in 1953 during the constitutional debates. Religious leaders had pressed for an amendment declaring the Ahmadiyya a non-Muslim minority. They maintained that the founder of the Ahmadiyya, Mirza Ghulam Ahmad (1835–1908), had proclaimed that he was a prophet and thus denied an essential Islamic belief, that Muhammad is the last of the prophets. Moreover, they demanded that Pakistan's foreign minister and other Ahmadi officials in the government and military be dismissed from office since, they argued, non-Muslims should not hold key positions in government or the military since members of a non-Muslim minority could not be fully committed to the state's Islamic ideology.

The situation exploded in 1953, resulting in widespread rioting and the murder of Ahmadis in the Punjab province. The report of a national court of inquiry, the Munir Report of 1956, revealed many of the deep-seated and divisive issues of identity that would continue to plague Pakistan's political development. The commission found that the ulama, self-proclaimed religious experts and staunch advocates of an Islamic state, proved incapable of agreement on the most fundamental questions of Pakistan's Islamic and political identity. They could agree on who was not a Muslim (the Ahmadi), but they were hopelessly divided on such basic questions as, What is Islam? Who is a Muslim? and What is the nature of an Islamic state?

Constitution-making proved to be a slow process, lasting from 1948 to 1956. Influenced by the legacy of its British colonial past, Pakistan in its nation-building relied heavily upon Western models of development—constitutionally, legally, and educationally. Jinnah's secular orientation was reiterated by Pakistan's Prime Minister Liaquat Ali Khan in March, 1949: "The people are the real recipients of power. This naturally eliminates any danger of the establishment of theocracy."[3]

The first draft of the constitution "contained very little, if at all . . . as to the Islamic character of the proposed constitution."[4] However, in response to growing agitation by Mawlana Mawdudi's Jamaat and the ulama for an Islamic state and constitution as well as to growing ethnic/regional divisions, the authors of the second draft constitution turned to religion as a means of national integration, incorporating the Objectives Resolution (1949), which had addressed the issue of Islam and the state. It began with a statement affirming the primacy of divine sovereignty: "[S]overeignty over the entire universe belongs to God Almighty alone, and the authority He has delegated to the State of Pakistan through its people for being exercised within the limits prescribed by Him is a sacred trust." Critics argued that this and other of its principles were contrary to Jinnah's desire to establish a secular democracy. Muhammad Munir, a former chief justice of Pakistan, observed critically: "From the sovereignty of Allah and the legislature acting within the prescribed limits [of God], is negatived [sic] the basic idea of modern democracy that there are no limits, except in a federation, on the legislative power of a representative Assembly . . . . The distinction between religious majorities and minorities takes away the right of equality which again is a basic idea of modern democracy."[5]

Pakistan's first permanent constitution, that of 1956, was both democratic and Islamic. Pakistan was an Islamic republic (the Islamic Republic of Pakistan) with a Westminster-style parliamentary democracy. On these principles most Pakistanis, secular modernists and religious leaders alike, agreed. However, with regard to the role of Islam in government, the makers of the constitution settled for a compromise between secular modernists and religious traditionalists. Islamic provisions were inserted into the constitution. The title of the state was the Islamic Republic of Pakistan, and divine sovereignty was affirmed; the constitution required that the head of state be a Muslim, and no law was to be repugnant to the injunctions of Islam. An Islamic Research Institute and Islamic Ideology Council were established to advise the government on its laws and development. The relationship of Islam to modern constitutional concepts such as democracy, popular sovereignty, parliamentary political parties, and the equality of all citizens was simply asserted, not delineated. This pragmatic compromise, which one scholar has called "rhetorical Islamization," failed to address the nature of Pakistan's Islamic identity systematically and effectively.[6]

Although many were content with slogans and an Islamic veneer, unresolved questions regarding both the role and function of Islam and democracy would resurface in Pakistan's subsequent history: What does it mean to say that Pakistan is an Islamic republic and a Muslim state? How is the state's Islamic character to be reflected in the ideology and institutions of the state? What is the relationship of Islam to democracy, multiparty politics, law, and minority rights? Of divine sovereignty to popular sovereignty? The relationship of Islam to the state remained a sensitive issue—marginalized, "finessed," or exploited by both government and opposition when convenient.

The diversity of Islam's implementation, its ambiguous relationship to issues of national identity and democracy, can be seen in three distinct periods or forms: Ayub Khan's "guided democracy" (1958–69), Zulfikar Ali Bhutto's populist Islamic socialism (1971–77), and Zia ul-Haq's Islamic authoritarianism (1977–88).

Ayub Khan: Martial Law, Modernist Islam, and Guided Democracy

Despite its constitutional creation as a Westminster-style parliamentary government, much of Pakistan's history (approximately twenty-five of its forty-seven years) has been spent under martial law. In 1958, Field Marshal Muhammad Ayub Khan established the first of what would become three martial law regimes in Pakistan. He established a precedent that would be repeated: the military's intervention when it believed the politicians were not in proper control. Seizing power in the midst of political chaos, Ayub rejected uncritical adoption of a Westminster parliamentary democracy as inappropriate for Pakistan's sociopolitical context, and instead advocated a more limited "guided" or "basic" democracy—guided by the hand of the military through the morass and chaos created by the politicians. Despite his reservations about democracy, Ayub was a Western-oriented modernist Muslim, primarily concerned with establishing a strong centralized government and fostering rapid socioeconomic change. As one analyst has noted, "Although Pakistan was officially declared an Islamic Republic, . . . in effect, it was an Islamic Republic in name only."[7] When useful or necessary, Ayub employed a modernist Islamic stance to rationalize and legitimate innovative change, arguing the need to "liberate the spirit of religion from the cobwebs of superstition and stagnation which surround it and move forward under the forces of modern science and knowledge."[8] Ayub turned to lay experts or scholars of Islam. The ulama, the traditional guardians and interpreters of Islam, found themselves minority and marginalized voices in what now became lay-dominated organizations and institutes, such as the Islamic Research Institute and the Islamic Ideology Council. Ulama resistance to this challenge to their traditional authority and to what they regarded as Ayub Khan's "Western Islam"—the use of Islam to foster Western-oriented, secular modernization—can be seen in their battle over legal and constitutional issues. At the same time, they criticized Ayub's "guided democracy" as political authoritarianism that frustrated the development of democracy.

The traditional religious establishment and Islamic organizations, led by Mawlana Mawdudi's Jamaat-i Islami, mounted a national campaign against government-sponsored reforms of family law (marriage, divorce, and inheritance), denouncing them as a blind copying of the West and contrary to Islam. Although Ayub Khan, with the support of women's organizations like the All Pakistan Women's Association (APWA), was able to enact the Muslim Family Laws Ordinance of 1961, the scope of reform was less than that originally envisioned. The law remained a subject of controversy that would reemerge two decades later during the regime of General Zia ul-Haq.

A second battle bore directly upon Pakistan's Islamic identity and state power. Pakistan's second constitution of 1962 changed the name of the state from the Islamic Republic of Pakistan to the Republic of Pakistan (dropping the adjective Islamic), and omitted the "divine sovereignty" clause that restricted the power of the state "within the limits prescribed by Him." However, in the end, Ayub was forced to yield to religious forces and in 1963 restored the omitted provisions. Finally, when elections were held under Ayub Khan's constitution, in which political parties were banned and the right to vote was given to 80,000 members in an electoral college, Ayub, who was challenged by Fatima Jinnah, the sister of Mohammed Jinnah, obtained a *fatwa* (formal legal opinion given by an expert in Islamic law) from the ulama that a woman could not be the head of state.

Writing in 1968, Freeland Abbott could observe that the government of Pakistan had been largely successful in keeping "the heart of the religious problem in Pakistan, the disparate views of modernists and traditionalists," in the background, but that "it will have to be faced some day."[9]

Zulfikar Ali Bhutto: Islamic Socialism

If previously Islam had remained a somewhat peripheral, although at times sensitive, factor in Pakistani politics, under Zulfikar Ali Bhutto (1971–77) it moved to center stage. Bhutto came to power with the resignation of General Yahya Khan, whose martial-law regime (1969–71) had succeeded that of Ayub Khan. Both Bhutto's socialism and promises of a restoration of democracy were to become major issues. Despite his personal secular-socialist orientation, political realities led Bhutto increasingly to appeal to religion in his domestic and foreign policy.

The 1971 Pakistan-Bangladesh civil war and the transformation of East Pakistan into Bangladesh testified to the failure of Muslim nationalism to provide a viable national identity that could bridge ethnic and linguistic differences. For many in Pakistan, it refocused attention on the issue of Pakistan's identity and raison d'être as a Muslim homeland. For more religiously minded, the disastrous loss was due not only to Pakistan's failure to achieve national integration—to realize the Islamic identity of its Muslim nationalism—but also to dependence on Western secular institutions and culture during Ayub Khan's regime. Voices, in particular those of the Jamaat-i Islami and the ulama, were raised, calling for a reaffirmation of Pakistan's Islamic roots and a restoration of democracy. At the same time, Bhutto turned to Arab oil countries (Iran, Libya, and especially those in the Gulf, such as Saudi Arabia, the United Arab Emirates, and Kuwait). Emphasizing their common Islamic identity and brotherhood, he sought foreign aid and an outlet for Pakistani products, laborers, and military advisors. The price for improved relations with the oil sheikhdoms included the public promotion of Islam. The Bhutto government obliged, sponsoring Islamic conferences and introducing Islamic regulations and laws restricting alcohol.

Bhutto's promotion of Islam outraged religious leaders, who regarded his appeal to Islam as personally hypocritical and politically opportunistic. Moreover, it impinged upon an area they regarded as their province and compromised their power and authority. Bhutto had attempted to Islamize his socialism by identifying it with Islam, equating socialism with notions of Islamic egalitarianism and social justice. His Pakistan People's Party (PPP) adopted Islamized socialist slogans such as Islamic equality (*musawwat*) and the equality of Muhammad. Government socialist policies, such as land reform and nationalization of banks, insurance companies, and many industries, were justified in the name of Islam.

Bhutto's attempts to Islamize his socialism proved divisive, and were roundly condemned by religious leaders such as Mawlana Mawdudi of the Jamaat-i Islam:

> They found that their socialism cannot dance naked. . . . After realizing this they started calling socialism "Islamic" . . . . If it is really based on the Quran and the Sunnah then what is the need for calling it socialism? . . . Now when they can see that this too does not work they have started calling it Islamic

equality (musawat) and Muhammadi musawat. The object is the same—pure socialism.[10]

The Jamaat-i Islami and many religious leaders mounted a campaign, the Fund for the Protection of Pakistan's Ideology. One hundred thirteen ulama issued a fatwa that condemned socialism and anyone who advocated, supported, or voted for it.

Bhutto's populist use of religion had been part of a broader consolidation of power, legitimated by an appeal to the masses. Like his predecessors, as well as his successor, Zia ul-Haq, Bhutto had not been elected president of Pakistan, and thus had tenuous political legitimacy. As Wayne Wilcox had observed earlier, "Surely, no democracy in history has been as innocent of elections as that of Pakistan."[11] Bhutto and his PPP had triumphed in national elections in West Pakistan in 1970, and, as a result, Yahya Khan had appointed Bhutto his deputy prime minister. Thus he was the logical choice to step into the political vacuum that existed after Bangladesh's secession in 1971. Having initially promised a return to democracy and constitutional government, he in fact moved swiftly to establish his authority and control of the political system. By 1973, he switched from a stance for a strong presidency with centralized authority to a parliamentary form of government "dominated by a chief executive, secure from assaults by both the legislature and the judiciary."[12] The new constitution of 1973 provided for a modified Western parliamentary democracy that concentrated power in the hands of the prime minister. By 1976, this populist prime minister would criticize even the constitutional limits of the 1973 constitution, and seek a new mandate from the people to extend his authority:

> In 1970, I promised you democracy. In 1973, I gave you democracy. . . . But there are people in this country [who] have attempted to put obstacles in our way; to stop us from building a new Pakistan. . . . Should we continue to permit them this freedom? Mustn't we change the rules of the game so that our progress towards a new Pakistan is not continuously thwarted?[13]

He would later bluntly denounce his opponents for "constraining him in the name of liberty and democracy—concepts that only a few people understand in a nation as poor as Pakistan and from which fewer could expect to benefit."[14]

Bhutto's use of Islam, along with socioeconomic reform, to broaden and reinforce mass loyalty and popular support for his government as well as counter his religious critics led him in 1974 to cave in to renewed anti-Ahmadiya agitation and demands to declare the Ahmadiya a non-Muslim minority and exclude them from the highest government positions. Pakistan's third constitution, of 1973, was amended so that the oath of office for the president and the prime minister required their public affirmation of the finality of Muhammad's Prophethood.

By the mid-1970s, Islam had become the idiom of political discourse and politics, a primary vehicle for mass politicization by both government and opposition.

In the general elections of March, 1977, a broad coalition of secular and religious opposition parties, the Pakistan National Alliance (PNA), placed itself under the umbrella of Islam, promising an Islamic system of government (*nizam-i-Mustafa*, the system of the Prophet) and advocating a return to parliamentary democracy and private enterprise. Support was drawn from both the traditional and modern middle class: urban intellectuals, traditional merchants and businessmen, teachers, doctors, and clerical workers. The middle-class character of the PNA was reinforced by the presence and leadership of the religious parties (the Jamaat-i Islami, the Jamiyyat-i-Ulama-i-Pakistan, the Jamiyyat-i-Ulama-i- Islam), whose primary base of support was the urban and town-based middle class.

When Bhutto and the PPP nevertheless scored an apparently impressive victory in national elections in 1977, the opposition, claiming widespread voting irregularities, utilized Islam and the mullah-mosque system of Pakistan for protest and political mobilization in an anti-Bhutto movement. The clergy found ready support from those entrepreneurs and others who had been affected by Bhutto's nationalization programs. At no time in Pakistan's history had there been so pervasive a mixture of religion and politics. The stage was set for General Zia ul-Haq's bloodless coup d'état ("Operation Fair Play") on July 5, 1977. In some sense, one could argue that during the Ayub Khan and Zulfikar Bhutto years (1956–77), Pakistan was an Islamic republic with a modernist bent. Under Zia, a more conservative Islamic orientation and attempt to Islamize state and society would prevail.

ZIA UL-HAQ: ISLAMIZATION OF STATE AND SOCIETY

Zia ul-Haq moved quickly to legitimate his coup and continued rule in the name of Islam. He pledged himself to the implementation of an Islamic system (*nizam-i-Islam*) of government. Islam became the core symbol of his regime, ostensibly informing both domestic and foreign policy. Zia employed Islam as a source of national identity, legitimacy, cultural integration, and public morality to a degree that exceeded that of any previous government. At the same time, Islam proved equally to be a divisive force, pitting secular and religious forces, Sunni and Shii, Muslim and non-Muslim, as well as proving impotent in subordinating ethnic differences to a sense of national identity and unity.

The politicization of religion in Pakistan was evident in politics, law, economics, and social life. Islamic symbols and criteria were often invoked so successfully by the government that those who opposed Zia were forced to cast their arguments in an Islamic mold. Zia skillfully legitimated his seizure of power in the name of Islam and coopted the PNA's Islamic banner. Seizing its slogan of *nizam-i-Islam* (the system of Islam), he invited members of the PNA to join his government. Individuals known for their strong commitment to an Islamic order were appointed to key cabinet positions, in particular members of the Jamaat-i Islami.[15] Religious ideologues were prominent not only in administrative and educational positions but

also in the state-run media and the military. Mawdudi's Jamaat, like other Islamically oriented parties, was caught between a government that espoused its goal and
agenda, implementation of an Islamic system of government, and its desire for the
restoration of parliamentary democracy.

Many, including Zia ul-Haq, had been influenced by Jamaat-i Islami leader,
Mawlana Mawdudi's ideological interpretation of Islam. Mawdudi's prolific writings provided an interpretation of Islam that appealed to many educated Pakistanis and, indeed, many throughout the Muslim world who did not belong to the
Jamaat or support its electoral politics. He has been one of the most widely read
authors in Pakistan, and his ideas penetrated society through his books, newspapers, lectures, and the work of his followers. It offered an interpretation that
demonstrated the relevance of Islam to every aspect of modern life: politics, economics, education, and law. The manifestos of the Jamaat, written long before Zia
came to power, reveal many of the beliefs and reforms that he later espoused.
Among these principles were the belief that Islam is a comprehensive way of life
and that Pakistan's failure to implement true Islam was the cause of its weakness
and failures; that the Quran and Sunnah must be declared the only source of law
and that all laws must be brought into conformity with the tenets of Islam; that the
oath of office of all key government leaders should include a pledge to observe
Islam in their personal lives; that anyone who did not accept the finality of
Muhammad's prophethood should be declared an unbeliever; that *salat* (prescribed five times daily prayers) be promoted in society and proper facilities provided; that the weekly holiday be fixed on Friday; that observance of Ramadan be
enforced.[16]

Zia and Mawdudi's Jamaat became allies in a marriage of convenience. Despite
the Jamaat's desire for national elections, in a bid to capitalize on its gains and
expand its political power, the Jamaat pragmatically compromised its position on
elections and accepted interim martial law as it assisted Zia in planning and
implementing his Islamization program. The Islamic orientation and legitimacy of
Zia ul-Haq's regime was formalized and promulgated in late 1978 and early 1979, as
Zia reaffirmed Pakistan's Islamic identity and announced measures ("Measures to
Enforce Nizam-i-Islam" and "Introduction of Islamic Laws) designed to implement Islam as the political ideology of the state and to enforce Islamic law. Reforms
were introduced that not only affected prayer and worship but also included political, economic, educational and judicial changes.

Zia ul-Haq's political use of Islam provided an excuse for military rule. In
October, 1979, Zia postponed elections indefinitely, banned political parties, and
imposed strict censorship of the media. His rule as chief martial law administrator (CMLA) and president were all justified in the name of Islam. Zia questioned
the compatibility of Pakistan's Western-inspired democracy, with its political
party system of government, with Islam. He referred these questions to the government-appointed experts of the Council of Islamic Ideology and the Islamic

Research Institute, in a move aimed at postponing if not burying these issues indefinitely.

Zia appropriated and expanded the scope of Bhutto's reforms, such as the banning of alcohol, gambling, and night clubs, and introduced a new series of Islamic legal and economic reforms. The government implemented Islamic penal laws, the *hudood* (*hudud*, or the "limits" of God), for crimes believed to be expressly forbidden by God and for which Allah has stipulated the appropriate punishment: drinking alcohol; false accusation of sexual crimes; theft; and adultery. While flogging did become a common form of punishment for a variety of crimes, amputation (for theft) was never carried out, since no medical doctor would agree to supervise the punishment. Similarly, although stoning was prescribed by a court for adultery, it was never carried out. The introduction of an alms (*zakat*) and agricultural (*ushr*) tax and interest-free banking were the more substantive and controversial Islamic economic reforms. The Islamic Ideology Council and the Federal Shariat Court reviewed Pakistan's laws to determine whether specific laws were repugnant to Islam.[17]

The government's reforms exacerbated sectarian tensions between Pakistan's Sunni majority and its Shii minority. Shii constitute approximately 15 percent of the population. Implementation of Islamic law raised the question: "Whose law"? Shii protested that while they welcomed the implementation of Islam, they would not tolerate the imposition of regulations that stemmed from Hanafi (Sunni) law school rather than Jafari (Shii) legal principles. Shii had also taken exception to the Sunni interpretation of the Islamic penal laws (hudood) regarding amputation for theft, which differs from that of the Shii.

Shii concerns had resulted in organization of the Movement for the Implementation of Jafari Law under the leadership of a prominent Shii cleric, Mufti Jafar Husain. In early July, 1980, Shii leaders convened a conference in Islamabad which drew more than 100,000 Shii. This was followed by a protest demonstration on July 5 of some 25,000 Shii against compulsory zakat. The government finally capitulated and passed legislation enabling a Muslim to obtain an exemption based on "faith and *fiqh* (interpretation of law)."

Zia positioned himself above the law, even Islamic law. The Shariat Court was barred from reviewing laws in three areas: the constitution and martial law ordinances, Muslim family laws, and fiscal laws. Second, with the cancellation of elections and extension of martial law, implementation of the Shariah Court's findings through legislative action meant, in effect, implementation at the discretion of the chief martial law administrator, General Zia ul-Haq.

Through such ploys, Zia created an Islamic facade for retention and consolidation of his power within a martial law regime. He was strongly supported by senior Punjabi military officers who held key positions in the cabinet and served as provincial governors. The Soviet invasion of Afghanistan in December 1979 enhanced Zia's position, both raising the specter of an external threat to Pakistan's security and attracting a significant increase in U.S. military and economic aid. For some observers, Zia's Pakistan had become a state dependent on the three "As": Allah, the Army, and America.

ISLAM AND NATIONAL INTEGRATION

Zia ul-Haq pledged that he would restore Islam as the cornerstone of the nation's Islamic-Pakistani identity. His intention was to foster national identity in the face of the threat of ethnic and regional factionalism as witnessed in the 1971 civil war and in Baluchistan, the Northwest Frontier Province, and Sind. A series of symbolic and real educational and cultural reforms were initiated to produce what Zia called "a new generation wedded to the ideology of Pakistan and Islam." Reforms ranged from language and dress to the media and education. Regulations requiring national language and dress were introduced to offset Western and regional influences. Television and film censorship increased, limiting Western films, local music, and dancing, and strictly regulating modesty in women's dress and programming. School curricula and textbooks were reviewed, both to eliminate un-Islamic materials and to reorient Western-generated and -oriented materials by including topics and books that emphasized Islamic-Pakistani history and values. However, these measures, like Zia's Islamization program in general, proved divisive.

Zia's implementation of "national-Islamic" language and dress brought resistance not only from more Westernized sectors, secular oriented bureaucrats, and educators, but also from religious minorities and regional/ethnic leaders, who regarded many reforms as further subordination to Urdu-speaking and Punjabi interests. The Punjab constitutes 60 percent of Pakistan's population, and Punjabis were a dominant presence in the military and bureaucracy. Ironically, increased emphasis on national culture in society and the media fueled religious criticism. The ulama denounced public performances of national dance and music programs, decried the sad state of public morality, and criticized the slow pace of Islamic reform.[18]

WOMEN AND MINORITIES

Pakistan's regime-imposed Islamic system of government had negative repercussions on women and minorities in particular. Greater emphasis on religion in public life unleashed proponents of traditional forces, who became more assertive in demanding more emphasis on what they regarded to be Islamic norms of modesty, in particular a restoration of the separation of the sexes in society, implementation of classical Islamic laws, and the repeal of the modern reforms enacted by the Muslim Family Laws Act of 1961. They regarded departures from traditional practices as Western-inspired deviations from true Islamic norms. Their demands for the veiling and seclusion of women filled Friday mosque sermons, newspapers, religious pamphlets, and parliamentary debates. Islamic moral ideals of purity and modesty were contrasted with caricatures of the West that focused selectively on its Western social mores and problems. The social ills of Muslim society were attributed to the Western penetration of Muslim societies, and were characterized as the products of European colonialism as well as the policies and influence of indigenous colonizers, the Westernized Muslim elites.

A series of government directives and laws in the early 1980s fostered the segregation and seclusion of women. There was increased pressure to ban women's photographs in the print media, to limit their presence on television, to require women broadcasters to cover their heads and to wear the *dupatta* (a thin cloth worn over one's garments), and to establish separate women's universities. Women were reprimanded and accosted in public for "un-Islamic behavior."

These restrictive measures and attitudes politicized women's organizations such as the All Pakistan Women's Association (APWA), the National Women Lawyer's Association, and the Women's Action Forum (WAF), which had sprung up as professional women in particular were increasingly mobilized in their concerns about the potential threat of Zia's Islamization program to women's status and role in society.

"Islamic" legal reforms (the Hudood Ordinance, the Law of Evidence, and the Law of *Qisas* and *Diyat*, or retribution and blood money) precipitated a confrontation between conservatives and modernists over the issue of women's place in Pakistani society. For adultery and fornication, the Hudood Ordinance stipulates maximum punishments of death by stoning for married persons and 100 lashes for the unmarried. The law recognizes only male witnesses, prevents women from testifying, and does not distinguish clearly between fornication and adultery or between rape and adultery.

Pakistan's Evidence Act in 1983 and the Law of *Qisas* and *Diyat* confirmed women's worst fears. The draft Evidence Act advocated the implementation of the traditional legal viewpoint that the evidence of two Muslim women equals that of one Muslim male. The law, enacted in October 1984, was a modified version that equates the evidence of two women to one male in specified cases, in particular those concerned with financial matters. The Law of *Qisas* and *Diyat* stipulated that compensation (*diyat*, blood money) for an offense against a woman be half that of a man, and that proof of a murder liable to retribution (*qisas*) require two male witnesses.

As in other parts of the Muslim world, the reassertion of Islam in public life has raised many questions regarding the status and role of non-Muslims in society. The Ahmadiyya or Qadiani issue provides the most sustained example. It precipitated a national crisis and Pakistan's first martial-law government in 1953, and the 1974 constitutional amendment that declared the Qadiani a non-Muslim minority. In 1983 it emerged again. A worldwide Qadiani conference that year which drew 200,000 participants to their headquarters in Rabwah outraged Sunni and Shii ulama, who in January, 1984, passed a series of resolutions which (1) called upon the government to enforce the punishment under Islamic law (death penalty) for apostasy and (2) demanded that Qadiani be prohibited from using Islamic terminology, that their literature and newspaper be confiscated, and that their members be removed from civil and military positions.[19] More than one hundred thousand people assembled at a conference on the finality of prophethood in Islam in Faisalbad on April 11 and issued similar demands. The government responded with the Anti-Islamic Activities of the Qadiani Group, Lahore Group, and Ahmadis (Prohibition and Penalty) Ordinance 1984, which was incorporated into the Pakistan Penal Code. The ordinance stipulated punishments for any Qadiani who called himself a Muslim, referred to his faith as Islam, preached or propagated his faith, used Islamic terminology such as masjid (mosque) or adhan (call to prayer) " . . . or in any manner outrages the religious feelings of Muslims."[20]

For Christians, who constitute about 1 percent of the population, the greater emphasis on Islamization of state and society under Bhutto and Zia ul-Haq meant nationalization of religious schools and concern about the greater emphasis on Islam as Pakistan's heritage, as well as the introduction of Islamic laws and required courses in Islamic studies. Christian leaders pressed for the inclusion of courses on their own tradition in the curriculum as an option for Christian students. A general concern of all minorities was that Pakistan would retreat to classical Islamic law's designation of non-Muslim "People of the Book" as *dhimmi* (protected people), a status that, however advanced relative to the past, by modern standards would amount to a second-class citizenship of restricted rights and duties in relation to Muslim citizens. Their fears seemed corroborated by the fact that most religious leaders believed that the ideological nature of the state should exclude non-Muslims from the higher policy-making positions of government.

MOVEMENT FOR THE RESTORATION OF DEMOCRACY

Restricted political participation drew strong criticism and opposition not only from Bhutto's PPP but also from many of the "defunct" political parties of the PNA, which joined together in February, 1981, in the Movement for the Restoration of Democracy (MRD). Religious leaders, who had initially favored Zia's Islamic reforms, found common cause with more secularly oriented political parties in calling for elections. To blunt his critics, Zia created an appointed, not elected, Federal Advisory Council (FAC) in 1982. The FAC was consultative and had no legislative powers; Zia, as CMLA, retained the right to legislate or issue decrees. The FAC was given an Islamic facade; the term or Islamic designation *majlis-i-shura*, or consultative council, derived from the early council of elders who selected/elected the first caliphs, and was to be a transitional mechanism to "create conditions in which the country could attain a democratic, Islamic polity."[21] The majority of Zia's critics charged that this was simply one more delaying tactic. By the spring of 1984, even the Jamaat-i Islami, which had continued to support Zia and had remained aloof from the MRD, called for a joint front to oppose martial law and campaign for the restoration of democracy. All agreed that a military government was un-Islamic, asserting that an Islamic government based upon consultation (*shura*) is one in which the head of state is subject to Islamic law and members of parliament are elected in party-based elections, not appointed by an unelected military ruler. The MRD's challenge to the legitimacy of Zia's martial law government and pressure for democratization were in large part responsible for the gradual erosion of Zia's power, forcing a movement to provincial and national elections.

In December 1984, Zia ul-Haq announced a referendum as a "transition of power to elected representatives." Although ostensibly a referendum on his Islamization program, Zia linked a "yes" vote with his continuance as president until 1990. In February, 1985, national and provincial elections took place on a non-party basis as Zia continued to steadfastly maintain that "shuracracy" (government by consultation, *shura*), his version of Islamic democracy which acknowledged the sovereignty of God, as distinct from Western democracy's emphasis on popular sovereignty, did not permit political parties, which he regarded as an un-Islamic institution.[22] By the end of 1985, martial law was terminated, civilian rule restored, press censorship lifted, and political parties permitted to function with some restrictions. The MRD, as well as the Jamaat-i Islami, continued to press for free elections on a political party basis and for Zia to resign as army chief of staff in order to be a truly civilian president.

The transition to civilian rule did not take place before Zia amended the constitution of 1973 to ensure his ultimate power as president (that is, that the president appoint the prime minister, who serves at the pleasure of the president, as well as all ministers of state on the recommendation of the prime minister and the heads of the armed forces) and to exempt from prosecution those associated with his martial-law regime. This amendment subsequently proved pivotal and controversial in post-Zia politics.

THE POST-ZIA PERIOD AND THE RESTORATION OF DEMOCRACY

On August 17, 1988, Pakistan's decade-long experiment with Islamization under General Zia ul-Haq came to an abrupt end with his death in an airplane crash. Though the MRD was not ultimately responsible for the end of Zia's regime or for a democratic victory, the movement did set a tone and expectations that all contenders for power felt the need to adopt. In November, 1988, in Pakistan's most open and democratic national elections to date, Benazir Bhutto and the PPP defeated the Islamic Democratic Alliance (Islami Jamhoori Ittehad, or IJI), a coalition of nine parties backed in large part by Pakistan's military—in particular the Inter-Services Intelligence (ISI), which wished to retain its influence and prevent a PPP victory. The IJI claimed the banner of Islamization and included the Jamaat-i Islami, the Muslim League, and the Jamiat-i-Ulama-i-Islam. The manifestos of the political parties, as well as the Islamic title chosen by the member parties of the Islamic Democratic Alliance (IDA), made political Islam an issue, but also reflected the common acceptance of democracy by all concerned as a necessary part of the political process. Benazir Bhutto became Pakistan's first freely elected prime minister in eleven years, and the Muslim world's first woman prime minister.

The post-Zia years reflected the continued influence of his rule. Islam and democratization continued to be political issues. While the IJI had found it necessary to incorporate the rhetoric of democracy, the PPP could not simply opt for a secular democracy but instead was constricted by the "Islamic climate" of Pakistani politics. Of equal importance, Zia's controversial eighth constitutional amendment of 1985, which strengthened the powers of the president vis-à-vis the prime minister, proved to have major impact on political developments. It enabled the president to play the IJI off against Benazir Bhutto, whose PPP victory (25 percent of the national vote) and plurality of seats in the national assembly were far from decisive and due more to her charisma and family name than strong, effective party organization and political program.

Benazir Bhutto also had to contend with the impact of more than a decade of "Islamic politics," initiated by her father and exploited on a grander scale by Zia and the military. While Zia's use of Islam fed the cynicism of many, for the majority of the electorate, Pakistan's Islamic identity was a given, however much its form and implementation might be subjects of contention. Thus, despite campaign promises, Bhutto's government did not make significant inroads in dismantling or countering the "Islamic legacy" of Zia ul-Haq. Moreover, Bhutto herself found it necessary to project a profile in accord with Pakistan's Islamic religio-cultural traditions. Shortly after her election she went on a much-publicized pilgrimage (umra, the lesser pilgrimage) to Mecca, had an arranged marriage, and began rearing a family. Although she had distinguished between a correct interpretation of Islam and Zia ul-Haq's Islamization program, political realities prevented her from changing substantially the Islamic laws introduced during Zia's rule or initiating substantive women's reforms.

Lacking the required parliamentary majority for bold leadership, forced to accommodate the wishes of a powerful military which was more sympathetic to Pakistan's president Ghulam Ishaq Khan and her IDA opposition, faced with significant provincial and ethnic political opposition in the Punjab, Baluchistan, and the Northwest Frontier provinces and rampant ethnic violence in Sind which brought it to the brink of disintegration, and hampered by charges of massive corruption in her government and family, Benazir Bhutto proved incapable of effective leadership. Bhutto and many of those who surrounded her seemed more attuned to the West, where they had studied and lived than to the realities of Pakistani culture and politics. This image was exacerbated by the fact that, in a weakened condition, the Bhutto government seemed very close to if not reliant on the

United States, fanning anti-American sentiments. The weakness of the Bhutto government, its lack of authority and inability to rule, seemed evident in late May, 1990, when Benazir Bhutto, the leader who promised democracy, sent 20,000 troops into Sind to restore order in her home province, where ethnic violence bordered on civil war.

On August 6, 1990, President Ghulam Ishaq Khan, a close associate of Zia ul-Haq and ally of the IDA's Nawaz Sharif, dissolved the National Assembly and dismissed Prime Minister Bhutto's government on charges of corruption and incompetence. New elections were scheduled for October 24, 1990. The perceived importance of both Islam and democracy in political discourse and mobilization were evident. The chief contenders were the Islamic Democratic Alliance (which included the Muslim League and the Jamaat-i Islam) and Bhutto's Pakistan Democratic Alliance. The campaign revolved around Bhutto and charges of corruption and incompetence. Although neither side seemed concerned with presenting a detailed platform, both pledged themselves to the implementation of an Islamic society in Pakistan. The Islamic Democratic Alliance swept the elections, soundly defeating Bhutto. Nawaz Sharif became prime minister.

Sharif was quick to assure other Muslim rulers, as well as the West, to which he would look for economic and military assistance, that he was not a "fundamentalist." Nawaz attempted to walk a fine line between secular and religious forces. Although he focused more on economic development, he could not escape the Islamic expectations of the Zia constituency who supported him; of the Jamaat-i Islami, which was a key member of his coalition; and of President Ghulam Ishaq, who had been closely identified with Zia's Islamization program.[23] Sharif and the IDA proved pragmatic on international and domestic Islamic issues. Sharif supported Saudi Arabia and the United States in the Gulf War, setting itself at odds with the masses and straining its relationship with the Islamic parties who belonged to the IDA coalition, as well as with some members of the military, such as General Beig, who publicly accused it of being anti-Muslim.

The issue of the Shariah Bill, initiated by Zia ul-Haq but tabled in parliament in 1985 by Prime Minister Junejo after martial law was lifted, became particularly important, symbolically and politically. The symbolic significance of the Shariah Bill and the continued importance of Islam as an issue of national identity for many Pakistanis was reflected in a Gallup poll which occurred immediately (April 12, 1991) after the Shariah Bill's introduction in parliament on April 10. Eighty-one percent of those polled supported it, while only 6 percent were opposed. Several months later, in the wake of criticisms from a variety of interest groups and government compromises, a majority of the National Assembly approved the bill (a somewhat milder, watered-down version), and polls still showed 65 percent in support and 18 percent in opposition.[24]

CONCLUSION

The role of religion in the Islamic Republic of Pakistan has been an enduring and unresolved issue. However, from 1971 through 1988, under Zulfikar Ali Bhutto and Zia ul- Haq, the relationship of Islam to state and society progressively moved from the periphery to the center, and was characterized by a pervasive use of Islamic discourse and symbolism as well as burgeoning Islamic laws, regulations, institutions, taxes, and educational and social policies. Initially feared by some but welcomed by many, Islamization under Zia ul-Haq moved from serving as an effective means of establishing the early legitimacy of his government, coopting religious forces and the Pakistan National Alliance, and mobilizing popular support to being a source of division, disillusionment, and, at times, oppression. Promises of a more authentic Pakistani state and society, Islamically rooted and unified, gave way to the reality of a state in which government use of Islam divided more than united, restricted and punished more than guided and liberated, and fostered cynicism rather than pride and respect.

Retrospectively, the greater deference to and profile of Islam in Pakistan, as in many Muslim countries such as Libya, Iran, and Sudan, raises a variety of questions: Whose Islam, what Islam, and why a negative Islam? Contemporary politics in Pakistan has witnessed both cooperation and cooptation in the relationship of the state to religious forces. The state under Zia skillfully manipulated religious forces. Yet these skillful maneuvers to assuage and coopt the ulama and religious organizations also created high expectations and, eventually, disillusionment and opposition. Those who at first winked at authoritarianism in order to realize a good cause, Islamization, became more disenchanted and joined their voices with more secularly oriented opposition leaders in denouncing martial law and in calling for the restoration of democracy and free elections. Many others, like Muhammad Munir, former chief justice of Pakistan, in assessing Zia's Islamization program or Islamic Order, observed: "The Order and Ordinances present a grim and dreadful picture of Islam and ignore the forgiving and merciful attributes of God."[25]

Although touted as a source of national identity, unity, and pride, Islamization exacerbated religious and ethnic divisions. Islamization intensified differences between Sunni and Shii as well as among diverse Sunni groups, and thus often fanned the fires of sectarianism. Unity of faith in Islam did not mean a common interpretation or understanding of Islamic belief and practice. Tensions between Sunni and Shii increased markedly after the Iranian revolution of 1979 – 80. Iran encouraged and helped Shii in South Asia (as it also did in the Middle East) to organize and assert their rights. At the same time, Saudi Arabia and other Gulf countries increased their aid to Sunni rulers such as Zia ul-Haq and to Sunni Islamic organizations to offset Iranian influence.

Growing Shii "assertiveness" exacerbated Sunni-Shii tensions which triggered demonstrations, riots, and armed confrontations. Thus, while Shii demonstrations in 1980 did lead the government to amend the Zakat Ordinance, it did not end but rather contributed to communal conflict. Shii religious and sociopolitical activism grew and became more visible, and included the construction of religious edifices, public religious processions, marching and demonstrations for Shii rights, and the formation of militant Shii organizations such as Tehrik-i-Nafaz-i-Fiqh-i-Jafria, led by Allama A. H. H. Husaini, and the Imamia Student Organization.[26] These activities in turn have brought a Sunni backlash, which has led to counterdemonstrations, violence, the bombing of mosques, riots, and government-imposed curfews.[27]

Similar divisiveness emerged in Pakistan's Sunni majority community. The Sunni Muslims of Pakistan include many schools of thought: Deobandi, Brelevi, and Wahhabi or Ahl al-Hadith. Their individual theological orientations constitute a form of Sunni sectarianism that remains an obstacle to any consensus on an Islamic vision and program for state and society. The zeal of these Sunni schools to purify and strengthen the Islamic community has not only contributed historically to anti-Shiism but also to inter-Sunni competition and rivalry for the mantle of the true defenders of Islam. These schools represent differing class as well as religious interests, which have found articulation in rival organizations or parties. Deobandi interests are represented in a religio-political party, the Jamiyyat-i-Ulama-i-Islam, and the Brelevi's in the Jamiyyat-i-Ulama-i-Pakistan. Their differences encouraged mutual vilification in polemical works and mosque sermons and, together with the competing personalities of their leadership, produced a Sunni sectarian atmosphere that has been both divisive and, at times, explosive.[28] I. A. Rehman, director of the independent Human Rights Commission of Pakistan, observed: "The present wave of sectarianism is the inevitable result of Zia's policy. He created a strong theocratic polity, and the politicization of religion carries the seeds of the most obnoxious intolerance."[29]

Old rivalries among established religious parties such as the JI, JUI, and JUP have increasingly been supplanted by more militant and violent factions and organizations who use violence and crimes such as bank robberies and kidnappings to finance their activities. Militants like the Sipah-i-Sahaba (SSP) believe that Shia are not Muslims, and thus advocate "the physical elimination of all Shias" in a Sunni Islamic state.[30]

Although the Bhutto government had resisted advice from some in the military and government to ban extremist sectarian organizations and seize their funds and arms, sectarian battles so threatened the stability of the state that in mid-February, 1995, the Bhutto government moved against both the SSP and the TFJ, arresting forty militants in Karachi and Punjab and driving hundreds of others underground.[31]

Islamization also failed to foster a national unity that transcended Pakistan's ethnic-regional divisions. Zia's government, with its Punjabi-dominated military and bureaucracy, continued to be beset by ethnic/regional conflicts growing out of the resentment of many in Sind and Baluchistan, who regarded the Punjabis as "a rapacious ruling elite that has acquired a stranglehold over national resources through its domination of politics and the bureaucracy".[32] Pakistan is a country which has long witnessed antagonism and conflict among major ethnic communities and active regional nationalist (Bengali, Sindhi, Pathan, and Baluch) movements. Part of Zia ul-Haq's legacy to his successors was a series of ethnic battles and killings among Baluch and Pathan in Baluchistan, and among Sindhi and non-Sindhi, Pathan and Muhajir, in the Sind; this was the product of what one government minister called in 1989 "the culture of Kalashnikov and heroin."[33]

Not since the secession of East Bengal and its re-creation as Bangladesh had Pakistan seen the intensity of ethnic violence that has occurred in Karachi and the Sind province. Sporadic ethnic violence has occurred in many areas, including provincial capitals such as Lahore and Peshawar, and in the Northwest Frontier Province, where several hundred people died in confrontations between tribesmen and paramilitary groups over a demand for the introduction of Shariah law. However, Karachi witnessed the most sustained and explosive conflicts. Battles between Sindhis and Muhajirs in this major city and economic center in 1994–95 alone killed more than 800 residents.

Muhajirs (migrants), Urdu-speaking Muslims who had emigrated to Pakistan from India at the creation of Pakistan and who controlled many urban centers in Sind, were resented as outsiders by Sindhi nationalists. Their alliance with the Punjabi military and political elite further incensed Sindhi nationalists. Zulfikar Ali Bhutto, a Sindhi, introduced pro-Sindhi economic and social policies that progressively inflamed relations between Sindhis and Muhajirs, who regarded these policies as discriminatory. As the Muhajirs' economic status continued to deteriorate during Zia ul-Haq's rule, they became more vocal in their objections to Zia's Punjabi-dominated military government's pro-Sindhi policies and to the expansion of the influence of the Punjabi and Pathan communities in Sindh. Muhajir disaffection was reflected in the defeat of Jamaat-i Islami candidates associated with the Zia regime in Karachi elections in 1985 and the formation of the Muhajir National Movement (Muhajir Qaumi Mahaz, or MQM).

The reintroduction of democracy in Pakistan after Zia ul-Haq's death has not only contributed to greater political participation but also to political fragmentation. Both the governments of Benazir Bhutto and the PPP and Nawaz Sharif and the IDA have had to court political parties for support. Ethnic parties such as the MQM have emerged as serious forces capable of playing national parties off against each other. The MQM became a major national as well as provincial power in national and provincial elections in 1988 and 1990. By 1992, in an effort to control the MQM, the government directed the army to impose martial law in Karachi, and the MQM was driven underground and its leader into exile. This did not stop, but contributed to, a spiral of violence, from drive-by shootings and kidnappings to mosque bombings, murder, and rape.

Pakistan in the 1990s not only experienced the impact of domestic terrorism but also was identified as a major center for the training of international terrorists.[34] Ironically, the Afghan resistance and war, a jihad heralded and supported in the Muslim world and the West, contributed to the growth of religious extremism and international terrorism. Both Zia ul-Haq's Islamic agenda and the Afghan resistance, which he strongly supported, yielded unforeseen results. Whereas between 1947 and 1975 870 new madrasas (schools) were established, between 1976 and 1990 an additional 1,700 sprang up, primarily as part of Zia policy. While many provided students with an Islamic education meant to prepare them to lead productive lives in society, others combined a revolutionary Islamic message and education with military training.[35] At the same time, Pakistan, with major assistance from the United States, other Western governments, Saudi Arabia, and other countries in the Arab and broader Muslim world, supported refugee relief and training for the Afghan mujahidin. Both Afghans and thousands of volunteers from the Arab world were given training and arms, generously provided by the C.I.A. and the Pakistani military intelligence organization, Pakistan Inter-Services. As a result, according to some, Pakistan joined Iran, Libya, Sudan, and Lebanon as a training-ground for revolutionaries and terrorists. So-called Arab Afghans, veterans of the war in Afghanistan or graduates of its training camps, were identified by Arab governments (Egypt, Algeria, and Tunisia) as a major source of terrorist activities in their countries. Pakistan's place as a capital for international terrorism seemed confirmed with the arrest of Ramzi Ahmed Yousef in Islamabad on February 7, 1995, for his connection to the New York World Trade Center bombing. This event highlighted Pakistan's role as a base for international terrorists and led to the Bhutto government's attempt to control their foreign funding and military training. In addition, Bhutto, citing the inability of her government to curtail so deeply rooted a problem, requested assistance from the United States and other countries to "close down suspected bases of Arab and Asian militants, including religious schools and other organizations that have been used as fronts for terrorist activities."[36]

Since its creation, Pakistan has struggled with the meaning and implications of its Islamic identity, from the Muslim nationalism of its early years to the "Islamic systems" of the 1970s and 1980s. Whatever the motives of political actors and their use or manipulation of Islamic rhetoric and symbols, however much one may debate the extent to which Islamization has been cosmetic, change did occur in the name of religion in politics, law, education, and social life.

Pakistan has never been a secular state or society. Religion has been an integral part of modern Pakistan's history, a component in its identity, ideology, and politics. For the ordinary people of Pakistan, Islam and Muslim are important and operative terms, signifying a sacred faith, identity, and values that are to be present not only in private life but also in society. Personal piety may vary considerably, and many may be leery of the manipulation of religion by clerics or governments. However, in principle, many if not most would accept the following propositions or presuppositions (although they will differ widely in their understanding or interpretations): Pakistan was founded to be a Muslim (which many would simply understand as "Islamic") state; thus, Pakistan is an Islamic Republic; Pakistan's national ideology is a Muslim, not simply secular, nationalism; Islamic law should play an important part in the legal system; the head of state and key senior positions should be held by Muslims; the state should support, defend, and promote Islam.

At the same time, despite Zia ul-Haq's attempt to delegitimate Pakistan's parliamentary political system and to replace it with his "shuracracy," the majority of Pakistanis, from secular to Islamic activist, demanded the reimplementation of democracy that included a parliamentary, political party system. Major religious organizations or parties, such as the JI, JUP, and JUI, were among those who were politically active and assertive in the name of Islam and of the restoration of democracy. They have demonstrated an ability to function within the political system, whether it in government or in opposition.

While they have not captured the electorate, Islamic parties have demonstrated their bargaining power as a political force to be reckoned with in national and local politics. Groups like the Jamaat-i Islami, whose leadership cadre is well educated, committed, well organized, and well funded, enjoy a following among the lower-middle and middle classes, among students, trade unions, businessmen, and middle-level civil and military bureaucrats. Their influence is often disproportionate to their numbers. Islam has proved an effective rallying cry not only in the past but also in the present. The cry "Islam in Danger," which proved effective in mass mobilization during the struggle for national independence, has also played an important role in mobilizing popular sentiment on transnational Islamic issues: Afghanistan, Kashmir, Salman Rushdie, and the Gulf War.

Yet the Zia period and its legacy of "Islamic rhetoric and symbols" has also contributed to a weakening of religious parties in electoral politics. With most political leaders and parties "playing the Islamic card," the major Islamic organizations/parties' lock on religious political rhetoric and legitimacy has been undercut. Thus, the extent to which other leaders and parties accommodate Islamic politics and the extent to which Islamic parties accommodate a parliamentary political system and have formed alliances with other parties has affected the ability of Islamic parties to claim a special role as defenders of Islam. Thus, in the 1993 elections, despite the Jamaat-i Islami's attempt to provide a third option or alternative with the formation of a Pakistan Islamic Front, it and other religious parties were routed. The election demonstrated both the inability of religious parties to unite and their lack of a distinctive agenda in a political arena in which others, too, conveniently and usefully appealed to Islam.[37]

However, as history has shown, while there may be a general consensus among the Muslims of Pakistan for Islam, there is no clear agreement on what that means at the level of national ideology and policy. Islam and democracy have proven pragmatically compatible, although their content and form have varied. Islamic politics in Pakistan clearly demonstrate that, beyond oppositional politics, religion can be more a divisive than a unifying force. Islamic activist leaders and parties divide rather than unite. At the same time, a more open political system has unleashed ethnic and religious forces that have proved difficult for recent governments to control. Any government will have to contend for the foreseeable future with the Islamic dimension of Pakistan's history and heritage in establishing and maintaining its legitimacy and mobilizing popular support, as well as with its ethnic and linguistic diversity and rivalries.

Six

Malaysia

The Politics of Multiculturalism

"Few Muslim countries in the world have gone as far as Malaysia in the attempt to use the power of the state to enforce for Muslims the prescriptions of the Koran and the Hadith."[1] However, fewer Muslim states are less well known than Malaysia.

Malaysia presents a unique Islamic experience. Malaysia is a multiethnic and multireligious society in which Malays constitute approximately 45 percent of the population but are the dominant political and cultural force. The remainder of the country consists of a variety of ethnic and religious groups, the largest being the Chinese (35 percent) and Indian (10 percent) communities. Islam and Malay national identity and politics have long been interconnected, as reflected in the popular belief that to be Malay is to be Muslim.

A distinctive characteristic of Malaysian political development is the role of political Islam in Malay politics. Malaysia is a federation of states, an officially pluralistic polity in which Islam is the official religion and Islam and Muslims enjoy a privileged position. Although the participation of Islamic parties in electoral politics and their ability to function as a legal opposition is a relatively recent phenomenon in most Muslim countries, for many years, Islamic political parties and organizations have competed with the ruling United Malays National Organization (UMNO) party, as well as with each other, but they have done so as legitimate opposition parties participating *within* the political process. In contrast to the Middle East, where some political systems have refused to allow Islamic political parties and some Islamic movements have engaged in violent opposition, the Malaysian system involves a dominant ruling party that accepts the existence and political participation of Islamic groups and Islamic organizations that function as nonviolent opposition. The acceptance and integration of revivalist Islam within Malaysia's evolving democratic process is witnessed not only by its ability to function within the system but also by the movement of the charismatic Islamic activist, Anwar Ibrahim, from the opposition to the government in the 1980s, in which by 1994 he had become finance minister and deputy prime minister.

ISLAM AND NATIONAL IDENTITY: THE FORMATIVE PERIOD

At the crossroads of Southeast Asia's trade routes, the Malay Peninsula became the home of many religious and cultural influences.[2] Indian, Arab, and Chinese merchants and traders as well as Portuguese, Dutch, and British colonizers brought Hinduism, Buddhism, Sikhism, Confucianism, Taoism, Christianity, and Islam to Southeast Asia, producing a rich cultural mosaic. The two most pervasive formative cultural influences were centuries of Indianization, followed by Islamization from the fourteenth century onward, when Arab and Indian Muslim merchants and mystics (Sufis) converted Malay rulers (sultans) and spread Islam throughout Southeast Asia.[3]

From its earliest period in Malaysia, Islam has had intimate ties to politics and society: "Traditionally in the Malay states, all aspects of government were, if not directly derived from religious sources and principles, cloaked with an aura of religious sanctity."[4] Islam served as a core element of Malay identity and culture, providing "an integrated perception of religion, traditional values, and village and family life."[5] Islam was a source of legitimacy for sultans, who assumed the role of head of religion, defender of the faith, and the guardians of Islamic and customary (*adat*) law, education, and values. Islam and Malay identity were intertwined; to be Malay was to be Muslim. The identification of Malay and Muslim can be seen today in the term used to refer to a non-Malay's conversion to Islam in Malaysia. The new Muslim is said to have become Malay (*masuk Melayu*).

British colonialism brought a clear distinction between religion and the state, with the introduction of a civil administration and a legal system distinct from the Islamic legal system and courts. At the same time, society also became more pluralistic as a result of the massive immigration of non-Muslim Chinese and Indians and the eventual growth and prosperity of their communities. Pluralism and the relationship of religion to Malay national identity became political issues as Malaysia moved toward independence in the post-World War II period. Initial British proposals for a united Malay Union, with equal citizenship for all, were rejected by Malays, who feared the growing population, economic power, and influence of Chinese and Indian communities, who enjoyed a higher economic and educational level than Malay Muslims. The pan-Malayan Islamic Party (PMIP; now called the PAS, Parti Islam Se Malaysia) emerged in 1951, with a message and platform that combined Malay nationalism and Islam and soon became the leading opposition party.

The Malay constitution of 1957 preserved and perpetuated the identification of religion and ethnicity—the special status of Islam, the sultans, and Malay Muslims. The constitution defined a Malay as "a person who professes the Muslim religion, habitually speaks the Malay language, and conforms to Malay customs."[6] Malays enjoyed special privileges that included a system of Malay quotas in education, government, and business. Islam was declared the official religion both in the federation and each of its states, and the sultans were recognized as the head of religion in their states, that is, as the defenders and protectors of Malay religion and culture, with the right to enforce moral and religious obligations. At the state level, sultans established departments of religious affairs and Islamic courts, levied and collected Islamic taxes (*zakat*, or wealth tithe), and controlled the preaching, communication (via news media), and propagation of religion. Religious regulations varied at the state level and covered a broad range of concerns: from fines for failure to attend Friday prayer at the mosque, drinking liquor, or violating the fast of Ramadan in public, to penalties for teaching false doctrines, being found in close proximity (*khalwat*) with a woman who is not a close relative, or showing contempt for religious authorities or for Islam.[7]

At the same time, the constitution accorded freedom of religion to non-Muslim communities. They had the right to practice their religions, own property, establish religious schools, manage their own affairs, and be governed in private matters by their religious laws and institutions. However, they were not permitted to preach or propagate their faith among Muslims; this was used to limit their growth and influence in other areas. Although non-Muslims were protected constitutionally and legally, non-Muslims and Malay Muslims were not equal since they possessed different duties and privileges.

The constitution embodied the political and social realities of society, reflecting the interrelated issues of national identity, religion, and ethnicity. As Fred R. von der Mehden has observed: "The first political and social fact of life of Malaysia is and has been the relationship of religion and ethnicity."[8] Malay politics reflected Malaysia's ethnic dichotomy and the resultant politics of accommodation. Politically, although the dominant Malay party, UMNO, initially excluded non-Malays from associate membership, the sheer size of the non-Malay population necessitated accommodation and cooperation. This was accomplished through the formation of the Alliance with the Malaysian-Chinese Association and the Malaysian-Indian Association, and later broadened to include other communal organizations in the National Front (Barison Nasional). However, Malaysia's ethnic dichotomy, with its communal accommodation and conflict would continue to play a major role in its political development and prove to be the major indigenous catalyst for the Islamic resurgence.[9]

1969: WATERSHED IN MALAY MUSLIM POLITICS

The internal tensions produced by the ethnic dichotomy of Malaysian society erupted in 1969. Ethnic riots between Malays and Chinese in Kuala Lumpur marked a turning point in Malaysian politics. While Malay Muslims, predominantly rural and agrarian, had dominated the government and politics, the urban-based Chinese and Indian communities prospered and excelled in the economic and educational spheres. Malay economic grievances over perceived disparities and resentment at the rising tide of "foreign" presence and ascendancy triggered anti-Chinese riots that left hundreds dead or wounded, the disbanding of parliament for almost two years, imposition of emergency rule, and a concerted government attempt to address the issue of communal equality. "The perception of Islam as the religion of an endangered indigenous population that has been primarily rural, poor, and noncommercial in its character has also fostered a sense of defensiveness that has been the foundation for Malay-sponsored politics, public policy, and attitudes."[10]

In contrast to most other Muslim countries, the Islamic revival in Malaysia was a religio-ethnic resurgence.[11] Many factors (indigenous and international) coalesced during the 1970s and early 1980s to produce an Islamic/Malay revival in which religion, economics, language, and culture were intertwined. The government implemented an economic reform program that targeted Malays and other "sons of the soil" (*bumiputra*). The National Economic Policy (NEP), an affirmative action–like plan of special rights, quotas, and subsidies for economic and educational uplift, was meant to alter the "imbalance" between Malays and other communities. Although the program's primary focus was Malay socioeconomic development, the promotion of Malay language and cultural values further strengthened the bond between religion and ethnicity. The process, with its emphasis on Malay language, history, culture, and religion, reinforced Malay pride, identity, and solidarity. Malay nationalism and Islam, already critical elements in Malay cultural identity, became an even more powerful ideological and political force.

The dynamics of a Malay-Islamic resurgence was particularly evident among the younger generation of Malay students and university graduates in the post-1969 period. As in Egypt and other Muslim countries, urban universities became centers for Islamic student activism, which replaced nationalist and socialist groups as the most effective actors. As a result of the NEP, thousands of Malays were admitted to secondary schools and universities at home or sent abroad for study. Many students were uprooted from the ethnic homogeneity, integrated life, and security of predominantly Malay rural environments. They were thrust into modern urban cities, which were far more culturally diverse and were experienced as both Westernized and dominated by Chinese "yellow culture." Malay youth at campuses like the prestigious University of Malaya and the Universiti Kebangsaan (National University) turned to their Islamic heritage to preserve their sense of Malay Muslim identity. The experience of an alien or foreign urban culture and of economic and educational disparities between Malay Muslim and Chinese and Indian communities reinforced a sense of inferiority, discrimination, and injustice. It fostered a belief that the system and policies of UMNO-led government had failed.

Islamic revivalism in Malaysia was further reinforced by Malay students returning from study in the United States and Great Britain, who were greatly influenced by exposure to students from other Muslim countries and to the writing and thinking of Islamic activists from the Arab world, Iran, and Pakistan. Whatever their differences, all proclaimed an Islamic alternative—a common reassertion of Islam as a total way of life and a God-ordained alternative to the excesses of capitalism and socialism. It was not uncommon for critics to comment that students went abroad for university education only to return as "Islamic fundamentalists." Indeed, the prime minister, Hussein Onn, having spoken adversely of such students, was chagrinned when "[a]fter he had criticized young women returning wearing 'curtains,' his own daughter stepped off the plane in traditional dress."[12]

Events in the Muslim world also influenced Malaysia's Islamic revival. The 1967 Arab-Israeli War (with its loss of Jerusalem) and the Arab oil embargo of 1973 brought an outpouring of popular Islamic sentiment and stronger governmental and nongovernmental ties with the Arab and broader Muslim world. Pakistan's Islamization program under General Zia ul-Haq (1977–88) and Iran's "Islamic revolution" of 1978–79 were well known to Malaysian leaders, who maintained contacts with fellow activists and participated in international conferences. Issues concerning Afghanistan, Palestine, the liberation of Jerusalem (and, more recently, the Intifada, the Gulf War, and the war in Bosnia) received wide news coverage and were the object of popular demonstrations of support and concern. International events, coupled with mass communications, contributed to a transformation in which Malays, who always believed that to be Malay was to be Muslim, expressed this consciousness in a more universal Islamic language. Thus, individuals became more prone to identifying themselves not just as Malay but as Muslim. Similarly, in the aftermath of 1969, when many Malays spoke of the survival of the Malay community they used the term *ummah*, which in fact refers to the worldwide Islamic community. At the same time, concern about the influence of Iranian and Libyan radicalism contributed to increased government concern and sensitivity to Islamic sentiments and issues.

THE ISLAMIC RESURGENCE AND THE DAKWAH MOVEMENTS

While Malaysia had previously had a number of prominent organizations, post-1969 political developments produced the growth of Islamic organizations that came to be called *dakwah* (Arabic *dawa*) movements. Dakwah means the "call" to Islam, and refers not only to proselytizing among non-Muslims but also to the call to those born Muslim to become more observant. During the 1970s, the more political- and reform-minded of these organizations put pressure on UMNO to be more assertive in the defense of Islam, Malay nationalism, and Malay-Muslim economic rights and privileges. They condemned dependence on Western and Chinese values, charging that it subverted Malay Muslim identity, integrity, and solidarity. They advocated a return to Islam as a total way of life combining worship and social activism, and called for a greater Islamization of Malaysian society. However, the *dakwah* movements embraced diverse groups, and interpretations of revivalist Islam had differing implications for personal and public life. Some simply emphasized greater attention to personal behavior: observance of prayer and fasting, the replacement of western styles with Islamic dress, and the avoidance of dances, nightclubs, Western music, drugs, alcohol, and other "foreign-inspired" activities associated with or attributed to "Western" or "yellow" cultural activities. More militant activists agitated for the establishment of Islamic government and the implementation of Islamic law and the separation of the sexes in education, sports, and public life in general. The variety of *dakwah* organizations and orientations can be seen in three groups in particular: Darul Arqam (the House of Arqam), ABIM (the Islamic Youth Movement of Malaysia), PAS (Parti Islam Se-Malaysia, or Islamic Party of Malaysia), and the Islamic Republic group.

Darul Arqam

Darul Arqam, in some ways, fulfills western stereotypes of Islamic activism as consisting of atavistic fundamentalist movements that wish to return to the seventh century. Established in 1968 by Ustaz (teacher) Ashaari Muhammad, it emphasized the importance of establishing an Islamic society prior to creating an Islamic state. Arqam has been critical of most Muslim governments and Islamic organizations outside and within Malaysia, attributing their lack of success to a failure to focus sufficiently on Islamic education and emulation of the model Islamic community governed by the Prophet at Medina. However, in its early years Arqam tended to be Sufi (mystical) and apolitical in orientation, focusing on the creation of model Islamic communities rather than engaging in political action.

Members live in communities that emulated the communal life of the Prophet's community. Both Western and traditional Malay forms of dress are eschewed. Men wear green robes (the color of Islam), and a turban and beard in imitation of the Prophet. Although historically women had not been separated from males or veiled in Malay society, members of Darul Arqam practice total segregation of the sexes; women are completely veiled in public.

The organization had seemed to go into eclipse when its leader left the country in the late 1980s. Among the early rumors were that its leader had quit the organization. However, under Ashaari's leadership from his self-imposed exile in Thailand, Arqam had become a powerful and wealthy organization with international branches by the early 1990s. Darul-Arqam ran some forty-eight communities in Malaysia, with its own schools and medical clinics. The Arqam communities in Malaysia ran educational, agricultural, manufacturing, and social service projects, as well as restaurants and publishing houses. Factories manufactured *halal* (Islamically permitted) foods, soap, and drinks.[13] Arqam existed in some sixteen additional countries, with a growing network of schools and universities in Indonesia, Thailand, Singapore, Brunei, Pakistan, and Central Asia.

In the summer of 1994, the government moved against Arqam, at first charging that Arqam and its leader, Ashaari Muhammad, were engaged in radical politics, from training a suicide squad in Thailand (where Ashaari lived in exile) to having conspired to overthrow the Malaysian government in 1986. In fact, Arqam's growth and prosperity, as well as the movement's transformation from an apolitical to a political force in Malaysia, contributed to the government's decision to curb the movement. Ashaari's downfall was precipitated by his having made a series of religious and political claims "to have regular dialogues with the Prophet Muhammad . . . forecasts [of] the eventual arrival of a messiah in Mecca with a caliph, or ruler, in Malaysia . . . [and the claim that] he and the Prophet discuss Malaysian politics, and [forecast] the downfall of Mahathir and Deputy Prime Minister Anwar Ibrahim within six months to two years."[14] Growing fear of Arqam, which spread among middle class students and professionals, its penetration of UMNO elite, and its political agenda, led to a government crackdown. Finally, the government arranged for Ashaari's extradition and arrested Ashaari under Malaysia's Internal Security Act (ISA) for teaching "deviant" Islamic teachings and as a threat to national security. Religious officials associated with the government-sponsored Islamic Council (Pusat Islam) issued a fatwa (religious edict) condemning Arqam as a deviant sect. Arqam was banned for propagating deviationist teachings in August 1994. Ashaari and some of the movement's core members were detained without trial under the Internal Security Act. However, amid criticism of the Malaysian government by international human rights groups, Ashaari and his followers made a public confession on national television.[15] Darul-Arqam was disbanded, its properties and institutions seized, and the group's members absorbed within the broader Muslim community.

ABIM

The most vital, effective, and politically successful *dakwah* movement in the 1970s and early 1980s was the Islamic Youth Movement of Malaysia (Angkatan Belia Islam Malaysia, or ABIM). Created in 1971–72, ABIM embodied the events, issues, and concerns of the post-1969 period that fostered religious revivalism in general and the mobilization of youth in particular. Under the charismatic leadership of one of its founders, Anwar Ibrahim, who served as its president from 1974 until his resignation in 1982, ABIM became the dominant Islamic movement in the 1970s and early 1980s, growing to a membership of more than 35,000. Ibrahim reflected what would become the profile of many ABIM members: young, secular- or Western-educated (Ibrahim was educated at the English language, British-influenced University of Malaya), emerging middle class, who in university years had "turned" to Islam as a modern religio-cultural alternative to Westernization and secularism, as well as to conservative or traditionalist Islam of the older generation. In contrast to more Westernized elites, ABIM asserted that Islam offered an indigenous, authentic identity and way of life that combined concern for religious ritual with social and economic reform. ABIM's Islamic orientation was modern reformist rather than a return to the Islam of the more traditionalist ulama and of PAS. Ibrahim himself proved to be a charismatic and formidable leader: bright, well-read, a superb speaker (with charm, a winning personality, and a sense of humor), energetic and with strong organizational and strategic skills and an accommodationist orientation. His role and significance can be seen both in ABIM's accomplishments and the extent to which it seemed to stall and decline after his resignation in 1982.

ABIM was not a political party. In theory apolitical, its mission and goal were to spread Islam and revitalize the Muslim community in Malaysia through preaching, communications, and education. As one of its former presidents observed, "ABIM is an Islamic movement which will continue to struggle to uphold Islam, guided by genuine Islamic principles pursued through *dawah* (the act of inviting a person to the faith) and *tarbiyah* (education)."[16] ABIM's audience was both Muslim and non-Muslim. It wished to call those born Muslim back to Islam, that is, to be more observant Muslims; and it also sought to attract non-Muslims. ABIM, through programs (seminars and conferences), publications, and audiotape cassettes, sought to develop a new generation of more Islamically aware leaders— modern-educated but Islamically oriented. It established schools that combined modern and religious education, preparing students for government examinations and other jobs. ABIM organized students studying abroad and mobilized Muslim students and young professionals at home to spread Islam in Malaysia and to bring about socioeconomic reforms.

Like Islamic movements in many parts of the Muslim world, ABIM advocated an Islamically oriented state as the corrective to secularism and Western-oriented development. Although it remained unclear regarding the establishment of a formal Islamic state, it called for the implementation of Islamic law and values. However, it remained consistent in its recognition and acceptance that Malaysia was and would continue to be a multiethnic and multireligious state. As for socioeconomic issues, ABIM denounced corruption, poverty, maldistribution of wealth, the penetration of Malaysian society and culture by a "decadent" Western pop culture, gambling, and alcohol consumption, and called for greater political and press freedom and respect for human rights.[17] Its indictment of the political and economic status quo and its call for social action were given a Malay-Islamic shape and idiom, as one member observed, in order to mobilize disillusioned and disaffected students

> disgusted by the hypocrisy in society. We were disillusioned with the leadership. . . . The leaders were condemning corruption, but they were enriching themselves. They talked about Malay nationalism, but they were alienated from the Malay masses. They were obsessed by the West. They were too accommodating to non-Malay sentiments. They were extremely slow in implementing national policies in education and language. We were impatient and angry about the plight of the Malays, their education, rural development, rural health. There was this huge University hospital, but no clinics

in the rural areas. There were schools with no laboratories, no libraries and no qualified teachers. We were very angry, disgusted and critical of the government. There seemed to be no moral foundation and no spiritual guidance. We turned to Islam to fill this vacuum and to look for solutions.[18]

ABIM formed study groups or cells (*usrah*), ran orientation programs for new students, conducted seminars and community projects, translated and distributed the writings of international activists such as Egypt's Hasan al-Banna and Sayyid Qutb, and Pakistan's Mawlana Mawdudi, into Malay, and recast its commitment to social justice in an Islamic framework. Islam was offered to students as an alternative to prevailing nationalist and socialist options. Thus, for example, groups such as the Malay Language Society for Implementation of Malay as the national language, as well as health and economic reforms, was now rooted not simply in Malay nationalism but in an Islamically informed Malay nationalism.[19]

Although influenced by outside Islamic activists, movements, and experiments in Pakistan (General Zia ul-Haq and the Jamaat-i Islami), Sudan (Jafar al-Numayri and the Sudanese Muslim Brotherhood), and to a lesser extent the creation of an Islamic Republic in Iran, ABIM's ideology and goals were primarily shaped to speak directly to Malaysia's specific history and context, to a multiethnic, pluralistic society. Anwar Ibrahim recognized that the experience of other Muslim organizations and governments might be learned from, but not uncritically copied and duplicated, in Malaysia's multiethnic and religious context.

ABIM's universal vision of Islam (the Islamic call [*dawa*] to Muslims and non-Muslims) made it critical of narrow expressions of Malay-Muslim identity, of the simple equation of Malay and Muslim, of Malay nationalism and Islam. It therefore rejected the UMNO government's promotion of Malay nationalism, in particular its Malay-focused bumiputra program. Anwar Ibrahim denounced communalism, racism, and sectarianism: "Islam regards discrimination as a criminal act because it is contradictory to the (Islamic) call to unite different communities and to encourage tolerance, friendship, and mutual respect among all human beings."[20] Sensitive to non-Muslim concerns, ABIM's advocacy of implementation of the Sharia was accompanied by condemnation of racism. Ibrahim insisted upon the preservation of non-Muslim rights within a pluralistic and democratic society, in a concerted effort to reassure the Chinese minority community in particular.[21]

ABIM maintained that the creation of an Islamic state would strengthen rather than hinder the development of democracy in Malaysia. Ibrahim was quick to emphasize that he favored a democratic and multiracial society:

> The future society should be more committed and have a better understanding of the Islamic struggle, with the aim of creating a fair society, one that respects human rights . . . a national policy that guarantees real justice for all. . . . Islam places high regard for the rights of minority groups, the freedom

of worship, . . . with a just economic system that will abolish class distinctions, and wipe out narrow communal feelings.[22]

ABIM swept Student Union elections in 1974, signaling its rise to prominence. It reached the height of its power in the late 1970s, as a result of its charismatic leader and its activities, as well as an alliance with its chief political rival PAS (Parti Islam Se-Malaysia, or Islamic Party of Malaysia).

PAS and the Islamic Republic Group

PAS, Malaysia's oldest and largest Islamic political party, was established in 1951 by ulama who defected from UMNO because of its "compromise policy towards non-Malays and also due to what they claimed to be an ambivalent attitude toward Islam."[23] With a rural base and support from the conservative ulama, PAS, which regards itself as both a political party and an Islamic movement, has participated in elections since Malaysia's first elections in 1955, when it officially became a political party. It has tended to fare better in state elections in Trengannu, Kelantan, and Kedah than in national elections. PAS has consistently advocated an Islamic state and social order accompanied by the introduction of Sharia law. PAS and ABIM shared many similar goals, such as the creation of an Islamic social order, and the denunciation of Westernization, secularism, materialism (conspicuous consumption), economic and social disparities, and political authoritarianism. However, in contrast to ABIM's more moderate, modernist image as an urban-based, Islamic reformist pressure group for Islamically rooted socioeconomic change, PAS has often been regarded as a more strident, confrontative, intransigent, Islamically conservative, religiously chauvinistic political party. It is far more sweeping in its denunciation of the West and traditionalist in its inflexible interpretation of Islam from general matters of Islamic law to specific issues such as women and non-Muslims. Indeed, PAS was often quicker to label its Muslim opponents as *kafirs* (unbelievers). In contrast to ABIM, PAS leaders tended to be traditional ulama, and many were graduates of Islamic universities in the Middle East (Cairo's al-Azhar University or those in Mecca and Medina).

PAS was quite clear about its desire for the Islamization of society (politically, economically, educationally, and socially). It accepted a parliamentary system of government and participated in elections, but criticized the control of the UMNO-led government. Somewhat similar to Iran, PAS advocated the creation of an ulama committee that would ensure that all laws conformed to Islam. It called for the Islamization of the educational curriculum, for a strong dose of religion plus "modern" subjects as long as they conformed to Islamic principles. In economics, it advocated interest-free banking. However, despite many years of existence, its platform and agenda tended to be vague regarding the means and methods with which to implement and achieve its goals.

PAS tended to advocate the implementation and enforcement of traditional or classical Islamic law rather than acknowledging, as did ABIM, the need for its reform. Moreover, although it insisted that non-Muslims had nothing to fear from the creation of an Islamic state, its equation of Islam and Malay nationalism, insistence on special privileges for Malay Muslims, and wholesale rejection of Western values, secularism, and "yellow culture," as well as its tendency to identify Chinese and Indians as a threat to Malay development and interests (that is, as the cause of economic disparities), raised serious questions about the future of non-Muslims in a PAS-dominated Islamic state. Public statements by some PMIP (PAS's earlier name) representatives during the elections of 1959 and 1964 that if the party were elected, "the non-Malays would be either sent back to China or dumped back into the South China sea," and, again in 1974, the proposal that the constitution be amended so that only Malays could become prime minister and chief minister (Menteri Besar) reinforced non-Muslim fears.

The late 1970s and 1980s brought significant changes in PAS orientation and leadership. The result of an alliance between PAS and ABIM in 1977 was that PAS and ABIM strengthened and reinforced each other. Members crossed organizational lines, especially as candidates in political elections—so much so that some within PAS entertained the idea that Anwar Ibrahim might also become its leader in the near future. By 1980, PAS began to be transformed, as its old-guard leadership was challenged by younger voices, many of whom were ex-ABIM leaders. In addition, more Islamically militant activists newly returned from study in Britain pressured the PAS leadership to adopt a purer, more systematic Islamic stance with less emphasis on Malay nationalism, and to devote more emphasis to organization, cadre training, and political action, in order to create an Islamic republic, as had occurred in Iran.[24]

Among the key figures in the new guard was Hajji Abdul Hadi Awang, who represented the new ABIM-PAS synthesis. Hadi Awang bridged the worlds of ABIM and PAS. In contrast to many ABIM leaders, and more like the PAS leadership, he was the traditionally raised son of a religious leader and was educated at Medina University and al-Azhar University in Cairo. His fluency in Arabic, training at leading Islamic universities, and ability as a preacher enhanced his credibility with the ulama and contributed to his popularity. More militant students found in him a leader who, in language reminiscent of Iran's Islamic revolution, denounced the government's un-Islamic colonialist policies and called for the creation of a true Islamic state, a struggle whose realization might require martyrdom. Here was an ABIM leader who had contested the 1978 elections as a PAS candidate and possessed the background, training, and rhetorical approach attractive to a PAS constituency. In 1982, the new guard joined with the ulama, and Hadi Awang captured the PAS party leadership.

The ranks of PAS increasingly attracted more militant students; in particular those students, professors, and young professionals who returned from study in Britain in the late 1970s and early 1980s. They were influenced by radical interpretations of the teachings of Pakistan's Mawlana Mawdudi and Egypt's Sayyid Qutb, to which they were introduced at British universities by Muslim faculty members or fellow students from other Muslim countries. In Britain, they had formed two organizations: Saura Islam (Voice of Islam), which was influenced by Pakistan's Mawdudi and his Jamaat-i Islami and the Islamic Representative Council (IRC), and was drawn to the example of the Egyptian Muslim Brotherhood. Saura Islam believed that an Islamic state could only be realized by a revolution led by an Islamic party composed of a trained, Islamically committed elite. The IRC sought to create a mass movement, organized as were the Egyptian Brothers, into secret cells (*usrah*). IRC's militant, underground organizational approach and straight-forward, unambiguous message proved attractive:

> Their black and white approach to the Islamic struggle—you are either a Muslim practicing Islam as a complete way of life or you are an infidel, you either fight for Islam or you are irreligious, you either join an Islamic group or you are not part of the movement—appealed, in particular, to the science students . . . [25]

Upon their return to Malaysia from Britain to take up positions in the universities, schools, government bureaucracy, and professions, Islamic activists were attracted to the more militant Islamic political language of PAS under its new leadership, rather than the moderate approach of ABIM. It mirrored their own condemnation of an illegitimate, "infidel" secular government, their anti-Western rhetoric, their call for a true, all-encompassing Islamic state based upon the Quran and Sunnah, their admiration and support for revolutionary Iran, and their strong emphasis on political activism. Whereas ABIM and PAS had both been early supporters of the Iranian revolution, ABIM's enthusiasm had cooled, while PAS continued its admiration and support.

Members of the IRC and Saura Islam became part of the younger guard in a PAS that seized the banner of Islamic opposition from ABIM. They also established a new student dakwah organization, the Islamic Republic group, which was committed to the establishment of an Iranian-type Islamic government in Malaysia and which replaced ABIM as the dominant Islamic student organization in the 1980s. The Islamic Republic group's ideology and political activism were radical in their rigid worldview, confrontational politics, and agenda. There were no gray areas. Both the individual and the state were either Muslim or they were not, Islamically committed or un-Islamic, believer or infidel, saved or damned. Malaysia's man-made constitutional government must be replaced by one based upon the Quran and Sunnah (model example) of the Prophet Muhammad, and guided by the ulama and Islamic law (the Sharia).

Emulating the organizational approach of the Egyptian Muslim Brotherhood and the Jamaat-i Islami, the Islamic Republic group, like all campus dakwah organizations, had as its chief means for achieving its goals the *usrahs* (cells), study-support groups that emphasized religious and political activism. The strength and success of *usrah* groups lay in the high level of ideological commitment and organization that often enables a minority to influence or dominate the majority. Students were organized into small cells, separated by sex, which met regularly to study (have religious talks, discussions, and debates) and to pray together as well as to provide a social support system, thus developing and reinforcing a strong sense of religious identity and solidarity. Student activists, who saw themselves as guardians of Islam and community morality, quietly spread their message through distributing publications and video and audio tapes, organizing orientation programs and religious courses for new students, gaining control of student organizations and hostels, and confronting university administrators and other students to demand that they ban "un-Islamic" activities such as dances, parties, concerts, and mixed socials. Those students or university officials who disagreed or attempted to block their actions often found themselves denounced as infidels (*kafirs*). While the approach of the Islamic Republican group attracted many, it alienated many others. As one student commented, "They're the 'no-no' faces who have made Islam into a 'no-no' religion."[26] Although it enjoyed a following among students and faculty, it failed to become a significant organization on the political scene nationally.

GOVERNMENT/UMNO TILT TOWARD ISLAM

While the ruling party (UMNO) and its politicians had always been sensitive to Islam, in its early years UMNO had tended to emphasize its role as the defender of Malay nationalism and of a pluralistic system. However, the climate changed markedly after 1969. The need to respond to the economic and cultural demands of its Malay base of support prompted a greater emphasis on Malay-Islamic identity and solidarity in its symbols, political discourse, and policies. As the political and social milieu changed, with the influx of Malays into urban areas, the increased emphasis on Malay language and religion, the activities and demands of PAS and ABIM organizations, and the presence of a more militant Islamically oriented younger generation, the elite culture itself changed. Politicians, some out of conviction and others out of pragmatic necessity, increasingly associated themselves more visibly with their Malay-Muslim heritage. The government and UMNO sought to project its Malay-Islamic credentials as well as to contain and neutralize the opposition.

The government response was one of coercion and cooptation. It moved to contain and silence its Islamic opposition, in particular its most effective leader: Anwar Ibrahim. Ibrahim was detained for one year. However, at the same time, UMNO's politicians increasingly employed Islamic rhetoric and slogans to bolster their Islamic image. By the early 1980s, Dr. Muhammad Mahathir (Mahathir bin Mohamed), elected prime minister in 1981, placed UMNO and the government firmly on a more Islamically oriented path, giving greater emphasis to Islam both domestically and internationally.

Mahathir was able to skillfully weave together past and present, to coopt and coerce his Islamic opposition, to use Islam in domestic, regional, and international politics. The UMNO-led government's Islamization program ranged from the use of Islamic symbols and rhetoric to the creation of Islamic institutions. UMNO politicians equated "Islamic values" with hard work, discipline, and progress, and linked the NEP's uplift programs with Islam: "UMNO tracts have urged the need to develop a more modern, competitive Muslim if Islam is to thrive in the modern world. If Islam is to be defended and develop, the Muslim must be able to compete with the Chinese and Indians."[27]

Most significantly and unexpectedly, Mahathir invited Anwar Ibrahim to join his government. Ibrahim's acceptance surprised and stunned many. Some argued that he had been coopted; others believed that he had seized the opportunity to work for the greater Islamization of society from within the government. His resignation as president of ABIM in 1982 was the beginning of his rapid rise to power. To the consternation of many UMNO politicians who had opposed (and continued to oppose) him, Anwar Ibrahim's broad base of support among the younger generation, even within UMNO itself, was reaffirmed almost immediately with his election as UMNO Youth President and, later, UMNO Vice-president. Many predicted that the longevity of Ibrahim's political career would be that of a shooting star, both because of strong opposition from within UMNO's political hierarchy and because he would prove ill prepared for high-level government positions. Ibrahim moved steadily upward through several cabinet positions: minister of youth, of sports and culture, of agriculture, of education, and, finally, minister of finance and deputy prime minister (1993).

Ibrahim himself had to bridge the gap between two worlds, that of Islamic activist and UMNO politician. He faced the criticism and cynicism of those who thought that he had been coopted by the government. Many later criticized the once-outspoken, charismatic voice of opposition for simply becoming "another compromising politician." Many senior UMNO leaders were both suspicious of this Islamic activist, whom they had once sought to suppress, and resented his meteoric rise in their party. Over the years, Ibrahim proved an asset to Mahathir— a loyal UMNO politician and an effective cabinet minister and politician, who diffused the challenge of PAS and reached out to Malaysia's non-Muslim minority communities, particularly the Chinese. He soon became Mahathir's choice to be his eventual successor as prime minister.

In moving to coopt its Islamic opposition, the Mahathir government testified to its growth and strength. Rather than simply yield to some of its demands, it sought to coopt or preempt its ideology and agenda. The government significantly expanded its involvement in Islamic affairs in a number of ways: by providing greater support for expanded coverage of Islam in the media and in school curric-

ula; by establishing a new International Islamic University, as well as Islamic studies faculties in existing universities; by creating an Islamic bank and insurance company; by increasing funding for the building of mosques, for social welfare programs, and for the propagation (dakwah) of Islam; and by convening international
Islamic conferences on everything from Islamic philosophy and law to economics
and the sciences. The government also became more visible in its participation in
regional and international Islamic organizations such as the Asia Pacific Mosque
Council, the Regional Islamic Dawa Council of Southeast Asia and the Pacific, the
World Assembly of Muslim Youth, and the Organization of the Islamic Conference.
To those who called for an Islamic state, Mahathir answered that, while it safe-
guarded its pluralistic system, for Malay Muslims, Malaysia was already in effect an
Islamic state and society.

Malaysian Islam has had both strong international and regional Islamic ties.
Historically, the Middle East, rather than Southeast Asia, has been the most influential source for the development of Islamic thought and institutions. Religious
leaders and scholars studied in Cairo at Al-Azhar University or at Islamic universities in Saudi Arabia. Prominent Islamic thinkers or ideologues such as Hasan al-
Banna, Sayyid Qutb, and Mawlana Mawdudi were translated into bahasa (bahasa
Malaya, the Malay language), and their writings widely disseminated in books and
pamphlets.

The 1970s and 1980s reinforced and expanded Malaysia's international Islamic
connection. International events mobilized Islamic identification and sentiment in
Malaysia as in the rest of the Muslim world. While the 1967 Arab defeat and the loss
of Jerusalem in the Six Day War had made Palestine an Islamic issue, the 1973 war
and oil embargo restored a sense of Islamic pride. Arab oil wealth became a source
of pride and reinforced a sense of identity and solidarity with the transnational
Islamic community (ummah). The heartland or motherland of Islam, the birth-
place of the Prophet and the revelation of the Quran, reemerged as a source of
wealth and power as witnessed by the impact of the 1973 Arab oil embargo. Arab
oil countries became a source of major employment and revenue; their petrodol-
lars supported Islamic projects, from the building of mosques and hospitals to support for Islamic institutions (schools, universities, and banks). Islam in Southeast
Asia benefited not only financially but also intellectually from contacts with the
Middle East. Scholars from the Middle East filled important positions in faculties
of Islamic studies at universities, in particular at the International Islamic University. The Iranian revolution of 1978–79 was hailed by ABIM and PAS and the Muslim masses in Southeast Asia as much as it was feared by governments. Shii
thought, from that of the Ayatollah Khomeini and other leading clerical leaders to
lay intellectuals such as Mehdi Bazargan and especially Ali Shariati, became a
source of inspiration and, for some, an object of emulation.

However, increasingly, in the late 1980s and 1990s, both the Mahathir government and Malaysia's Islamic organizations like ABIM and PAS had developed their

own paradigms: "Southeast Asian Muslims have become an integral part of the worldwide Muslim intellectual resurgence and are gaining the tools to provide their own interpretations of Islam to the *ummah*."[28] Islam in Malaysia (and in Indonesia) has increasingly taken on a more regional flavor, as scholars trained in the Muslim world and the West apply their knowledge and skills not only to communicating the more highly developed tradition of Islamic scholarship in the Middle East but also to developing more local Islamic interpretations and applications, to making them accessible in local language and idiom and thus more relevant.[29]

ABIM's Decline and Reorganization

ABIM did not fare as well as its former president. By the late 1970s, it had already been challenged by more militant Islamic activist students and professionals recently returned from Britain. The loss of its charismatic leader in 1982 and the subsequent move of other ABIM leaders into the government, as well as ABIM's moderation of its criticism of the government, made ABIM more vulnerable to critics' charges of cooption and accommodation. ABIM's changing image and role were signaled by PAS's return as the leading Islamic opposition group. ABIM also lost its dominance on the campuses to the more radical voices of the Islamic Republic group, a close ally of PAS which in 1983 wrested control of the Islamic Student Society, the most important student dakwah organization, from ABIM. At the same time, what ABIM lost visibly, in terms of its organization and in terms of its dominance of campus politics, it seemed to gain invisibly, as ex-ABIM leaders and members increasingly joined the government and its bureaucracy—resulting in what some called the "ABIMization" of the Malaysian government.

Democracy, Pluralism, Islam and the New World Order

The late 1980s and early 1990s witnessed greater political concentration of power and, some would charge, greater authoritarianism, in the hands of Prime Minister Mahathir; his projection of a stronger profile as a regional and international Muslim leader, especially vis-à-vis the West; and an economic upsurge under the leadership of Finance Minister Anwar Ibrahim that reversed a recession. Today, like many of its Pacific rim colleagues in ASEAN, Malaysia possesses a strong leadership and economy. Mahathir bin Muhammad, who became prime minister in 1981, employed a strong, "hands-on" approach to government to accelerate the process of nation-building and industrialization. His aggressive leadership style included capturing control of UMNO and thus leadership of the ruling coalition, Barison Nasional, and consolidation of the prime minister's central authority over the administration and political institutions of the country. Although faced in 1987 with a nearly successful challenge by several other UMNO leaders that split the party and led to the formation of an opposition party, Semangat (Spirit) of '46,

Mahathir demonstrated his remarkable political skills, weathered the storm, and by the early 1990s enjoyed solid control of the government and its ruling party.

Several issues have emerged, or perhaps more accurately reemerged, in the 1990s which have threatened to exacerbate Malaysia's always tenuous politics of ethnic and religious pluralism: reintroduction of an international language, and an attempt in Kelantan by a PAS-led government to implement Sharia for Muslims and non-Muslims alike. Mahathir approached these issues, as he had others, by balancing emphasis on the importance and interconnectedness of Malay as the national language for national unity with acknowledgment of the value of English for international business and economic development. As his deputy education minister observed: "We should recognize the different roles played by the languages. One is to do business, the other establish an identity."[30] With regard to PAS's desire to implement Sharia, and, in particular, the hudood, Mahathir declared that Malaysia's laws were in conformity with Islam, reaffirmed the values of pluralism and tolerance, and warned of religious extremism. At the same time, the government continued to espouse a positive, reformist understanding of Islam and Islamic values, portraying Islam as a dynamic religion with a strong work ethic, to support Malaysia's aggressive approach to business and industrialization. This policy is embodied in Vision 2020, announced in 1991 as the successor to the National Economic Policy (NEP), the twenty-year Malay uplift program initiated in the aftermath of the 1969 riots. Its goal is a modern and industrialized Malaysia by the second decade of the twenty-first century.

If Anwar Ibrahim somewhat tempered his Islamic profile, Mahathir seemed comfortable in increasing his and that of Malaysia within Southeast Asia, the Muslim world, and the broader international community.

Mahathir has long been a frank critic of the West, both of European colonialism and of modern Western neoimperialism as well as of Western support for Israel. His relations with Britain as well as the United States, although generally cordial, have been strained on numerous occasions. For Mahathir, the impact of Western imperialism (of "the non-Muslim countries of the West"), its political, economic, and cultural domination of the Muslim world, is both a past reality and a present challenge or threat. It is a history of exploitation and injustice that continues to affect the Muslim world: "Islam is suppressed almost everywhere in the world even though the world alleges that it subscribes to the principles of justice and the rule of law."[31] Just as European colonialism shaped and imposed its values on much of the world, the process is perpetuated today, as the West in the name of a New World Order and in the name of justice seeks to impose its definitions of (or brand of selective) democracy and human rights:

> They speak eloquently of the rule of law, human rights, democracy or the voice of the majority, without taking account the existence of certain man-made laws that are unfair, excessive human rights, and unwise majority voices. Hence, the

laws in the West place too much priority on the individual's right that allows him to do anything he pleases even though his actions may threaten the peace and security of the society. International laws, meanwhile, were formulated to provide the mighty with the right to suppress the weak. The same applies to human rights which are highly valued to the extent that group, in the name of democracy, are given protection even if their activities threaten society, peace and progress.[32]

Thus, in speaking on the New World Order before the United Nations, Mahathir charged that

> what is actually happening is similar to the nineteenth century colonial empirialism [*sic*], where "might is right." The "Big Powers" are still there, brandishing their heavy sticks in the face of the smaller nations to defend their vested interests even at the expense of what is basically just and fair. . . . All members of . . . the United Nations should participate in the shaping of the New World Order if we are to avoid a return of a new colonial rule.[33]

Mahathir's critique of Western imperialism, past and present, and his concern that the New World Order not be a mere contemporary expression of Western hegemony extends to his position regarding democracy and democratization. Thus, while he has insisted that "[d]emocracy, and only democracy, is legitimate and permissible now," he has also been quick to ask, "But is there only one form of democracy or only one high priest to interpret it?"[34] The Malaysian government, as reflected in statements of its prime minister and deputy prime minister, has warned of the dangers inherent in those who not only preach but also seek to impose their brand or interpretation of democracy: "Hegemony by democratic powers is no less oppressive than hegemony by totalitarian states."[35] For Mahathir, there are many forms of democracy, and just as there are differences in practice among those who preach democracy, so too "[c]annot the converts too interpret the details, if not the basics?"[36]

Thus, while Mahathir affirms the desirability, indeed necessity, of democracy, he rejects a blind acceptance of "universal" notions or definitions of democracy or human rights that are in fact primarily the product of an Old Order, dominated by big powers—from a United Nations in which all are equal but five are more equal than the other 166 to a New World Order defined by the few rather than the many. True democracy should exist both within states and between nation-states. States must have the ability to determine a form of democracy and human rights appropriate to their culture and values. This is particularly true where Western interpretations of democracy prove problematic:

> If democracy means the right to carry guns, to flaunt homosexuality, to disregard the institution of marriage, to disrupt or damage the well-being of the

community in the name of individual rights, to destroy a particular faith, to have privileged institutions which are sacrosanct even if they indulge in lies and instigations which undermine society, the economy and international relations . . . cannot the converts opt to reject them?[37]

Mahathir derides a Western democracy that, in the name of the voice of the majority, enables Serbs in Bosnia to suppress Bosnian Muslims and that continues to be highly regarded in the former Soviet Union and Eastern Europe, although it has led to the breakdown of law and order, widespread poverty, and repression. He is especially critical of what he regards as the hypocrisy of a West that does not hesitate to disregard out of self-interest the very principles of justice it espouses. Thus, although the West intervened in defense of Kuwait on ostensibly humanitarian grounds, it offered "a thousand and one excuses" for not protecting the rights of the Bosnian Muslim minority: "The truth is that they acted in Kuwait because they wanted to protect their source of petroleum. Since they have no interest in Bosnia, they are willing to allow the Serbs to kill, terrorise, and suppress the Bosnian Muslims."[38] It is the West's, and indeed the majority of the world's countries' systems of ethics and justice, based on "might makes right," that are causes of the oppression of Muslim countries internationally: "today, certain countries and races, such as the Serbs and Jews, dare and are able to suppress and terrorise . . . because Islamic countries are all weak."[39]

Mahathir had shifted Malaysia's traditional pro-West view to a "Look East" policy that emphasized a South-South, rather than North-South, orientation. Malaysia's "Look East" policy, which is national and regional in scope, is driven both by its critique of the West and its emphasis on indigenous Asian values (the implementation of the Confucian values of Japan, Korea, and Taiwan) and Islamic values to strengthen the Malay Muslim community and Malaysian development.

Mahathir's turn to the East is rooted in his rejection of Western imperialism and secularism and belief that the East possesses a more integrated approach to life. The root of the West's failure is that "Christian Western societies" have "secularized their religion," that is, have confined religion to private personal life. Modern Western societies' secularization of religion and a resultant valuing of unlimited individual freedom at the expense of societal needs have led to the the West's "moral decadence."[40] Thus, Malaysia has sought a Western standard of development without its social problems. As Malaysian society has felt the social consequences of rapid development and urbanization, the West has provided an easy scapegoat: "Western culture is held responsible for most social ills. Rock music in particular has been blamed for drug addiction, promiscuity, alcoholism, abandoned babies, teenage runaways, and loafing." As Malaysia's information minister noted: "Decay in the West started at Woodstock."[41]

Mahathir praises Asian societies, such as the Japanese, the Korean, and the Chinese in Singapore, Taiwan, and Hong Kong, that integrate values into work and professional ethics. By contrast, he believes, although Muslim societies have remained firm in their faith, and indeed are experiencing a religious resurgence, they have generally been unimpressive in economic development. Mahathir maintains that, in contrast to the past, when the Islamic community's emphasis on truth and justice, its integration of "both the physical and spiritual aspects of life in all spheres," enabled Islam to rapidly spread its influence and generate the many accomplishments and contributions of Islamic civilzation, modern Muslim societies have thus far failed to provide an integrated model for development.

Mahathir sees Malaysia, with its Islamic heritage and economic prosperity, as possessing the opportunity to offer an integrated indigenous Muslim model for development. In the midst of Malaysia's economic boom, with its rapid modernization and social dislocation, Mahathir has attempted to opt for modernization but not the secular modernity of the West. Thus, the Malaysian government has reemphasized the need to "return" to eternal religious truths and values in the midst of change and as a counterweight to the secularization of society and to Western materialism and a consumer society: "People who are affluent tend to forget God. We know that as we become more prosperous we tend to relegate religious life to the background. That is why we keep stressing the need to cling to religious values."[42]

Mahathir's rejection of a post-Enlightenment Western secular view that restricts religion to personal life, and his more comprehensive interpretation of Islam, has pleased some Muslims but also contributed to a feeling of unease among many non-Muslims (Chinese, Indians, Hindus, and Christians). Although the government has continued to emphasize pluralism and has not imposed a single system, minorities have remained nervous about the implications of such a direction. Minorities often see a Malaysian landscape that includes a 53 percent (seven million) Muslim population, Islam as the official religion, a deputy prime minister who was an Islamic activist (remembered by some as a radical activist), and a Malay Muslim-dominated government and educational bureaucracy.

While Mahathir has emphasized Malaysia's commitment to a pluralistic, democratic path that includes respect for the rights of minorities, his distinction between majority rule and minority rights has at times been ambiguous and thus not always a source of reassurance:

> The minority must have their rights, but do these include the denial of the rights of the majority? Admittedly the majority may not oppress the minority, but if the minority exercise their rights without responsibility, become the agents of foreign democracies, and try to weaken their own country so as to make it a client state to certain democratic powers, must the majority in the name of the democracy submit to the minority?[43]

Mahathir has coopted the holistic vision of the leading Islamic opposition party, PAS, by declaring that Islam is not merely personal piety and ritual, but also social and civilizational in its scope and impact. At the same time, the Malaysian government has both supported its own development plans and countered the conservative, antimodernization image of PAS by espousing a moderate, modernizing Islam. The Mahathir government has defined Islam, in particular Southeast Asian Islam, as a progressive civilization that emphasizes both material success in this life and spiritual values and reward in the next. Islam is portrayed as a faith and way of life that can inform modernization and development; a system of values that encourages and supports reason, science, and technology; and as a strong work ethic, as well as racial and religious tolerance and harmony. The government has institutionalized this view in a variety of ways, seeking to implement its vision gradually rather than to impose it unilaterally from above. While Anwar Ibrahim was minister of education, both curriculum reform and teacher-training institutes and programs were introduced that stressed the importance of Islamic values and the religious, moral values of other Malaysian communities. In 1993, the government created the Malaysian Institute for Islamic Understanding (IKIM) in Kuala Lumpur, a religious think-tank whose mandate is to promote better understanding among Muslims and non-Muslims, as well as to develop and promote a modern Islamic ideology that will legitimate the government's sociopolitical agenda among Malay Muslims. It has the additional benefit of both emphasizing the government's Islamic identity and distancing the government from Western values. Thus Mahathir hopes to counter PAS's tendency to associate the government with Western dependency and to reinforce the government's alignment with a "modern Islam" in contrast to PAS, which it portrays as a primarily conservative, rural-based organization, the bulk of whose ulama and constituency cling to a medieval Islam that cannot keep pace with Malaysia's rapid economic and social change. At the same time, a pluralistic vision of indigenous values has been utilized in domestic and regional politics.

Malaysia's critique of Western values and its distancing from the West with its "Look East" policy and emphasis on indigenous values has had regional implications as well. The government's talk of Asian values has emphasized Chinese and Islamic values in particular. In 1995, an international conference was held at the University of Malaya on Confucian and Islamic values which drew more than a thousand participants, including substantial representation from Singapore, Hong Kong, and China. Deputy Prime Minister Anwar Ibrahim drew a standing ovation when in opening the conference he used not only Bahasa and English but Mandarin Chinese. More specifically, the program explored the values of the two traditions, including those they shared in common. The university subsequently announced that it would establish a permanent center for Islam and Confucianism.

The "Look East" policy is also embodied in a younger leadership in Southeast Asia which increasingly emphasizes regional identity and economic cooperation. It is epitomized by government ministers such as Malaysia's Anwar Ibrahim and Indonesia's B. J. Habibie and new professional organizations such as Malaysia's

Writers Academy and Indonesia's Association of Indonesian Muslim Intellectuals (ICMI), which bring together businesspeople, intellectuals, and government officials who, despite differences, share a common emphasis on an Asian rather than Western alternative for development. They emphasize the need to reaffirm and reappropriate the centrality of their Asian identity and heritage, to work toward greater regional cooperation and economic integration, and to root technological and social development in indigenous Asian values.

Whatever its strengths, this more indigenous, regional approach also has potential weaknesses in terms of issues of pluralism, identity, and democratization. In fact, its major leaders and organizations tend to be Muslim; many are former Islamic youth leaders and activists who are now in their thirties and forties and in leadership positions. However much they may assert a pluralistic understanding of Asian culture and values, non-Muslims, in particular the non-Muslim ethnic Chinese of Malaysia and Indonesia, who have long been regarded by many Malay Muslims as a dominant minority economic elite, worry that this new ideological alternative will pander to those Muslims who believe and resent that "[l]iberal, pro-Western economists whose policies allowed equal opportunities for all allowed our economies to be dominated by the Chinese."[44] Having witnessed a contemporary resurgence of Islam not only in Southeast Asia but also in the broader Muslim world, in which reaffirmation of cultural identity and faith have gone hand-in-hand with Islamically inspired or legitimated sociopolitical and economic demands or reforms, non-Muslim minorities may well fear the implications of this new direction for their future in Muslim-majority nonsecular states. Thus, they fear in the long run the promotion and imposition not of a common Asian culture but of Asian Islamic culture and values. Although couched in somewhat less religious terms, current calls for a "Look East" policy will seem to some a more subtle, perhaps "non-fundamentalist" but no less threatening, form of Islamic revivalism.

Despite reassurances to non-Muslims through an interpretation of Islam that emphasizes pluralism, harmony, moderation, and tolerance, the attempt to wed indigenous spiritual values with industrialization and material development has its risks. Both non-Muslims and more conservative Muslims may find reason for concern. Many of the former may continue to be concerned that the emphasis on spiritual values will still mean the further privileging of Islam and Islamic values and an erosion of Malaysia's pluralist traditions. The latter, especially the more conservative ulama, may regard the high-profile linkage of religion with material progress as further eroding the essence of Islamic spirituality. Ulama concerns will find a ready audience, especially in rural areas and mosques, and a political voice in PAS. While PAS has participated in the democratic process and subcribes to notions of power sharing, many Muslims and non-Muslims alike have been concerned about the nature of its true agenda. Is the electoral process merely a means to an end? What would a PAS government implementation of an Islamic system of government and of Islamic law mean? The example of PAS in Kelantan, with its proposal to enforce the hudood on Muslims and non-Muslims alike, is, for many, cause for concern. These concerns are reinforced by the statements of some PAS leaders that "power sharing is itself not the primary objective of Islamic movements. It is just a strategy and a mechanism through which the ultimate objective, i.e. the establishment of an Islamic system of government, may be achieved."[45] The fact that in recent years PAS has sent students to study in Qum (Iran) reinforces, in the minds of some, concerns about PAS's true long-term agenda, allowing its opponents to charge that PAS does indeed wish to establish an Iranian-style Islamic republic.

National elections in April, 1995, epitomized the strengths and risks of the Malaysian political system. Prime Minister Mahathir and the UMNO-dominated fourteen-member National Front (Barison Nasional) coalition scored a runaway victory, soundly defeating its opposition, including PAS and the Democratic Action Front, which suffered a crushing defeat in its stronghold of Penang, the "hometown" of Anwar Ibrahim. A major part of the Front's platform or election manifesto had been "religious freedom." Yet, it is a circumscribed freedom. The manifesto, while recognizing Islam's status as the official religion, affirmed religious freedom and tolerance, noting that there was to be no coercion on religious matters. However, much of the section on religious freedom emphasized the government's task to "curb and eliminate all forms of religious deviation and extremism and safeguard the teachings of Islam; enhance the true understanding and teachings of Islam through schools, dakwah [Islamic missionary] classes, higher institutions of learning, and research institutions, [to] . . . ensure no misinterpreatation or abuse of religions for the benefits of individuals or groups."[46]

In a post-election followup, the government pressed its electoral advantage as the prime minister, declaring, "We are responsible for Islam," clearly warned PAS that the government might take action against it, as it had done to the Darul Arqam movement, on the grounds that it too had clearly deviated from true Islam teachings and threatened national security.[47] The Home Ministry set up a special committee, headed by its security division secretary, to monitor PAS leaders and activities, warning that the government would take action under the Internal Securities Act if PAS were found to be "creating tension, causing splits among the people or spreading deviationist teachings."[48] Although the government was quick to maintain that this action was not politically motivated but was to block any threat to security or manipulation of religious teachings, its actions underscore the politicization of religion in Malaysia and the potential pitfalls as government and its PAS opposition each maintained that it was the defender of "true Islam" and accused the other of deviationism.

CONCLUSION

Although Malaysia is considered a Muslim country, it is a pluralistic state in which a significant minority of the population is non-Muslim. Historically, Islam has been an integral part of Malay national identity, history, and culture. However, as a result of British colonialism, demographics changed, with the influx of Chinese and Indians. The sensitive multiethnic, multiracial, multireligious balance in Malaysian society has been tested by Malay reaction to the growing presence and power of non-Malays (Chinese and Indian) and the government's attempt after communal riots in 1969 to redress perceived imbalances and injustices. While UMNO and the national political elites in general have defined "Malayness" in terms of race, language, and customs or culture, with Islam an implicit factor or ingredient, the impact of contemporary Islamic revivalism and the activities of dakwah organizations produced a more explicit equation of Islam, language, and race. At the same time, international events, contacts, and communications have increased Malay awareness of and pride in its international Islamic identity and the issues and concerns of the broader Islamic community. As a result, Islam has become a more visible symbol in Malaysian politics, and one finds a greater emphasis on Malay-Islamic identity. Thus, despite the fact that non-Malays form a majority and enjoy significant economic power and educational status, Islam and Malays enjoy a privileged position:

> It is a state with a national flag showing a star and crescent, a Constitution that describes Islam as the official religion, a prime minister who gives highest priority to uniting Muslims, a government whose top ministers are all Muslims, and a national ideology . . . that is clarified by a government that claims that it is the "sacred duty of a citizen to defend and uphold" a constitution that guarantees a special position to the Malays, the role of the sultans, and the maintenance of Islam as the official religion.[49]

The effect of urbanization and modernization upon Malays, with concurrent challenges to lifestyle and cultural values, has seen a greater emphasis on religious and ethnic identity and privilege. However, Islamic revivalism in Malaysia has had many voices and interpretations. Common appeal to Islam has masked a variety of ideological interpretations, agenda, and strategies influenced by personalities and differing socioeconomic contexts, from the UMNO-led government's political elite to PAS's more rural constituency.

Both Islamic activist organizations and a government-sponsored program for Malay uplift have had a significant impact upon Malaysian society, influencing the Islamization of state and society. The challenge of Islamic revivalism, in particular from ABIM and PAS, has led to greater government appeal to Islam and to its role as the protector of the Malay-Muslim community. The moderate, "nonpolitical" reformism of ABIM proved to be a catalyst for Prime Minister Mahathir's government-sponsored Islamization program and the incorporation of Anwar Ibrahim and other ABIM members into the government. At the same time, a more pronounced turn to Islam included the more strident voices of a new PAS, which tried to combine its traditional rural base of support with a new generation of members, modern-educated but militantly Islamically oriented, and extended their penetration of urban areas. The government's response has been to meet the challenge on its own grounds, through government sponsorship and promotion of Islam, rather than, as in some Muslim countries, through suppression. While government tilt toward Malay-Muslim identity and concerns is a source of concern for some, Malaysia has been free from the radical politics and confrontation that government repression has produced in other parts of the Muslim world.

The development of ABIM and PAS demonstrates the extent to which faith and sociopolitical realities combine to determine the makeup, ideology, and political activism of Islamic organizations, as well as to influence their changing configuration and fortunes. ABIM's more modernist ideology and politics have been heavily influenced by its urban, educated leadership and base of support, while PAS's more conservative approach has reflected its more rural constituency and traditional Islamic, ulama leadership. However, changes in PAS have occurred as it experienced the influx of a new, younger and more urbanized modern-educated generation of university graduates. ABIM and PAS also demonstrate the ability and willingness of Islamically oriented parties and organizations to participate within the system. Their political and social challenges have varied. However, although they have pressured and at times confronted the state, even in their militant moments they have resorted to electoral politics (the ballot box rather than bullets) to achieve their goals.

The experience of Anwar Ibrahim and ABIM highlights a particular issue faced by moderate Islamic activists who seek to bring about change from within the system. If they accept the invitation to join an incumbent government rather than come to power independently, they run the risk of being coopted or being perceived as having been coopted. The case of Anwar Ibrahim reflects the positive and negative aspects of cooperation. Although a government portfolio presents the opportunity to influence Islamization measures and effect change, activists are identified with (and are used to give legitimacy to) all government policies, good and bad, even in situations over which they have little control. They leave the more righteous enclave of the opposition and contend with the pragmatism of political power and governance. Their new position requires political compromises that they never would have made when out of government, and association with the limitations of government in addressing social issues, undermining their former role as social critics. The strength and credibility of ABIM as an organization was strongest when it was viewed as an independent pressure group or member of the opposition, and declined precipitously after Anwar Ibrahim joined the government. However, the impact of ABIM, through many of its former members in government (service in government required resignation from ABIM) and other sectors of society, from the universities to the media and corporate sectors, remains significant and an important factor in the continued strength of Islamization in Malaysia.

Throughout its history, Malaysia has managed to build a pluralistic state, but one that promotes Islam and Malay Muslim privileges and, as a result, reinforces and perpetuates religious and ethnic communalism. The pluralism of Malaysian society has been a source for compromise, accommodation, and tolerance as well as communal tension and conflict. Ethnic particularism has retarded national unity and also created a tension between the religious particularism of Malay Islam and the universalism of Islam. The insistence of Islamists that Islam replace Malay nationalism as the basis of national unity alienated both Malay nationalists and non-Muslim communities. Yet, in contrast to Islam in many areas of the Middle East, Malaysian Islam has been more flexible and fluid in recognizing its sizeable and powerful minorities. Thus, while in other areas the fast of Ramadan or bans on gambling are enforced upon Muslims in public places, in Malaysia restaurants are teeming with non-Muslim patrons, as are the casinoes. Similarly, while PAS has advocated imposition of the Sharia and the hudood, in particular, the Mahathir government and UMNO have countered that Malaysia's laws are in conformity with the principles of Islam and that "a partial application of the Shariah is a necessary compromise in Malaysia's multiracial and multireligious society."[50] Although there have been tensions and flash-points in the relationship of the Malay Muslim community with non-Muslim communities, "[b]y comparison with many other states in the world, Malaysia practices a high degree of religious liberty and her population exhibit a remarkable amount of religious toleration."[51]

However, the growing tilt toward Islam by the Mahathir government has been a cause of concern for minorities. Increased emphasis on Malay-Islamic consciousness and identity and the expanded role of Islam in public life have often strained the delicate communal balance. While some argue that Malaysia's Islamization is cosmetic, long on symbolism but short on substance, nevertheless, it has fed the fears of non-Muslims and thus posed a challenge to nation-building among Malaysia's diverse, heterogeneous population. Calls by PAS for an Islamic state and the imposition of the hudood, the growth of state-sponsored Islamization, intemperate statements by religious activists regarding the limited rights of non-Muslims in an Islamic society combined with sporadic attacks on non-Muslim religious sites, have constituted a clear cause for concern for non-Muslims and influenced the growth of Chinese and Indian ethnic and religious revivalism as well as emigration.

SEVEN

Algeria

Democracy Suppressed

Much of the 1980s was dominated by fear of Iran's export of revolution. The question asked was invariably, will country X be another Iran? Is so-and-so another Ayatollah Khomeini? In the early 1990s, as surveillance and vigilance against "radical Islamic fundamentalism" continued, many in the Muslim world and the West were stunned by the prospect of an elected Islamic government. Algeria embodies the failures, hopes, and fears of the West's encounter with political Islam.

Although many witnessed the reassertion of Islam in contemporary Muslim politics in Iran and elsewhere, the consensus in the first half of the 1980s, was that it could never happen in Francophile and Francophone North Africa. Governments were controlled by strong rulers (Bourghiba in Tunisia and King Hassan in Morocco) and in Algeria by a single party, the FLN (Front de Liberation Nationale), that had dominated the political scene. In the late 1980s failing economies and the wave of political liberalization that accompanied the fall of the Soviet Union ushered in new realities. In 1988, governments in Egypt, Jordan, Tunisia, and Algeria, among others, experienced street demonstrations and food riots in response to food shortages, high unemployment, and corruption. Less out of a desire to democratize than to steady shaky regimes, rulers caused a crack in their otherwise authoritarian regimes, as they promised elections. However diverse the country contexts, electoral results sent a collective shiver up the spines of governments and ruling elites when Islamists emerged as the leading opposition in Egypt, Tunisia, and Jordan. In addition to 32 of 80 seats, the Muslim Brotherhood in Jordan held five cabinet portfolios. However, it was Algeria that stunned governments, policy makers, and experts alike. The Islamic Salvation Front (FIS) swept municipal and later national parliamentary elections. The unthinkable now seemed to be on the horizon: an Islamic movement would come to power not through bullets but through ballots, not by violent revolution but by working within the system.

ISLAM AND ALGERIAN NATIONALISM

Islam had played an important role in the political development of Algeria. It is not only the faith of the vast majority of Algerians but, as in much of the Muslim world, it also historically has been a source for national solidarity and unity. This was particularly true during the French occupation (1830–1962). Islam was an integral component of the independence/nationalist movement. It provided a refuge and a battle cry, a sense of inspiration and organization: "From the moment of the French intrusion in the 1830s, Islam provided a refuge of collective identity for Algerians, and Islamic sentiment was a constant source of anti-colonial resistance."[1] Islamic reformers such as Abdul Hamid Ben Badis (1890–1940) founded, in 1931, the Algerian Association of Ulama (AAU), whose motto was "Islam is my religion; Arabic is my language; Algeria is my Fatherland." The AAU combined Islamic reformism and nationalism and disseminated its message through a network of mosques and schools. Avoiding direct political involvement, it escaped French suppression. Through its educational work and the involvement of the ulama and mosques, Algerian nationalism was firmly planted in the minds of a new generation. Modern reformers were able to provide Islamic legitimacy and mobilize support by joining with the traditional Islamic leadership in developing and spreading a nationalism that was not simply Arab but Muslim. They found fertile ground in a society whose popular culture was deeply rooted in Islam.

The Algerian revolution of the 1950s and 1960s was particularly informed by Islam. Islamic ideology, symbolism, rhetoric, and institutions were central to the struggle and an antidote to the identity crisis triggered by the political, military, economic, and cultural threat of French imperialism. The slogan of the revolution was "Algerie Musulmane," (Muslim Algeria) not simply "Algerie Arabe" (Arab Algeria). The struggle was declared a jihad, its fighters were called mujahidun (holy warriors) and its journal *El Moudjahid* (*The Holy Warrior*). The leaders of the revolution, secular as well as religious

> took up Islam and reintroduced it as a strategic weapon . . . in order to rally Algerians against the French. People were told not to drink, not to smoke, not to eat during Ramadan. Religious rules were made compulsory for political purposes. A puritan, violent Islam was used against the spineless, the unconvinced and the unfaithful. Algerian and Muslim were made synonymous. Revolutionary chiefs frequently made use of threats and reprisals in the name of Islam. There were moments when a "religious terror" was put in force. Algerians responded to it though they did not all agree with it.[2]

ISLAM AND THE POST-INDEPENDENCE STATE

Modern Algeria is a nation of some 20 million people of Arab and Berber background. In 1962, more than a century of French occupation (1830–1962) was brought to an end after a particularly bloody eight-year revolution. After independence, the Islamic reformism that had been one of the components of the nationalist movement receded in political life. The FLN (Front de Liberation Nationale), which had led the war of independence, consolidated its power and "until the 1980s, a sturdy triple alliance of army, state, and a single party controlled Algerian politics."[3] Although called the Democratic and Popular Republic of Algeria, Algeria emerged as a populist-authoritarian state. It was ruled by successive autocratic FLN governments, first by President Ahmad Ben Bella, who was overthrown by Houari Boumediene in a June, 1965, military coup. Boumediene, upon his death in 1978, was succeeded by Chadli Benjedid (who ruled from 1979 to 1991), a former senior member of the military in a state in which the military remained a dominant force.[4]

Algeria's Arab socialist state was legitimated constitutionally by a thin veneer of Islam: "The building of socialism in Algeria is identified with the full development of the Islamic values which are a basic constituent in the personality of the Algerian people." The National Charter of 1976 of the Algerian Popular Democratic Republic identified Islam with Algeria's socialist revolution:

> The Algerian people is a Muslim people. Islam is the state religion. . . . the Muslim world has only one way out of its predicament to regeneration: it must go beyond reformism and commit itself to the path of social revolution. . . . The Muslim peoples are coming to realize more fully that it is . . . in adopting resolutely the path of socialism that they respond best to the imperatives of their faith and make their action accord with its principles.[5]

The state monopolized religion as it did power, nationalizing religious schools, institutions, and officials in the name of a national, socialist Islam. In fact, the FLN, in the guise of Islamic socialism, pursued an essentially secular path of political and economic development implemented by a Western-oriented ruling elite. However, in the social sphere, tensions did exist, owing to a bifurcation in society between a Francophone secular elite and the more Arabized masses, for whom Arabic language and culture were primary components of Algerian identity.

Owing to the prolonged presence of France and its cultural penetration, French, in Algeria, as in the rest of the Maghreb, had become the language of the elites. Historically, Algeria, more than Morocco and Tunisia, felt the tension between French and Arabic language and culture. Algeria witnessed the most extreme form of France's "mission to civilize." Through its policy of "naturalization," France had attempted to impose total political and cultural assimilation. French was made the official language and the language of instruction in schools. Arabic was reduced to a foreign status. The French "attempted to eradicate Islam and impose French culture. Most of the Quranic schools and madrasas (high schools) were shut down. Mosques were turned into churches. Those who wanted education had to turn to the French; and the French opened the schools only to a small number of Algerian children who thus learned about the French cultural heritage—their ancestors the Gauls, Corneille, Racine, and the French revolution."6 The school curriculum, from language to history, oriented students to France rather than to Algeria and North Africa. Thus, issues of religion, identity, and authenticity became central in the battle for independence.

After independence, the interconnectedness of language, religion, and national identity and authenticity continued to be an issue. Algeria's ruling and cultural elite pursued a more Western secular orientation. Pursuit of the French curriculum was a key to advancement. Although Western language education was necessary for upward mobility, the government also fostered an Arabization program for education, the judiciary, and the administrative systems. Arabic, with its deep religious and nationalist roots, continued to be a source of contention between the graduates of the French and Arabic curricula. The Arabic curriculum produced an educated although more traditional sector, for whom Arabic language and culture remained central to Algerian identity and nationalism. For the more Arabized and Islamically oriented, French language and culture were the remnants of European colonialism and symbolized continued foreign occupation—political, economic, and cultural dependence on the West. Many resented, in addition to this threat to Algerian identity and autonomy, the continued status and advantages that these products of an "alien" French language and culture had in elite society. The tensions and potential dangers of the state's attempt on the one hand to coopt and use Arabization and Islamization and on the other to be "Europeanized" in its models of development and elite orientation were evident:

> [T]echnical or technocratic Westernization goes along with a Westernization of morals in the cities and of manners within the ruling elite.... This widens the gap between official ideology and political speeches of the leaders, highlighting "islamization," Arabization on the one hand, and on the other social life and economic habits which tend to imitate the "European model."7

THE ISLAMIC MOVEMENT

The first Islamist student movements grew out of this cultural clash. During the late 1960s and early 1970s, individuals and organizations like Al-Qiyam (Values) emerged. Their writings and thought were eclectic, reflecting the influence of transnational Islam. They drew on the Islamic modernism of Afghani, Abduh, Muhammad Iqbal, and Shakib Arslan as well as Hasan al-Banna and Sayyid Qutb of the Muslim Brotherhood and Mawlana Mawdudi of the Jamaat-i Islami. In contrast to the conservative ulama, who tended to simply reject Western culture and thought, reformers spoke French and mastered modern science. Like the Islamic modernist movement in Egypt and South Asia, their knowledge of modernity was to both empower them and provide them with a vantage point from which to critique the West. Such an attitude was exemplified by Malek Bennabi, French educated and an admirer of modern science and engineering, who reasserted the central importance of Algeria's Arab-Islamic heritage. Like Iqbal, he called for a reconstruction of Islam.

By the late 1970s, the conflict between Arabophone and Francophone students became acute. Realization that Arabophone education was generally not as helpful as Francophone education in obtaining the best jobs exacerbated the polarization. The Arabic educated tended to dismiss the French educated as secularists or Marxists, and from time to time clashes occurred. The cultural lines, Arab-Islamic versus French, were further drawn over the family law reforms debate that extended from 1975 through 1984, as students and women's organizations demonstrated and clashed.

In the late 1970s and throughout the 1980s, a transition occurred from a focus on issues of culture and ritual to a more comprehensive Islamism that stressed life in a more Islamic political and social order. Small groups congregated and shared ideas at mosques: "These were no longer lessons dealing with how to pray or perform a fast and all that. No, these were lessons at a high level in which we explained, or we searched for a method by which we could. . . . And we touched on all the problems which the Algerian nation was confronting. We spoke about everything. Of all the situations, the economy, of all aspects of life."[8]

FAILURE OF THE STATE

Algeria's state-run economy and socialist programs, which took responsibility for education, employment, housing, and social services, benefited from the country's strong petrochemical resources, which supported material and social development or modernization. However, in the mid-1980s, Algeria (whose oil revenues accounted for more than 90 percent of its exports), like many countries, suffered the impact of the world economic crisis precipitated by the oil glut and consequent fall in energy prices. Failure of the state-run economy, a growing national debt (which would rise to $24 billion accompanied by a 30 percent inflation rate and 25 percent unemployment rate), along with the decline of hydrocarbon revenues, severely impacted industrialization and agricultural projects and public and social services. Algeria's demographics, with its large population of unemployed youth, exacerbated social tensions between the ruling elite and the majority of the population, who felt the full impact of imposed austerity measures and were increasingly critical of government failures.

In October, 1988, Algeria was rocked by massive street protests and "food riots." A wave of public demonstrations swept across the country, precipitated by a dramatic fall in living standards (high unemployment, severe food and housing shortages, corruption, and inefficient government). Beginning in Algiers, the demonstrations quickly spread to many other major cities, including Oran and Constantine.

It was in this context that the Islamic Salvation Front (FIS), a coalition of groups, emerged as a political actor, gaining legitimacy and credibility. FIS activists were among the most visible and organized leaders, and were seen by some as the instigators of a popular revolt and protests, as well as being among the chief victims of the military's brutal suppression, which resulted in an estimated 500 civilians' being killed.[9] The message of Algeria echoed that of other parts of the Arab world. The "ruling Bargain" of many regimes had failed:

> Under this arrangement, the ruled traded their rights to independent political activity in return for the rulers' guarantee of social welfare and job security. To provide these benefits, the state relied on oil revenues, foreign remittances, tourist spending, and foreign aid to finance huge government bureaucracies and inefficient state-run enterprises, institutions whose primary mission was to provide guaranteed employment and a minimum level of social equity rather than efficient capital accumulation and production.[10]

It is against this background of nationwide political, economic, and cultural unrest that the rise of Islamic movements in Algeria and the subsequent "war" must be understood.

THE ROAD TO REFORM, THE PATH TO DESTRUCTION

The Benjedid government of the late 1980s, like that of many of the states in the region, promised greater political liberalization and democracy to counter public discontent. Benjedid's political reforms included a national referendum and, in 1989, a revision of the constitution which retreated from Algeria's socialist tradition. It ended the FLN's monopoly of the state, transforming Algeria's one-party state into a competitive multiparty political system. While liberals called for greater political and economic freedoms, it was the Islamists who emerged in the late 1980s as the self-proclaimed voices of the oppressed masses. Thirty years of one-party rule and the absence of opposition parties made the FIS the only formidable challenge to the authoritarianism and legitimacy of the government. The growth of "street mosques, and prayer rooms in factories, schools and government offices" threatened the power and secularism of a faltering state.[11]

The FIS, drawing its support from the poor and middle class, denounced the failure and corruption of the regime, called for greater Arabization and Islamization of society, and effectively penetrated state institutions, especially schools and universities. Their proclamation of Islam's message of social justice—in particular, their condemnation of societal failures in education, housing, and employment, and of government corruption—proved especially popular among Algeria's unemployed youth and rural-urban migrants. With more than 60 percent of the population under 25 years of age and with a high percentage unemployed, young people proved ready recruits, exchanging idleness and boredom for a sense of direction and hope as they swelled the crowds at mosques and engaged in political action.

The living conditions of many in 1991 stood in stark contrast to the lifestyles of ruling and bureaucratic elites. As one observer noted: "Half of the young men and women joining the labor market each year cannot find jobs. Devaluation of the dinar (whose official rate is down by 94 percent since August 1990) has sent consumer prices soaring. In the capital's poor districts people live seven or eight to a room."[12]

POPULIST ISLAM

As previously indicated, Algerian rulers, like their counterparts in many Muslim states, although embarking on an essentially Western, secular path of development, did employ Islam selectively, identifying it with Algeria's socialist national ideology to strengthen their own legitimacy. The state's bureaucracy also attempted to control official Islam through government supervision of educational institutions, the ulama, and mosques. However, in the 1980s, as in other parts of the Muslim world such as Egypt, Tunisia, Jordan, and Kuwait, populist Islamic groups surfaced and grew, creating a network of "independent" mosques (freed from government control) and social welfare agencies that became increasingly important as state institutions faltered in the the late 1980s. Given the role of Islam in the nationalist movement and revolution and its roots in popular culture and the nonelite sectors of society, Islamists offered an attractive populist message. They proclaimed an Islamic alternative and critique of the failures of the government and of Algeria's Western-oriented secular elite. Their social services were an implicit critique of the government's failures. When Algeria was hit by an earthquake in 1989, the Islamists were the first to respond and did so effectively. They, rather than the government, supplied blankets and medicines and thus scored further points while the government reinforced its image of ineffectiveness.

Among the almost sixty opposition parties that quickly sprouted in response to the opening up of the political system in 1989 were several Islamic parties or associations, among them HAMAS (Mouvement de la Societe Musulmane), Ennahda (Renaissance), and the Islamic Salvation Front (Al-Jabhatu al-Islamiyyatu Lil'inqadh, whose French acronymn was the FIS, for le Front Islamique du Salut). The FIS was an umbrella organization or coalition established in 1989 under the leadership of Shaykh Ali Abbasi Madani (b. 1931), a moderate, religiously and Western-educated professor at the University of Algiers, and Ali Belhadj, a younger, more radical preacher.

Abbasi Madani was born in southeastern Algeria, the son of a religious leader and imam. He studied Arabic and Islamic subjects. Madani possessed both nationalist and Islamist credentials. A political activist in the early 1950s, he joined the National Liberation Front and was imprisoned for eight years by the French during the occupation, and later by Benjedid for four years. Like many Islamists in the Arab world, disillusionment with the failures of Arab nationalism had led him to turn to an Islamic alternative. In 1963, he joined the Al-Qiyam (Values) Society, which advocated a reassertion of Algeria's Arab-Islamic heritage. He took part in demonstrations in 1966 against the execution of Sayyid Qutb, the ideologue of the Egyptian Muslim Brotherhood. Disillusioned by the Arab defeat in the 1967 Arab-Israeli Six Day War, and increasingly critical of the FLN's socialist policy, he returned to school, earning degrees in psychology and philosophy. In 1978, he received a British doctorate in education and taught at the University of Algiers.

In 1982, Madani became embroiled in campus and national politics during clashes between students and governmant forces at the University of Algiers. Islamic political activism became more visible in the early 1980s on the campuses and in urban neighborhoods. Student activists and Islamic pamphlets called for political, educational, and social reforms, from the abrogation of the National Charter and the establishment of an Islamic government to curriculum reform, separation of the sexes on campus, and the prohibiton of alcohol. The activists' growing force became evident when in response to a government sweep and arrest of more than 400 students in Algiers after the murder of a socialist student, more than one hundred thousand Islamists demonstrated at the University mosque: "Governors and people were astounded at the magnitude and passion of what they saw. It was the greatest challenge to state authority since independence."[13]

Madani, who had become a professor known for his lectures condemning the government's failures and advocating an Islamic alternative, was arrested and imprisoned for two years when he joined several other prominent religious leaders, Shaykhs Sahnoun and Sultani, in a public statement calling for the promotion of Islam in government and society. After his release, a more liberal government policy enabled Madani and other Islamists to preach and organize in mosques, schools, and universities. The members' numbers grew significantly, as did the network of mosques and charitable organizations. The growing presence and potential power of the Islamists was seen in the government's attempt to reform family law. Despite a demand by Algerian feminists in 1981 for substantive reforms in the family code, the law finally approved in 1984 reflected the government's sensitivity toward Islamist influence. The code incorporated a substantial amount of Islamic and traditional Algerian law that reinforced a Muslim woman's dependence on her family and husband, forbade her marriage to a non-Muslim, and made divorce the prerogative of the husband.[14]

As the government's economic programs had failed, so too its religious policy proved impotent: it was incapable of controlling the spread of populist Islam. As a front, the FIS was able to attract and include a cluster of orientations and constituencies under its umbrella. However, the organization of the FIS proved both a strength and a weakness. On the one hand, it was broad enough to include a wide diversity of individuals and orientations; on the other hand, it lacked unity of leadership and vision on critical issues. Nowhere was this clearer than in its two most prominent leaders, Madani and Belhadj. While both were critical of the system and called for substantive Islamic reforms, Madani projected the image of reason and was moderate in his discourse and publically supportive of democratic elections and pluralism.

Ali Belhadj, on the other hand, was more confrontative in his rhetoric. Belhadj, who was born in Tunisia in 1956, lost both his parents in Algeria's war of independence. Unlike Madani, he is the product of a completely Arab-Islamic religious education. He became a secondary school teacher of Arabic and an imam, or mosque preacher. He was imprisoned from 1982 through 1987 during a crackdown against Islamists. In contrast to Madani and many modern Islamic activist leaders in other Muslim countries, Belhadj had no exposure to the West or to the world outside Algeria. As a result, he tended to be dogmatic and militant. His call for immediate imposition of the Sharia and his denunciation of the Algerian government and of the West proved popular among many young Algerians.[15] In contrast to Madani, Belhadj was dismissive of democracy, which he saw as but another tool of the West.

FIS IDEOLOGY

Abbasi Madani was the FIS's primary leader and chief ideologue. While the FIS leadership represented a variety of positions, Madani's intellectual vision and worldview embodied its general thrust and orientation. He described the FIS as a popular front and political party. Rather than capitalism or communism, the FIS espoused an Islamic solution, based upon the belief that Islam offered a comprehensive ideology for state and society. While advocating participatory democracy, Madani believed that justice, freedom, equality, and moral political principles can be best realized in an Islamic democracy based upon Islamic principles, which, in contrast to Western democracy, is less pragmatic and more socially just:

> Democracy in Algeria cannot be given the same philosophical and political interpretation as that of pragmatic philosophers like Adam Smith, Kant, and Dewey, who define it as the right to exercise capital freedom, even if it exceeds the needs of other classes of society, i.e., the working class or the poor. Democracy in the U.S., in a liberal and pragmatic sense ... has given the individual more rights to personal freedoms at the expense of the group. It has given more rights to the powerful and less to the weak. This is freedom at the expense of social and economic justice. . . . Liberal democracy is not free of contradictions, nor is socialist democracy free of oppression and injustice. Democracy in the socialist and communist sense is nothing but emptiness and historical marginalism.[16]

Madani identifies the FIS's brand of democracy with Islam. The Islamic model of democracy precedes modern forms ("new thought"), and is a system in which individual and social freedoms do not oppose each other; they are "two faces of a single coin."[17] Islam provides a complete and just political system in which individuals are free to vote, compete for elective office, and govern. The Sharia is the cornerstone of justice and freedom, the means to achieving a system that balances the rights and duties of the individual with those of society. Thus, Madani maintains, the Islamic model is more perfect than liberal and socialist democracy; it is the best model to confront the ideological crises of civilization.[18]

At the heart of Madani's interpretation of Islam is an emphasis on Islam as the religion of the people and as social justice, as capable of producing and guiding a just political and social order. His populist Islam gives political and economic primacy to the people over individual self-interest. Although he accepts a multiparty system and power-sharing, in which the rights of the minority are to be affirmed and safeguarded, Madani dismissed Algeria's political parties as failures. Just as he accuses the West of fostering individual rights at the expense of the community, so too he sees Algeria's political parties as narrow, elite organizations, driven more by self-interest and partisanship than by the needs of the people. A former member of the FLN, he charged that it had departed from its noble principles and become a party dominated by presidential personalities and elite interests that produced a system that was "politically and morally bankrupt." Despite the fact that other political parties such as the Movement for Democracy and the Front for Social Forces called for democracy, Madani also charged they were "founded for selfish or partisan reasons and not for . . . guaranteeing the self-determination of the people. . . . They are like museums and are not able to face the historical crisis confronting us."[19]

Madani often presents an Islamic ideal in which the world is one of white and black, right and wrong, self-interest and altruism. It is a world of transcendent principles and "shoulds." The FIS presumptively embodies this ideal, an ideal that is used to discredit and judge its rivals. Thus, the FIS views itself as the party of the people, of self-determination, of all Algerians. All other parties are seen as flawed and driven primarily by narrow self-interest and power. While a multiparty system and power-sharing are affirmed, it is not always clear whether those who are judged "misguided and elite" will be permitted to participate. The place of religious, ideological, political, and social differences is not clear. The assertion of an ideal or a mythic unity of the Muslim community seems at times to counter an affirmation of diversity and pluralism. Despite the fact that the electoral success of the FIS did not enjoy universal acceptance, Madani generalized about Algerians' "current lack of doubt about the capabilities of Islam in solving their problems and their readiness to apply Islamic solutions."[20]

As in politics, so too in economics. The FIS agenda attempted to balance individual and societal interests as it sought to address both Algeria's chronic unemployment and the maldistribution of wealth. The FIS did not offer a blueprint for economic reform. It did, however, reject the discredited socialist system of the past and advocate a free enterprise system: "The Islamic Salvation Front has proposed programs of free investments and private enterprise in agriculture, industry, commerce and banking. . . . It is proposing an economic model based on justice which provides assurances for the investment of capital and the creation of a climate for the human resources to flourish by the investment of technological skills and expertise."[21] Madani attributed Algeria's stagnant economy to government monopoly and restrictions: "While the liberal motto of 'laissez faire' has moved the liberal economy, in socialist Algeria we find that the motto 'don't do' has hindered the economy."[22]

The FIS advocated economic reforms that would preserve Algeria's oil reserves and exploit instead its other resources. The failures of Algeria are attributed not only to the FLN and its bureaucracy but also, more broadly, to a Western neocolonialism and imperialism that has dominated the oil market and adversely affected the economies of developing nations such as Algeria. Madani accused the FLN of mortgaging Algeria's future for its present by making Algeria dependent on an oil market controlled by the West and selling its national mineral treasure to Western markets at a cheap rate: "The neocolonialist imperialist policy that is controlling the oil market and other major markets, has forced our countries to sell the more expensive commodities at a low price and buy the cheaper commodities at a higher price—and that's the way to poverty. . . . We are buying expensive eggs and selling cheap oil."[23]

As with most Islamic movements and, for that matter, Third World populist movements, European colonialism and Western neocolonialism loom large as the reputed sources of failure and oppression. America, in particular, in its role as a superpower is seen as a political and economic threat. Its oil policy, which makes it dependent on outside sources, results in a strategy that "does not exploit its oil reserves but adds to its oil stock from the world oil supply. . . . the oppression of America . . . puts its interest at the expense of others and wants to get richer while we get poorer."[24] For Madani, America's economic and political oppression go hand in hand. Its domination of the world market and "neocolonial greediness," coupled with a "cowboy" foreign policy, has deepened the plight of the oppressed in the Islamic world. Madani believed that the Gulf War and American attitudes toward the Middle East were due to Zionist influence, the media, and a "colonial crusade" reminiscent of the Crusades—a regression to the Middle Ages and religious warfare.

Like most Islamists the world over, Madani regards secularism and related ideologies as a major cause of Muslim decline and impotence. It is a foreign import imposed first by colonial powers and then by the state and Western-oriented Muslim elites through state institutions and media. The conflict between Islam and secularism is not one initiated by Islam. Thus, Algerian secularism, which dismisses

Islamists and fundamentalists, has waged an ideological war that Madani characterizes as an attempt to pressure the Algerian people to "abandon their Islamic identity and moral values."[25] Although critical of the United States, Madani maintained that he desired a constructive cooperative relationship based upon recognition of Algeria's autonomy: its right and that of the Muslim world to determine its destiny. Madani maintained that the FIS economic programs "open the doors for American investors. They will be given an equal opportunity to participate in Algeria as long as their presence is not of a neo-colonial nature. . . . The American incursion in the Gulf makes some of us have reservations about dealing with U.S. companies or U.S. backed development programs."[26]

From Oppositon to Electoral Politics

On June 12, 1990, Algeria had its first multiparty elections since its independence. Municipal and regional elections tested both the government's new direction and the strength of Islamists. In contrast to Egypt, Morocco, and Tunisia (where Islamic political parties were banned and Islamists had to run as individual candidates), the Benjedid government permitted the FIS to participate as a political party. Given the FLN's control of the political process, the power of the ruling elite, and opposition from Algeria's feminist movement, the question seemed not to be whether the FLN would win but how well the Islamists would do. The clear expectation of government officials, experts, and the media in Algeria and internationally was that the combination of secular forces and Algeria's long political and cultural association with the West would limit the performance of the FIS. The government and Western-educated critics warned of the fundamentalist threat to Algeria's secular orientation, to democracy, pluralism, and women's rights. Few were prepared for the outcome. With 65 percent of the electorate voting, the FIS swept the elections, controlling 55 percent, or 853 of the 1,551 municipal councils, and two-thirds (32) of the 48 regional assemblies, in contrast to the dismal showing of the FLN, which won only 32 percent of the municipal and 29 percent of the regional elections. The FIS won a majority in all the major cities: "64.18% in Algiers, 70.50% in Oran, and 72% in Constantine."[27] Algeria, North Africa, and the West stood stunned; the unthinkable had happened. This was not an Iranian-style Islamic revolution but an overwhelming victory at the ballot box that defied the secular presuppositions of modernization theory and the vision of Algeria as a modern state.

For Islamists, the electoral victory was part of a broader ongoing ideological battle between Islam and Westernization. "The secularists are not the only ones to be sad over an Islamic victory. There are also the Western planners and enemies of Islam. This victory is a rejection of Western and secular values, which were implanted in the heart of the Muslim Arab country and reinforced by colonial masters and their stooges [a minority secular Muslim elite who perpetuated the legacy of French occupation]."[28] Rulers' fears of the election's international impact and implications were fed by Islamists who declared:

> Algeria stepped forward to usher in a new era. . . . This situation will soon become a common denominator in the entire Arab homeland, incessant demonstrations, rebellion and protests by hundreds of thousands of people everyday will become a real problem for Arab governments, regardless of their ideology. The importance of Algeria as a pioneering and leading case in this universal Arab economic and political transformation lies in the experience it will provide other peoples and other countries.[29]

The FIS victory was due to a discredited FLN—its European models of development and its failure to permit a strong secular opposition to develop, together with actual support for the FIS. While public apathy kept some voters away from the polls, many others turned out. In many ways, the elections were a repudiation of an ideologically and materially failed system by a popular movement that brought together disparate groups in opposition to the government. The FIS provided the core and backbone of the movement, attracting a broad base of support across the country, but particularly in urban areas. They brought a level of organization and ideological commitment lacking in other sectors of society and an impressive record of social responsibility and social welfare. The FIS network of medical clinics and charitable associations served the poorest and most crowded urban neighborhoods, providing housing and free tutoring in mosques, creating shops and jobs, and cleaning up neighborhoods.[30] Standing in the void created by the abysmal failures of the government and the FLN, the corruption and growing gap between rich and poor, the FIS offered an indigenous alternative. Their religious ideology and values had deep nationalistic ties and were integral to Algerian society, in particular the mass of Algerians as distinct from the Western, secular-oriented minority who had guided and dominated public life.

The FIS possessed an agenda with broad appeal: denunciation of the failures of the regime and its Western models of development; reassertion of Algeria's Arab-Islamic identity, heritage, and values; the championing of popular political participation and economic reform (jobs and housing); effective delivery of social services; denunciation of political and moral corruption; espousal of the rights of the economically oppressed and the promise of a more equitable redistribution of wealth; and reemphasis of family values. At the same time, the lack of any other viable alternatives meant that the FIS also benefited from those who abstained and, more important, from those who cast their vote for the FIS less out of support for their party than as a protest vote against the FLN, reflecting a high level of frustration and outrage with the prevailing political and social order.

The FIS's rise to power and victory was all the more impressive if one considers the movement's relative youth and isolation from the outside world and from other movements. In comparison to many other Islamic movements, such as the

Muslim Brotherhood, the Jamaat-i Islami, or Tunisia's Ennahda, the FIS did not take shape as an organization until the late 1980s. Algeria's Islamists tended to be more intensely nationalistic and less influenced by outside forces. Algerian Islamists were aware of and influenced by the Iranian revolution; the mujahideen's struggle against Soviet occupation in Afghanistan; Palestine; and the reassertion of Islam in Muslim politics worldwide. They were clearly in touch with and inspired by Islamic activists and events in North Africa, and in particular by Rashid Ghannoushi, a leader of Tunisia's Ennahda (Renaissance) Party, and Hasan al-Turabi, the internationally active charismatic head of Sudan's Muslim Brotherhood, who both had visited Algeria and whose organizations were in contact with their Algerian counterparts. As with other movements, there were reports, denied by Madani, of support from Saudi Arabia and the Gulf nations who wished to contain Iranian influence.

In general, the vision and concerns of Algerian Islamists tended, more than most other Islamic organizations, to be local, and were more nationalist than international in scope. Madani, reflecting on FIS's relationship with other Islamic movements in the Arab world, noted, "They are our brothers in sentiment. . . . We cannot benefit them with anything further than sentiments until now because we are weak. If one lacks something one cannot give it to others. We have nothing to give them except prayers. And they have nothing to give us except prayers."[31]

Government Counterattack

In the aftermath of the elections, the government moved aggressively to cut off funds to the municipalities, thus hindering elected FIS officials' ability to provide adequate services. Despite charges that the FIS would bring radical change and Iranian-style government, local councils proved more interested in local governance and improvements and in "small-scale symbolic issues such as dress, alcohol consumption and gambling than radical changes in state, society and economy."[32] Moreover, with few exceptions, the FIS did not impose the veil, ban public bathing, close bars, or prevent women from voting or working. They did pass more conservative regulations in areas that were amenable to such measures.[33]

As the rescheduled June, 1991, multiparty elections drew near, the government introduced in March a new election law that gerrymandered or redrew voter districts to weaken the performance of the FIS and favor the FLN in the upcoming national elections. When the FIS leadership called for a nationwide general strike in May 1991, the government responded to public demonstrations with force. The president declared a state of siege and called in the army to restore order. FIS leaders called for demonstrations in opposition to the government's attempt to introduce new electoral laws. Madani and Belhadj were arrested on June 30, as were some 5,000 of their supporters, and elections were postponed. Madani and Belhadj were tried before a military court and sentenced to twelve years in prison, charged with conspiracy against the state. If some charged that the FIS was challenging the system and undermining state security, others noted that "the FIS demonstrations in June were not an attempt to 'obstruct' the democratic process but were calling for the abrogation of an undemocratic law implemented by the government. Virtually in uninterrupted fashion since its legalization in 1989, the Islamic Salvation Front has adhered to democratic procedures if not principles, the same principles which those in and out of government vigorously defend."[34]

In addition to providing a breathing space in which the government and secular forces could regroup, the arrests caused other Islamic organizations to come to the fore in a move some hoped would produce a more divided Islamic front. Shaykh Mahfoud Nahnah, whose Movement for Reform and Guidance (also called HAMAS), like the Association of Algerian Ulama, had avoided direct involvement in politics, and founded the Islamic Alliance, a coalition of religious and social organizations. Nahnah had originally opposed religious organizations such as the FIS's becoming political parties. Many Algerian secularists and Western observers saw Nahnah and the Alliance as a liberal alternative to the FIS which would severely hamper FIS electoral fortunes.[35]

On December 26, 1991, Algeria held the first multiparty parliamentary elections in its thirty-year history. Despite the advantages that the government and the FLN enjoyed, from gerrymandered voter districts and control of state institutions and the media to the continued imprisonment of Madani and Belhadj, with 59 percent of Algeria's registered voters casting ballots, the FIS won 47.54 percent of the vote and 188 of the 231 seats, 28 short of a majority, in the first round of Algeria's parliamentary elections.[36] Its closest rival, the Socialist Forces Front, managed only 26. The FLN was routed, as it finished third with just 16 seats. The remainder of the seats in a parliament that totalled 430 seats was to be determined in a runoff election in January of 1992.

The euphoria of the FIS and the exhilaration that swept through Islamic movements throughout the Islamic world were matched by the disbelief and apprehension of many Muslim rulers and Western governments. If Islamists saw the FIS victory as a vindication of the representative nature of their movements and the extent to which they had successfully become institutionalized and part of the mainstream, socially and now politically, their opponents charged that the FIS had "hijacked democracy." While the FIS denied this charge and claimed to recognize the importance of the electoral process, critics charged that the FIS was simply using the democratic process to come to power and then in turn impose an Islamic system of government with little tolerance of political pluralism and the rights of women. The statements of FIS leaders did not effectively counter these charges. However much the FIS might be united in slogans such as "Islam is the solution," differences abounded. As a front or coalition, the FIS included leaders and followers with diverse orientations and attitudes regarding Algeria's future and democratization. The statements of FIS leaders were often vague or contradictory. For some, political participation did not translate into a democratic political process. Abbasi Madani, while ostensibly supporting the democratic process, nevertheless seemed to equivocate and respond tactically when he stated: "Yes, the way is the elections; it is the way for all those who wish to yield to the will of the people. There is no other way at the present moment. All other ways have been obstructed by Allah. Therefore, the way to power is elections which are decided through the popular will of the people."[37] A similar note of pragmatic accommodation could be heard in a statement by another prominent FIS leader, Abdelkader Hachani's (a petrochemical engineer): "We say to you Algeria [Algeria's new rulers], Our constitution is the Koran and the Traditions, but we will go down the path of your constitution, not because we believe in it, but because we would give you a pretext [to crack down if we disregarded it.]"[38] Hachani seemed to accept a multiparty system: "Within the framework of our values and our own civilization, several parties will be allowed to exist. Politics will be enriched by this."[39] In contrast, Ali Belhadj categorically rejected democracy as an un-Islamic concept, and Imam Abdelkader Moghni declared, "Islam is light. Why do you fear it? It is in democracy that darkness lies. . . . Individual liberties will be respected in the general interest, but liberty must not be confused with permissiveness."[40] The range of statements made by FIS leaders, their seeming equivocation about democracy and equal rights for women, left them vulnerable to criticism and skepticism regarding the true nature of their ultimate agenda.

Islamist attitudes in Algeria, as elsewhere, toward democracy must be seen within the broader context of their reactions to the West and to dependence on Western institutions. Many Muslim leaders in the early twentieth century denounced nationalism, democracy, and pluralism, judging them less in and for themselves and more as foreign, un-Islamic concepts introduced by the West to further divide and weaken Muslims and thus perpetuate a process of political and cultural dependency. Similarly, many mosque preachers in Algeria regarded democracy as an alien ideology, equating it with secularism or "godless unbelief." The policies and legacies of European colonialism and Western neocolonialism were perceived as undermining the credibility of democracy.[41] Many argued that the West, during the Cold War and more recently with regard to democratization in Middle East and the Bosnian war, has demonstrated a pragmatism and selectivity that constitute a "double standard": democracy for itself and selected allies, but a willingness to tolerate authoritarian regimes in the Muslim world for the sake of oil, arms sales, and support for the Palestinian Accords. Thus, the West is perceived as supportive of governments that are antidemocratic (authoritarian, repressive, guilty of the flagrant abuse of human rights), much as it tolerated anticommunist dictatorships in Latin America and Africa during the Cold War.

MILITARY INTERVENTION: DEMOCRACY ABORTED

On January 12, 1992, the Algerian military, disregarding the majority of voters, intervened in what was a de facto coup to prevent the FIS from enjoying the fruits of their democratically elected and earned power. In many ways, Algeria and its neighbors had laid the groundwork for rationalizing intervention when several months earlier North African governments had met and established a task force to combat "radical Islam." As one expert has noted:

> Their message, aimed in part at the West, was unmistakable and could be encapsulated as follows: "The governments in power are worth preserving. For no matter what their shortcomings, ranging from political exclusion to severe human rights violations, they form the only barrier against fanatics who want to confront the West." According to this interpretation, local forms of authoritarianism are regrettable, but they are the only road toward western-style political pluralism.[42]

In the name of preserving state security and stability, the military acted just days before the second round of parliamentary elections, in which it appeared that the FIS was poised for another electoral victory that would give them a two-thirds to 80 percent majority in parliament.[43] The military forced President Benjedid, whom it feared had accepted the FIS electoral victory and intended to enter into a power-sharing agreement with the FIS, to resign. Although the head of the National Assembly should have succeeded Benjedid, the Assembly had been secretly dissolved at the end of January, "as the Parliament's president was considered to be too close to the fundamentalists."[44] A ruling coalition, a figurehead Council of State or High Security Council, was appointed by the military to govern. Algeria's democratic experiment was suppressed and a process of massive repression of the FIS initiated. On February 9, 1992, the Council replaced a budding democratic process with a state of siege. It declared a state of emergency, annulled the results of the December elections, cancelled the second round of parliamentary elections, and postponed all elections indefinitely. Journalists (non-Islamist and Islamist) were arrested and several newspapers were closed. The government moved to dismantle the FIS. In subsequent months the FIS was banned (March 1992), and leaders, members, and those suspected of membership or sympathy with the FIS were arrested and tortured. More than 10,000 Islamists were detained in desert concentration camps in the Sahara, and FIS's mosques and social welfare centers were closed and their assets seized. Imams sympathetic to the FIS were replaced by state-approved clergy, while others were arrested "for using the pulpit for political purposes."[45] One international magazine commented: "Now it seems to be official. Torture has made a comeback in Algeria."[46] John Entelis, a leading expert on Algeria, wrote: "The military's cancellation of the elections in January represents nothing less than a political coup and, most likely, the end of Algeria's democratic experiment for the immediate future. Despite government contentions to the contrary, the stability of the state was not in danger. The stability of the regime, to the extent that it was a regime to the army's liking, is a different matter."[47]

The military's swift move to crush the FIS raised serious questions about the nature of Algeria's democratic path. They denied the FIS the power they had earned through participation in the political system, purportedly to safeguard the security of the state. At the same time, the FIS became an example of the difficulty most regimes in the Muslim world have defining and tolerating opposition. The initial response of FIS leaders was to call for moderation and avoid violence. Hachani reminded FIS members that, as a result of the elections, the FIS "has achieved a legitimacy that nothing and no one can take away from it."[48] However, the military's attempt to decapitate the movement and provoke confrontation, coupled with the arrest of moderate FIS leaders like Abdelkader Hachani, set in motion a spiral of violence that would eventually lead to a virtual civil war.

While the cancellation of elections was applauded by members of the ruling secular elite, other secular opposition politicans, such as Hocine Ait Ahmed, leader of the Socialist Forces Front, an opponent of the FIS, observed that Algeria was experiencing a coup "if not in form, then certainly in fact. . . . They won't make anyone believe that stopping the electoral process is a democratic advance."[49] It also led to international human rights organizations' criticism of "mounting human rights abuses" and their call for the release of Abdelkader Hachani and Rabah Kebir, "arrested . . . for acts of peaceful expression, as well as all those who have been arrested for offenses involving nonviolent speech or association."[50] The gains that had been made from 1989 to 1991, with an opening of the political system—the introduction of a multiparty system, release of political prisoners, lifting of press censorship, termination of arbitrary arrests and torture—were reversed. While the FIS was the primary target of the government's repression, its secular opposition (intellectuals, politicians, and journalists) was also silenced.

From Legal Opposition to Guerilla Warfare

Arrests and confrontations between the government and the FIS escalated. Having functioned first as a legitimate opposition, contesting and winning handily both in municipal and parliamentary elections, the FIS had been denied its democratically earned place in the government. The military's crackdown drove the FIS to change from a legal opposition to a combative, and, in some segments, revolutionary, movement. With many of its leaders in prison or exile, the coalition fractured. Government repression transformed the FIS from a reform to a revolutionary movement. An organization that had challenged the regime from within the system became a polarized and fractured movement whose more disaffected followers, responding to state repression and violence, moved from a defensive to an offensive position and thus became a militant threat.

In a scenario somewhat reminiscent of Egypt's Muslim Brotherhood during the rule of Gamal Abdel Nasser in the 1960s, the FIS split into moderate and more militant factions. Repression and torture spawned extremist guerilla groups, drawn from radicalized elements of Algeria's Islamist movement: former FIS members, other Islamists, the "Afghans" (Algerians who fought in Afghanistan during the Soviet occupation). Rejecting participation in the political process, they espoused armed struggle (jihad) and terrorism, and were bent upon the violent overthrow of a "corrupt, anti-Islamic" government and the imposition of their version of an Islamic state. Armed paramilitary and clandestine groups such as Hizbollah and the Armed Islamic Group (GIA) inaugurated their own reign of violence and terror with bombings, ambushes, and attacks on army barracks, police stations, and prisons. The GIA explicitly condemned the FIS for its moderation, rejected any compromise or reconciliation, and pressed for an all-out jihad against the government and its supporters, Algerians, foreigners, and foreign powers. The FIS also spawned an unofficial military wing, the Islamic Salvation Army (AIS), which, in the absence of dialogue, pursued an armed struggle against the regime. As the insurgency spread, the situation deteriorated into virtual civil war—what some American officials called "low intensity warfare"—and the military and armed Islamists became locked in mortal combat. Extremists attacked and killed not only government officials, military, and police, but also civilians, leading secular intellectuals, "unveiled" women, and schoolgirls. If security forces saw the beard and headscarf as symbols of fundamentalist terrorism, militants now targeted unveiled women and secular intellectuals as symbols of state oppression and terrorism. Algiers became an armed camp "with 15,000 troops brought in to fight the (invisible) enemy."[51] By late 1993 and early 1994, many outlying areas were controlled by militants who seemed able to strike at will.

As both the military and extremists ruthlessly engaged in a "no-holds-barred" war with innocent civilians caught in the middle, some moderate elements of the FIS attempted to distance themselves from the terrorist actions of groups like the Armed Islamic Group. When the Algerian military killed the leader of the Armed Islamic Group, known as Gjafar al-Afghani, although FIS leaders denounced the action, it was reported that he had been betrayed by another group loyal to FIS. At the same time, rumors flew that the government, having in the past steadfastly refused to include the FIS in any national dialogue, was in conversation with Abbasi Madani and Ali Belhadj.[52]

Attacks on civilians also reflected an underlying cultural and class conflict. The FIS and other Islamists, who drew heavily from the unemployed Arabophone, urban lower class, represented, should they come to power, a direct threat to the power and privilege of the Westernized, Francophone, educated urban elite. The military crackdown and attempt to crush the FIS was seen and experienced by many in the FIS as being tied to the preservation of the interests and lifestyle of Algeria's secular, Western-oriented elite, who generally supported military intervention. The conflict was transformed into a jihad between secularism and Islam, Westernization and Islamization. However, these generalizations about the profile of contending social forces should not obscure the diversity of Algerian responses, from secularists (French and Arabic speaking, elite and nonelite) who deplored military rule to FIS support not only from unemployed youth but also from modern educated professionals: doctors, engineers, teachers, and even elements in the military.

The spiral of violence deepened the polarization in society. The government and the army, reflecting the broader society, split into two factions: those convinced of the need for dialogue and national reconciliation (les reconciliateurs) and entrenched hard-liners (les eradiateurs), who continued to support the total suppression of the FIS. The former were led by President Liamine Zeroual, many secular and Islamic parties, and younger military officers. The latter included the senior military and many elites motivated more by self-interest than ideology: "many with much to lose, hold out against real negotiations for the basest of reasons—greed."[53] At the same time, anti-Islamic death squads, like the Organization of Free Young Algerians and the Organization Secrete de Sauvegarde de la Republique del'Algerie, emerged. Believed to be composed of members or former members of the security and armed forces, they have countered "fundamentalist terrorism," and have claimed responsibility for attacks on and the murder of Islamists.[54]

The power and threat of political Islam exacerbated ethnic tensions, and the army increasingly found itself caught between two flanks, Islamists and Berbers. The Berbers predated the coming of Islam to North Africa and, although they have converted to Islam, have remained fiercely loyal to their language, culture, and independence. Antigovernment and even more antifundamentalist, more militant Berber leaders such as Dr. Said Saadi of the Assembly for Culture and Democracy (RCD) denounced the government and called for armed resistance against what he charged was fundamentalist genocide against fellow Algerians.[55]

As the situation continued to deteriorate, France pressured the military-backed government to stay its course and not acknowledge the FIS; the United States quietly pressed for a national reconciliation that included the FIS. However, the government remained ambivalent, with President Zeroual and the military leadership at odds. On May 8, 1994, a march was called by secular and Islamic parties to support President Zeroual's policy of national reconciliation. Only ten of an expected one hundred thousand turned out, demonstrating the weakness of legal parties and the continued strength and influence of the FIS, which had boycotted the march. Exiled FIS leaders continued to demand that a prerequisite for talks was recognition of the FIS as a political party, release of political prisoners, and a fresh commitment to new elections.

FROM RECONCILIATION TO ERADICATION

1994 saw a dramatic increase in the level of violence and terrorism, as well as signs of behind-the-scenes contact between the government and the imprisoned FIS leadership. In September, 1994, the government released several FIS leaders and transferred Madani and Belhaj from Blida prison to house arrest in what looked like a first step toward a negotiated settlement. However, Madani refused to participate in a national dialogue until certain conditions were met: "the installation of a 'neutral' government until a 'legitimate' government was elected; the re-legitimization of the FIS; the lifting of the state of emergency; proclamation of a general amnesty; the cessation of all judicial proceedings against Islamists; and the army's return to its barracks."[56] President Zeroual flatly rejected the response. In December 1994 and January 1995, FIS representatives joined with other Algerian opposition parties (including the FLN) in a summit sponsored by the San Egidio Catholic community in Rome. They produced an agreement or proposal, which included many of the measures Madani had previously demanded, calling for the end of the military's intervention in politics, the lifting of the ban on the FIS, the release of FIS prisoners, and the convening of a national conference that would lead to free and pluralistic elections. The United States praised the agreement and France, a longtime supporter of the Algerian government, also responded positively. The Algerian government refused to recognize the meeting and regarded it as a non-event. It rejected the proposal, returned Madani and Belhaj to prison, and pressed on in its war to "eradicate" the Islamists.

CONCLUSION

Few countries have experienced as sustained an attempt by a colonial power to totally transform and dominate political and cultural life. Algeria withstood French hegemonic designs and waged one of the longest and bloodiest modern wars of independence in the Islamic world. Islam proved to be a unifying populist force in Algeria's resistance and independence movement. However, post-independence Algeria, like many Muslim countries, revealed a complex profile in which both the popular will and religion were subordinated to authoritarian rule, to a one-party state based upon a triple alliance of the FLN, the government, and the military. Beneath the unity and stability of Algeria's socialist program, deep cultural and class cleavages continued to exist. In the late 1980s, the economic and political collapse of the FLN unleashed forces that few had anticipated or could fathom. In what appeared to be a sudden turnabout, Algeria went from a one-party socialist state whose security was dependent upon the military and socioeconomic stability guaranteed by a Western-oriented Francophone elite to "a soon-to-be Islamic state." The introduction of an open political system and subsequent municipal and parliamentary elections unleashed an Islamic tide that confounded government officials and experts as it seemingly swept across state and society. Islam moved from the periphery to the center, as the FIS seemed poised to come to power through the electoral system.

Many charged that the FIS was out to hijack democracy; that it was not prepared to work within the system, to recognize individual and group rights and to leave the ultimate control of the political system to the people. However, the disruption of the electoral process by the military and the subsequent wave of repression clearly signalled the continued impact and legacy of decades of authoritarian rule and the resultant absence of a democratic tradition in Algeria. Algeria's decades-long secular authoritarian tradition, deprived of its political and cultural predominance by FIS electoral victories, moved through military intervention to safeguard their power and privilege and save the state from "fundamentalist" religious authoritarianism. Rather than risk the testing of Algeria's "democratic experiment" or the evolution of civil society with its trials, errors, and successes, the process was interrupted, indeed, halted, and an elected representative government replaced by an unelected, unrepresentative, military-appointed council.

The Algerian experience or experiment raised as many questions about the nature and agenda of secular elites—their commitment to political liberalization, democratization, pluralism, and power sharing—as it did about that of the FIS or "fundamentalists" on such issues. If the charge was that fundamentalists were out to "hijack democracy," the actions of the military supported a counter-charge that ruling elites only believed in "risk-free democracy." While some feared that the FIS only believed in "one man, one vote, one time," others countered that secular elites believed in elections as long as the opposition remained weak and thus their victory assured. As John Entelis observed,

> That the government, army, and FLN were unwilling to allow that process to evolve naturally speaks volumes to the strong residue of authoritarianism which continues to permeate Algerian political culture, attitudes, and behavior. . . . [I]t is only by abandoning its traditionalist commitment to an authoritarian and autocratic state that Algeria may proceed with its democratic experiment.[57]

Algeria demonstrates the extent to which both a secular and a proposed Islamic state can be the source of division and conflict between secularists and Islamists, among Islamists, between Arab and Berber, and between Francophone and Arabophone visions and values. Having survived a long and bloody war of independence, the Algerian people became locked into what some termed a war of identity, a defining or redefining of the nature of Algerian national identity. A spiral of state violence and Islamist counter-violence, of government-directed death squads and radical Islamist terrorism, produced a civil war that threatened the very fabric of civil society. It resulted in social polarization and radicalization and secular and religious extremism in which the majority of the Algerian people were victims—

a political situation with no clear winners and no resolution in sight. Both Algeria's government and its opposition, Islamist and non-Islamist, are challenged to create an environment within which the discussion and debate over redefining or reconstructing national identity occurs within a context of mutual acceptance of political participation, pluralism, and compromise.

EIGHT

Egypt

Governmental, Populist, and Extremist Islam in Conflict

Egypt has often been regarded as in the vanguard of political, social, intellectual, and religious development in the Arab and broader Muslim worlds. For more than two decades, Egyptian rulers have grappled with a resurgence of Islam that has significantly challenged the state and ruling elites.[1] Contemporary Islamic revivalism ("Islamic fundamentalism") in its origins and manifestations has strong roots—indeed, formative roots—in the Egyptian experience. This experience has had a regional and international impact on transnational Islam and on the West. The Muslim Brotherhood has provided ideological and organizational models for the growth and development of Islamic movements across the Muslim world, from North Africa to Southeast Asia. Islamists in the Sudan, Tunisia, Algeria, the Gulf, South Asia, and Southeast Asia acknowledge the formative influence of the Brotherhood, in particular of Hasan al-Banna (1906–1949) and Sayyid Qutb (1906–1966). Pamphlets, books, and tapes disseminate their ideas to this day.

In the 1990s, Egypt provides a primary example of the dynamic and diverse relationship of religion to society, its challenge to the state, and its impact upon the democratization process. The Egyptian experience has witnessed radical, violent revolutionary Islamic activism and the institutionalization of Islam socially and politically; diverse state policies toward Islam in the struggle of government and ruling elites to maintain their legitimacy and their world, with its lifestyle, power, and privileges; the growing polarization (as in many Muslim societies) between Islamists and secularists and government officials; advocacy of, and then reneging on, the government's official commitment to democratization, justified by the charge that "fundamentalists" are out to "hijack" democracy; and, finally, the widening of a confrontation between state security forces and Muslim extremists to include moderate as well as violent revolutionaries.

ISLAM AND MODERN EGYPTIAN POLITICS

Much of the character and politics of contemporary Egypt has been influenced by the revolution of 1952 and the subsequent emergence and rule from 1952 to 1971 of

Gamal Abdel Nasser. Nasser redefined the nature of Egyptian nationalism and promoted Arab nationalism and socialism both at home and abroad. He centralized and refined the apparatus of an authoritarian, "security" state and projected himself as a regional and world leader.

Although Nasser and the revolution initially enjoyed the support of the Muslim Brotherhood, after the revolution, the Brotherhood opposed it, when it became clear that Nasser did not intend to establish an Islamic state but instead promoted a secular Arab nationalism and socialism. As relations with the Brotherhood deteriorated, the government and the Brotherhood became entangled in sporadic battles that on several occasions erupted into violence. Both Nasser and his ministers were subjects of assassination attempts that the government attributed to the Brotherhood and which resulted in mass arrests and suppression of the Brotherhood. Finally, in 1966, Nasser moved decisively to eradicate the Brotherhood, executing Sayyid Qutb, its chief ideologue and others, arresting and imprisoning thousands, and driving many others underground or into exile. By the late Nasser period, the state had coopted the religious establishment and silenced its Islamic (and indeed any and all) opposition.

Anwar Sadat, who ruled from 1971 to 1981, inherited a defeated and demoralized Egypt. He took power in the wake of the Arab defeat of 1967 and the subsequent death of Nasser, a charismatic leader who was mourned by millions in Egypt and the broader Arab and Muslim worlds. Sadat sought to forge his own political identity and legitimacy, using Islam to blunt the power of the Nasserites and leftists as well as to enhance his legitimacy and mobilize popular support. He both utilized the state-sponsored religious establishment and fostered the reemergence of the Islamic movement, a step that led to the reassertion of a politicized Islam, the resurrection of a rehabilitated Muslim Brotherhood, and the emergence and proliferation of more militant Islamic organizations.

In the 1970s Egypt saw the government turn markedly toward Islam, as piety and the presidency were intertwined. Sadat employed Islamic symbols and rhetoric generously. He referred to himself as the "believer-president"; was photographed regularly at Friday prayer; promoted the building of mosques on an unprecedented scale; waged and legitimated the 1973 Egyptian-Israeli war as a jihad; released Muslim Brothers from prison and allowed them to function in public life; and supported the creation of Islamic student organizations on campuses to counter the influence of Nasserites and leftists.

Sadat's more open political and economic policy witnessed the development of a diverse and multifaceted Islamic movement. The Muslim Brotherhood emerged from prison and exile a seemingly broken, tamed, and aged remnant of the past. They reconstituted themselves. Although still an illegal party, the Brotherhood reestablished its publications and activities and was initially supportive, although at times critical, of the government. Chastened by repression, imprisonment, and torture, the Brotherhood under Omar Tilmassani took an unequivocal position against violence and adopted a clear policy of working for change within the system.

At the same time, younger, radical Islamic groups emerged. Many were led by former Muslim Brothers whose prison or underground experience had reinforced their belief that the government was anti-Islamic and that the only option was its violent revolutionary overthrow. By the mid-1970s, radical groups were active. They espoused a combative, violent antigovernment strategy, recruiting, mobilizing, and attacking government institutions and assassinating officials. Among the major groups were the Islamic Liberation Organization (also known as Muhammad's Youth, or Shabab Muhammad), Jamaat al-Muslimin (the Society of Muslims) or, as it was more popularly known, Takfir wal-Hijra (Excommunication and Emigration), Jamaat al-Jihad (Society of Holy War), and Salvation from Hell. The Islamic Liberation Organization successfully seized Cairo's Technical Military Academy in April, 1974. However, government forces foiled its attempted coup d'état, whose goal was to assassinate Anwar Sadat and declare an Islamic republic. In July, 1977, Takfir wal-Hijra kidnapped and subsequently killed Husayn al-Dhahabi, an Azhar shaykh and former Minister of Religious Endowments, who had been a strong critic of extremists. Although leaders of both Muhammad's Youth and the Takfir were executed and others imprisoned, many militants went underground and became active in other radical groups such as the Jund Allah (Soldiers of God) and Jamaat al-Jihad (Society of Holy War) the latter of which subsequently assassinated Anwar Sadat.

Sadat's Islamic initiatives proved counterproductive as he discovered what many have realized in other contexts—that Islam is a two-edged sword, capable of legitimating and delegitimating, of mobilizing support but also of mobilizing opposition. Government-supported Islamic student organizations quickly became a major force on campuses and began to sweep student elections as well as to strike a more independent posture. Increasingly, the regime found itself taken to task by the Brotherhood and the militant Gamaa Islamiya (Islamic Group), an umbrella organization for student groups. They criticized Sadat's visit to Israel and the signing of the Camp David Accords, his support of the Shah of Iran and condemnation of the Ayatollah Khomeini, and his enactment of family law reforms. Islamists ridiculed and dismissed these legal reforms as Western-inspired. They were called Jihan's laws, a reference to Jihan Sadat, whose mother was British and who was regarded as Westernized. Sadat's "open door" (*infitah*) economic policy was seen as increasing Egypt's economic dependence on the West, and promoting Western cultural penetration, from dress and behavior to television, music, and videos, benefiting an economically privileged, Westernized elite and thus contributing to a society in which the rich got richer and the poor became poorer.

Having let the genie out of the bottle, Sadat attempted to put the lid back on, declaring the separation of religion and politics, tightening the reins on the Brotherhood, banning Islamic student groups, and attempting to nationalize Egypt's mosques. During the 1970s, the number of private mosques had doubled from approximately 20,000 to 40,000. Sadat's early policy encouraged the building of private (*ahli*) mosques, which included not only formal buildings but also thousands of other structures and rooms added to hotels, hospitals, apartment complexes and other private dwellings. Out of 46,000 mosques in Egypt, only 6,000 were controlled by the Ministry of Religious Endowments. Private mosques and their preachers, in contrast to state-supported mosques, did not come under government control and thus were financially and politically independent. The religious establishment and the government-controlled media were often seriously undermined by fiery sermons in private mosques delivered by charismatic preachers.

Sadat's growing authoritarianism and suppression of dissent broadened to include secular as well as religious critics of his domestic and foreign policies. Critics called him the "new pharoah." The process reached its apogee in 1981 when Sadat imprisoned more than 1,500 people from a cross-section of Egyptian society: Islamic activists, lawyers, doctors, journalists, university professors, political opponents, and ex-government ministers. The arrests left in their wake a more radicalized Islamic terrain, and ultimately culminated in the assassination of Anwar Sadat on October 3, 1981, by members of the Organization for Holy War (Jama'at or Tanzim al-Jihad) as he reviewed a parade commemorating the 1973 war.

MUBARAK AND POLITICAL ISLAM

Vice-president Hosni Mubarak, having witnessed the assassination of Anwar Sadat, assumed the presidency with a vivid and personal sense of the power of militant Islam. Both the styles of new Egyptian president Mubarak and of Islamic revivalism changed in the 1980s after the death of Sadat. If Islamic revivalism or fundamentalism in Egypt during the 1970s seemed to be a movement of controntation and violence, the 1980s witnessed the entrance of Islamists into the mainstream and the institutionalization of Islamic activism.

Mubarak pursued a path of political liberalization and tolerance while at the same time responding quickly and firmly to those who resorted to violence to challenge the authority of the government. He distinguished more carefully between religious and political dissent and direct threats to the state. Religious critics were allowed public outlets for their opposition, and could compete in parliamentary elections, publish newspapers, and voice their objections in the media. The Mubarak government sponsored television debates between Islamic militants and religious scholars from al-Azhar University to represent the religious establishment. Government-run television and newspapers regularly featured religious programs and columns that were often independent in their tone and criticisms. Mubarak's policy led one expert to note: "A major reason why the government of President Hosni Mubarak has been so willing to seek an accommodation with its religious opponents is the realization that . . . the 'Islamic awakening' is not an alien and inherently subversive force but the continuation of long-standing movements . . . that contain many elements compatible with the development of capitalism and democracy."[2]

However, in the late 1980s, Mubarak's flexible policy, which failed to effectively coopt or silence his Islamic opposition, gave way to more aggressive response to the challenge of both religious extremists (those who advocated the violent overthrow of the government) and moderates (those who participated within the established political and legal framework). The Mubarak government became less discriminating and broadened its battle beyond the militant, clandestine Gamaa Islamiyya, Jihad, and other radical groups, using harassment and imprisonment to curb the growing strength and challenge of more moderate Islamist movements such as the Muslim Brotherhood.

THE INSTITUTIONALIZATION OF THE ISLAMIC MOVEMENT

The violence and disruptive acts of a more vocal and militant minority and Sadat's assassination overshadowed or eclipsed the growth of a broader based, Islamic alternative, a "quiet" or "silent revolution." The breathing space of the early Mubarak years had enabled Islamic political and social activism to grow more rapidly, to expand its institutions and to become part of mainstream society. The revivalist spirit, including increased religious consciousness and observance, was evident throughout much of society and had become normalized and institutionalized, as witnessed in personal religious observances, the growth of Sufi mysticism, the proliferation of Islamic institutions (banks and investment houses), and social welfare services, publishing houses, and media.

During the 1980s, a number of prominent intellectuals and professionals, secularist and Marxist, "returned" to Islam. Muhammad Amara, Tariq al-Bishri, Adil Hussein, and Anouar Abdel-Malek, as well as the respected Islamic scholar Khalid Muhammad Khalid, who had decades earlier gained attention when he argued for a secular state, now recast their thought within an Islamic idiom that advocated an Islamic political alternative. Islamists could also be found among prominent journalists such as Fahmy Howeidy and Adil Hussein, editor of Liberal Party paper *Al-Shaab*.

Similarly, during the 1980s wearing new forms of Islamic dress, a phenomenon that had begun in the 1970s, now became more widespread and prominent among Muslim women in urban areas, especially among students and professionals in the middle and upper-middle classes. While some women took up forms of dress that completely covered their face and bodies and withdrew from public life, most preferred modern forms of Islamic dress, which they believed enabled them to function more freely in their professional lives and in urban areas that were overcrowded and in which the close proximity and contact between the sexes in public transportation and the workplace were frowned upon. If wearing Islamic dress was a source of curiosity in the 1970s, by the 1980s it had become so widespread and fashionable that women no longer had to make their outfits but could purchase them in boutiques. Indeed, by the 1990s Islamic dress had become a popular fashion purchased and worn by some Muslim women in Egypt (and even by non-Muslim in the West) simply as an attractive garb. At the same time, more and more students and professional women were joining study groups, often conducted by women at mosques, to study the Quran and Islam and to address women's issues and concerns.

Perhaps the most significant development was the extent to which the Muslim Brotherhood and other voluntary (philanthropic) Islamic organizations became effective agents of social and political change, developing alternative socioeconomic institutions and participating in the political process, demonstrating their strength in institution-building and popular mobilization. They attracted members from the middle and lower-middle classes (businessmen, bureaucrats, doctors, engineers, lawyers, and journalists) and revenue from members working in the oil-rich countries of the Gulf and Iraq as well as from patrons in Saudi Arabia. They engaged in a broad range of social and political activities, from the creation of Islamic charitable associations (Jamiyyat Khayriyya) to participation in parliamentary and professional association elections. Their network of mosques, hospitals, clinics, day-care centers, youth clubs, legal aid societies, foreign language schools, banks, publishing houses, and drug rehabilitation programs multiplied.

Although many were apolitical, Islamic private volunteer organizations (PVOs) filled a void and thus were an implicit critique of the government's inability or failure to provide adequate services, in particular for the nonelite sectors of society. Their network of services provide an alternative for the middle class to expensive private institutions and for the poor to overcrowded public facilities. As the Egyptian sociologist Saad Eddin Ibrahim has commented,

> This strand of Islamic activism has therefore set about establishing concrete Islamic alternatives to the socio-economic institutions of the state and the capitalist sector. Islamic social welfare institutions are better run that their state-public counterparts, less bureaucratic and impersonal. . . . They are definitely more grass roots oriented, far less expensive and far less opulent than the institutions created under Sadat's *infitah* (open-door policy), institutions which mushroomed in the 1970's and which have been providing an exclusive service to the top 5% of the country's population. Apolitical Islamic activism has thus developed a substantial socio-economic muscle through which it has managed to baffle the state and other secular forces in Egypt.[3]

A stinging indictment of the government, and public testimony to the effectiveness of Islamists in responding to social crises, occurred in October 1992 when they, rather than the government, were the first to respond to a devastating earthquake.

Professional associations also felt the influence of Muslim Brothers and other Islamic activists. They became dominant voices, capturing the leadership in professional organizations of lawyers, doctors, engineers, and journalists. Operating within the political system, moderate activists such as the Muslim Brotherhood couched their criticisms and demands within the context of a call for greater democratization, political representation, social justice, and respect for human rights.

DEMOCRATIZATION

The clearest testimony to the mainstreaming and institutionalization of Islamic revivalism or activism was the emergence of the Muslim Brotherhood as a political force in electoral politics. Anwar Sadat introduced democratic socialism as a counter-ideology to Nasser's scientific socialism, and had replaced Egypt's one-party state with a multiparty electoral system. However, the growing authoritarianism of the late Sadat years produced an Islamist and secular opposition that criticized his democratic initiative as more rhetoric than reality. Under Mabarak, the Egyptian government has continued to be a "presidential state," with presidential elections in which Mubarak won by 94 percent of the vote with no opposition candidate; although he served as Sadat's vice-president, Mubarak has found excuses (the appointment or election of a vice-president would be divisive, would encourage the press to exploit issues and differences and divide the nation); the People's Assembly and the bureaucracy has continued to be dominated by the government's national democratic party; and the government has absolute control over the creation and continued existence of political parties. Thus, it has been able to refuse legal recognition of the Muslim Brotherhood as a political party.

In the 1980s, moderate Islamic activists in Egypt, North Africa, and Jordan demonstrated a gradualist, bottom-up approach to political change, and a willingness to participate within the political system.[4] Islamic movements participated in electoral politics and, relative to the expectations of some, scored stunning successes. Although banned as a political party in Egypt, the Muslim Brotherhood formed coalitions with other political parties and emerged as the strongest political opposition group.

Egypt's Islamists in recent decades have spanned the spectrum in their politics as in their tactics and use of force. Radical organizations like Muhammad's Youth, Takfir wal-Hijra, Jamaat al-Jihad, and the Islamic Group have sought to overthrow the government and would reject democracy outright. The attitude of the Muslim Brotherhood toward democracy has varied over the years. In the early decades of its existence, the Brotherhood's ambivalent attitude toward democracy was part and parcel of its belief that the Islamic world struggled to survive in the midst of the global civilizational threat of the Cold War. Muslims were caught between a capitalist West, with its emphasis on secularism, individualism, and materialism and a communist/socialist, atheistic East marked by dictatorship and tyranny.[5] Both alternatives, which possessed systems of political participation, were judged as doomed to failure and at the same time regarded as a threat. The Muslim Brotherhood believed Islamism was the authentic, indigenous Muslim alternative to imitation (loss of identity and failure) of West and East.

The Brotherhood's criticisms of democracy were of Western democracy, or perhaps more accurately dependence on foreign ideologies or forms of government. Hasan al-Banna and early Muslim Brotherhood leaders accepted principles of representative government and political participation. However, they rejected political parties or partyism (*hizbiyya*), believing that partyism creates disunity and had been used by Egyptian rulers to perpetrate tyranny. They believed that "[p]arties are not necessary for a representative form of government; democracy requires only that there be guarantees of freedom of opinion and the participation of the nation in government. Without 'partyism,' parliamentary life is perfectly compatible with Islam."[6]

The Brotherhood employed election processes internally in its organization and participated (or, when not permitted, demanded the right to participate) in national politics. For the Brotherhood, political participation or democracy was at best a means to an end, for everything is to be subordinated to the struggle to preserve and spread Islam. Increasingly, as the Brotherhood after its reemergence in the 1970s clearly choose participation rather than violent revolution, it invoked democracy both to critique the government and as a means to achieve its goal or to best wage the struggle for Islam.

When the political system permitted, the Brotherhood had participated in the system and in electoral politics: "The early record of the Muslim Brotherhood showed that it could play according to democratic rules."[7] In 1941, Hasan al-Banna and the Brotherhood had decided to participate in elections, and did so in 1945 parliamentary elections, although they failed to win any seats in this government-rigged contest. Nasser's authoritarian regime interrupted this experiment. Under the Sadat and Mubarak governments, the Brotherhood sought recognition as a political party and to participate within Egypt's multiparty system. The Brotherhood joined with the Wafd Party in the 1984 elections, and the coalition won sixty-five of 450 seats to become the largest opposition group in the Parliament. In the 1987 elections, the Brotherhood formed a new coalition, the Islamic Alliance, with the Labor Party and the Liberal Party. Campaigning with the slogan "Islam is the solution" and calling for the implementation of Islamic law, they won 17 percent of the vote, and emerged as the chief political opposition of Mubarak's government. Brotherhood candidates held thirty-eight of the Alliance's sixty seats.

The moderate, gradualist approach of the Brotherhood was reflected in a platform which, while critical of the status quo, did not reject society as un-Islamic. It did not call for revolution but rather for a process of Islamic reform in which Islamic values would inform the political, economic, social, and educational spheres as well as the media. The Islamic Alliance was inclusive rather than exclusive. It included Copts on its list of candidates, and in its 1989 program affirmed that "brother Copts in particular and the people of the book in general have the same rights and obligations as Muslims."[8]

Islamists in Egypt were divided in their responses to the Gulf War. The state-supported religious establishment (the Mufti of Egypt and leadership of al-Azhar) and a number of prominent ulama and Muslim intellectuals, such as Shaikh Shaarawy and Khalid Muhammad Khalid, supported President Mubarak and the Arab states that supported the U.S.-led anti-Saddam/Iraq international coalition. The Brotherhood vacillated between condemnation of Saddam's invasion and criticism of the Western-led armada and the dangers of a Western military presence in the Gulf. At the same time, a new Islamist-oriented opposition emerged under the leadership of the Liberal Party's Adel Hussein and Ibrahim Shukry, former socialists who had turned to Islam. The Liberal Party and its newspaper *Al-Shaab* became the most vocal opposition to Egypt's participation in the international coalition's military action ("invasion") and bombing of Iraq.[9] The debate and diversity of responses within Egypt over the Gulf War, as indeed in the broader Muslim world, revealed their ambivalence, opposition, and participation within the political system, and countered facile monolithic images of Islamist attitudes toward democratization: "The partisan contests, in which democratization figures as an issue for Islamists, speak against any facile assumptions, expressed more recently, about what democratization would mean for the relationship of the world of Islam and the West."[10]

MUBARAK'S WAR AGAINST EXTREMISM

Radical, violent alternatives, more silent in the early Mabarak period, boldly and directly challenged and attacked the regime in the late 1980s and 1990s. Islamic student organizations once again dominated university student unions. In Assyut, Minya, Cairo, and Alexandria, they pressed for an Islamic revolution: the implementation of Islamic law, curriculum reform, separation of the sexes in classes, restriction of mixed socials, and the banning of Western music and concerts. Their growth was fed by the government's inability to address continued chronic socioeconomic realities that had a disastrous effect upon the more than half of Egypt's 50 million citizens below the age of twenty. Hundreds of thousands of university graduates found jobs and housing impossible to obtain. Young couples often lived with their families or delayed marriage for years until they could find adequate housing.

Islamic organizations offered a new sense of hope and of community, a society organized into cells called families (*usrah*). More important, their community was based on an Islamic ideology that provided a sense of identity, community, and religio-cultural continuity. It offered a critique of modern Egyptian society and an agenda for radical corrective change, rooted in a religious worldview. Radical groups, like their more mainstream counterparts, extended their influence through a network of educational and social-welfare societies. Quran study groups for the faithful and social centers offered food, clothing, and assistance in obtaining housing. Student organizations at universities assisted with free books, clothes (including "Islamic dress" for women), tutoring, and housing.

The government attempted to control Egypt's private mosques, a breeding ground for Islamic militancy. The vast majority of Egypt's mosques were private (and thus independent in terms of their preachers, content of sermons, and activities) rather than state-controlled. During the Sadat years, government policy at first tended to encourage the building of mosques large and small, which were frequently separate buildings and small rooms attached to apartment complexes, and office buildings. In terms of sheer numbers, Cairo became the city of mosques. However, the overwhelming majority were private mosques outside government control. Although both Sadat and, later (1985), Mubarak announced plans to take control of private mosques, given the enormous number of mosques and limited resources, results were limited. In October, 1992, Mubarak's ministry of religious affairs announced that all sermons at state-controlled mosques would be subject to approval by government-appointed officials and that the building of private mosques would be curbed. On November 10, 1992, Muhammad Ali Mahgoub, the minister of religious affairs, announced once again that all private mosques would be brought under the control of the ministry.

The chief militant Islamic challenge to the Mubarak government has come from the Gamaa Islamiyya (Jamaat Islamiyya or Islamic Group) and Jamaat-al Jihad, who have been locked in a deadly battle with security forces and police during the 1990s. The spark was the assassination (the mysterious death) of Ala Mohieddin, a young physician and Gamaa leader reputedly appointed spokesman for the Gamaa by Sheikh Omar Abdel Rahman in 1991. The Gamaa blamed the government, and in return assassinated Rafaat Mahgoub, speaker of the Parliament or People's Assembly and set in motion a pattern of political violence and counter-violence between the government and the Gamaa Islamiyya.

The Gamaa Islamiyya evolved (or perhaps more accurately "devolved") from student groups active on university campuses and in politics in the early Sadat days to a front or umbrella organization that includes a host of underground extremist groups active in Cairo, Alexandria, Asyut, Minya, and Fayyum. Its membership, in contrast to the past, is younger (including a heavy component of adolescents, as well as university students and graduates), less educated, living in more desperate conditions of poverty and unemployment, more radical ideologically, and more random in its use of violence. Whereas the Gamaa in Sadat's days was urban and university-based, today it is a clandestine movement, many of whose members are high-school age and are active in small villages and towns as well as urban areas in Egypt. The Gamaa regards Sheikh Omar Abdel Rahman, the blind cleric who was arrested and tried but released in the trial of the assassins of Anwar Sadat, and was found guilty of bombings in the United States, as its spiritual leader. Bent upon destabilizing the Egyptian economy and overthrowing the government, the Gamaa has attacked and murdered foreign tourists, Coptic Christians, and government officials, as well as bombed banks and government buildings. They attack the cinema, theater, magazines, books, and associations that popularize modern concepts such as individualism and Western culture.[11] Militants believe that the liberation of Egyptian society requires that all true Muslims undertake an armed struggle or holy war against a regime which they regard as oppressive, anti-Islamic, and a puppet of the West.

The Islamist strategy has been to undermine the economy and thus domestic stability. They have targeted tourism and hit visible symbols of the government and elite Egyptian society in order to undermine the stability of the regime. Tourism, which in 1991 brought in more than three billion dollars, represents the most important source of Egypt's foreign revenues and is supported by an extensive infrastructure that provides income for millions of Egyptians. At the same time, government ministers have been killed or wounded, and prominent secular critics of fundamentalism have been attacked. The columnist Farag Foda, who had been outspoken in his criticism and ridicule of fundamentalism, was assassinated in July, 1992. A prominent judge and intellectual, Muhammad Said Ashmawi, who has countered Islamist claims with a liberal secular interpretation of Islam, has had to live under twenty-four hour security.

The Egyptian military, although generally loyal to the government, has not proven impervious to Islamist penetration. Despite attempts to weed them out, the military has proved vulnerable to infiltration by Islamists. In December, 1986, thirty-three activists, including four military officers, who were allegedly connected to Jamaat al-Jihad (Sadat's assassins), were arrested and charged with plotting to wage a holy war in order to overthrow the government. The government has continued to quietly purge those suspected of being "fundamentalists," thwarted several apparent attempts on Mubarak's life by officers, and used its military courts to secretly try and execute those who have challenged the regime. However, despite government vigilance, some argue that there remains a surprising degree of Islamist presence and sympathizers in the military among junior officers and soldiers. While the bulk of the army remains loyal, there continue to be signs of fundamentalist infiltration and presence in the military, including in the officer corps. Tight press control regarding both the military courts and dissent has not prevented stories of attempted coups, including a report that there was at a military trial "a white robed defendant, brandishing the Koran and screaming for President Mubarak's death. He turned out to be an army lieutenant."[12] In March, 1994, three officers were found guilty of an attempt to blow up the president on an airstrip near the Libyan border.[13]

Islamic movements and associations (moderate and extremist) in Egypt, as in many other Muslim countries, have received support from a broad spectrum of governments (Libya, Saudi Arabia, the Gulf, Iran, and Sudan). In the aftermath of the Gulf War, in which Islamists generally sided against Saudi Arabia and Kuwait, government funding has dried up. Today, Iran and Sudan may indeed provide limited financial support and some training for extremist organizations. However, given their economic and domestic problems and, in the case of Iran, logistics, substantial assistance is unlikely. It would not be surprising to find that more substantial funding comes more from outside individual patrons than from governments. In any event, the bulk of support generally comes from within rather than outside society. Although outside assistance can serve as a catalyst and can support activities, the strength and credibility of Islamic organizations is rooted in domestic conditions and actors rather than outside agitation.

The Mubarak government has aggressively responded to what it clearly perceives as a major threat of Islamic radicalism to the stability of the government and to regional security. In the process, the lines between radical and moderate Islamists, state security and the limits of state authority, prosecution of criminals and human rights, have often been blurred. In its war against "terrorism," a broad government crackdown and massive arrests of suspected extremists and sympathizers has included not only extremists but also moderate Islamists and family members of suspects, in an attempt to silence and intimidate any and all Islamic opposition. In 1989, for example, as many as 10,000 Islamic militants were arrested. Thousands were held without charge; the Arab Human Rights Organization accused the government of routine torture.[14]

Too often in the 1990s both extremists and the government have been locked in a "holy war" in which the government's police and security forces as well as the militants, had a "hit list" for murder and assassination rather than for arrest and prosecution. An Amnesty International report noted that security forces "appear to have been given a license to kill with impunity."[15] Special military courts, which do not permit defendants a right of appeal, have been created to try civilians accused of terrorism. Courts quickly, and often quietly, mete out swift, harsh sentences; the number of those executed has vastly exceeded those executed in the past for politically motivated crimes such as the attempt to kill Nasser or the assassination of Sadat. Lawyers for the defense have often charged that they have been permitted limited access to their clients and that their clients have been victims of torture. Lawyers for suspected militants have themselves been arrested. The death of a "prominent Muslim militant lawyer" Abdel Harith Madani, one day after his arrest, prompted the Egyptial Bar Association and international human rights groups to call for an investigation, suspecting "that security guards had tortured him to death."[16] The U.S. State Department's human rights report on Egypt on February 1, 1994, noted that the government "perpetrated many abuses, including the arbitrary arrest and torture of hundreds of detainees, the use of military courts to try accused terrorists, the failure to punish officials responsible for torture."[17] Systematic torture, long-term detention without charge, the taking of family members of suspected Islamists or terrorists "hostage" to force their relatives to surrender, and press censorship have led officials of international nongovernmental human rights organizations to declare: "This poor human rights record has yielded resentment, the narrowing of civil society, religious intolerance and erosion of the rule of law in Egypt—and fertile ground for the growth of extremist alternatives."[18]

PROFESSIONAL ASSOCIATIONS

The Mubarak government's attempt not only to eradicate violent extremism but also to counter and control the institutionalization of Islamic activism was starkly reflected in its changing policy toward professional syndicates. Egypt's syndicates—democratic and voluntary associations of teachers, lawyers, doctors, journalists—are a pillar of Egyptian civil society. During the 1980s, Islamists emerged as a major force in the syndicates. The successes of Islamic activist sociopolitical mainstreaming included a significant increase in an Islamically oriented professional class, reflecting the numbers of young professional graduates. Their presence and impact were felt in professional associations or syndicates in which Islamists captured the leadership of the physicians', engineers', and finally lawyers' organizations. Professional syndicates "are the most advanced sectors of public life in Egypt, enjoying high status and speaking with an autonomous and respected voice. The lawyers' syndicate has been at the forefront of the campaigns for human rights and the rule of law."[19] The Brotherhood's winning of a majority of the board seats in Bar Association elections, long regarded as a bastion of liberalism, in September 1992 signalled its growing strength and influence. Muslim Brotherhood successes reflected the growing number of younger Islamist-oriented professionals, the appeal of the Brotherhood to professional classes as the only credible opposition, the indifference and reluctance of many professionals to vote in association elections, and the ability of a well-organized, highly motivated minority to "get out the vote" and work with purpose and persistence.

In February, 1993, the government changed the election laws that govern associations and seized control of professional associations in order to counter the Muslim Brotherhood's control and influence. Evidence Law 100, passed by the People's Assembly, placed stringent quorum requirements on syndicate elections. If the requirements were not met, syndicate board members were to be politically appointed. Despite this move by the government, which was denounced by Islamists and non-Islamists alike, the Brotherhood retained control of the lawyer's, medical, and engineering syndicates.

However, government attempts to control or silence syndicate opposition continued. On May 10, 1993, a protest rally by lawyers over the death in police custody of Abdel Harith Medani, a leading lawyer for the Gamaa Islamiya and a member of the Egyptian Human Rights Organization, was broken up by police, who used tear gas and arrested thirty-three lawyers, who were charged with inciting violence. The government denied allegations of torture, returned the body in a sealed coffin, and refused to permit an autopsy. Although the public prosecutor subsequently conceded on May 12 that Medani's death was due to foul play and authorized a suit against the police for death by torture, nevertheless, the judiciary on June 17 extended the lawyers' detention for an additional fifteen days.[20] Abdel Aziz Mohammed, the head of the 70,000-member Cairo branch of the lawyer's syndicate (not an Islamist and, in fact, a lawyer defending a Cairo University professor accused of apostasy) charged that the government aimed "to weaken the syndicate as an institution of civil society in the guise of waging a fight against militancy."[21]

In a somewhat similar vein, in a move widely seen as an attempt to weaken the influence of Islamists, the government-controlled People's Assembly passed a new educational law, Law 104, on May 31, without warning or consultation, which cancelled the right of Egyptian professors to elect their faculty deans and allows the rectors of universities to appoint them instead. Opponents charged that despite the fact that the Brotherhood has not been particularly active or successful in university faculties, the law is "one step in the government's attempt to eliminate any possibility of the Islamists capturing any more key positions . . . [and that if] university professors are not to be trusted with electing their own representative, then there is no point in talking about democracy."[22] Government attempts to control Egyptian professional associations had the unforeseen result of driving Islamists and secularists into an uneasy alliance in a common defense.

More ominously, in June, 1994, in a move reminiscent of the actions of Tunisia and Algeria, the Mubarak government extended its war not just against the terrorism of the Gamaa Islamiya but against Egypt's strongest opposition group, the Muslim Brotherhood. In what seemed like an all-out, indiscriminate war, it moved "to curtail not only those movements that have carried out violent attacks, but also one that has come to dominate many municipalities, professional and labor associations and university faculties."[23] Egypt's prosecutor first ordered and then revoked a warrant for the arrest of the Muslim Brotherhood's Supreme Guide, Hamid Abu Nasser, and security forces arrested eleven Brothers in four governorates, who were charged with plotting to overthrow the government.[24] Although some feared violence, the Brotherhood continued to eschew confrontation and violence and instead responded by appealing to principles of democracy and human rights.

EDUCATION (CONTROL OF MOSQUES AND SCHOOLS)

Recognition of the size of its younger population, and the extent to which youth, unemployment, and lack of housing have created conditions for recruitment by Islamists and have made for an explosive mix, the Ministry of Education introduced a series of educational reforms to control a "breeding ground" for extremism. Historically, education and other issues concerning youth have long received primary emphasis by Islamist organizations. The goal of the founders of Egypt's Muslim Brotherhood and the the the Jamaat-i Islami in the Indian subcontinent was future oriented—the transformation of society through the creation of a new generation of modern educated, more Islamically oriented Muslims. Thus, priority was given to education. Hasan al-Banna and Sayyid Qutb were both former educators, as are Tunisia's Rashid Ghannoushi and Sudan's Hasan Turabi. Thus, influence, if not control, of education has been a clear and stated goal. Many Islamists have been teachers and university professors, recruiting and working closely with student organizations. When in a position to serve in government, Islamists have tended to emphasize domestic cabinet portfolios such as the ministries of Education, Youth and Culture, and Religious Affairs rather than Foreign Affairs or Defense.

The degree and extent of the Mubarak government's concerns were reflected in a statement by Hussein Kamel Baha Eddin, Minister of Education: "Terrorism starts in the mind.... The fundamentalists are planning to brainwash our children to seize power."[25] The government designated education as an issue of national security and initiated a number of policies designed to counter its "Islamist threat." The budget for education was quadrupled; teachers suspected of being Islamists or having Islamist sympathies were dismissed, retired, or transferred—many to clerical positions in remote areas; a national curriculum was imposed; and, in a reversal of previous policy, an attempt was made to introduce English language and Western secular values, to provide a window on development as well as "a 'culture shock' to upset the wave of fundamentalism sweeping Egypt's schools."[26]

Such policies resurrected memories of colonial rule and of early Egyptian modernists, whose approach to modernization was one of progressive Westernization and secularization. Islamists and some secular nationalists found a common basis for resistance which they regarded as a threat to cultural identity and authenticity, now coupled with existing economic and political dependence. Some secular critics charged that the government had overreacted to fears of a fundmentalist threat, creating a climate in which "[i]f a teacher just talks about the greatness of Omar Bin Al Khattab, the second caliph, he is considered a terrorist."[27]

MINORITY RIGHTS

Egypt, with the largest population in the Arab world, is predominantly Sunni Muslim. Although unrecognized by law (that is, no special legislation exists for minorities), religious and ethnic minorities exist, including Christians, Bahai, Jews, Shii Muslims, Nubians, Greeks, and Arabic-speaking Bedouin. Christians make up approximately 10 percent of Egypt's population of 60 million. The vast majority of Christians are Coptic Orthodox Christians, whose presence in Egypt predates the rise of Islam and its spread to Egypt, and who in large part share a common language, identity, and culture with Egyptian Muslims.

While some tensions have existed between the majority Sunni Muslim and minority Coptic Christian community, like other minorities, Copts have generally been able to practice their faith, and to live, work, and prosper. However, since the early 1970s, the resurgence of political Islam has strained relations between the communities and exacerbated majority-minority relations. The situation began to degenerate during the Sadat years, as Copts became caught between the government's manipulation of Islam as a source of legitimacy and mobilization and the growth of Islamic extremism.

Riots erupted in March, 1972, in Alexandria, where rumors spread that Pope Shenouda had initiated a plan to take over Egypt by converting Muslims to Christianity. In March, the celebration of a mass by Copts in protest over the burning of a church in Khanka, a village near Cairo, resulted in anti-Copt demonstrations in which Copt houses and shops were burned.[28] The situation exploded again from 1978 to 1981, with riots and demonstrations in Assiut, Minya, and Cairo in which Muslim militants burned churches and attacked and killed Copts.

At the same time, Sadat was challenged both by Islamists (radicals and moderates) and by many secular critics on domestic and foreign policy issues, from Camp David and Iran to democracy and growing authoritarianism. Islamists charged that Sadat's public piety and use of Islam was a sham, and demanded the imposition of Islamic law. Underground extremist groups attempted to overthrow the government. Sadat attempted to counter his critics. A draft amendment in 1977 to make apostasy punishable by death was followed by a constitutional change which declared the Sharia the basic source, rather than a source, of Egyptian law (1980). Equal citizenship and status under the law seemed further threatened by extremist demands that non-Muslims be considered dhimmi, protected people, rather than full citizens. Statements by Muslim Brotherhood and Sadat further exacerbated the situation. The Muslim Brotherhood vacillated in its attitudes, sometimes speaking of "our brothers" and at other times alleging "that foreign influences were trying to make the Copts a fifth column of the West in Egypt."[29] Such statements played on popular resentments and stereotypes. In addition to early historical conflicts such as the Crusades, in the nineteenth century the British had used the excuse of protection of (fellow) Christians from Muslims as one of its rationalizations for intervention in Egypt's internal affairs. President Sadat and his ruling party's newspaper also exploited this stereotype on occasion. As previously noted, Sadat had manipulated Islamic symbols and rhetoric to enhance his legitimacy and mobilize support; he also had a low tolerance for criticism. Pope Shenouda, the Coptic Patriarch, who, like Sadat came to power in the early 1970s, was a forceful leader who spoke on political as well as religious issues, criticizing the government's failure to assure and protect the rights and safety of Copts. Furious at criticisms from Shenouda and at overseas Coptic communities, particularly those in the United States, who demonstrated when Sadat visited the United States and gained international media attention for the plight of Egypt's Copts, Sadat lashed out at his critics with statements that tended "to reinforce the image of minorities as unpatriotic and ready to collaborate with foreign enemies against the nation's interests."[30] Sadat forced Pope Shenouda to retreat from his seat in Cairo to a desert monastery from which he guided his church.

Tensions between Muslims and Copts were also affected by deteriorating socioeconomic conditions, which provided a receptive audience for demogogues. Muslims charged that while Muslims were economically marginalized in terms of jobs, employment, and educational opportunities, the Coptic minority prospered, and Copts charged increased discrimination and exclusion in employment and education, especially at the more elite levels. If some Muslims wished to emphasize their majority elite status, Copts in return defensively spoke of their pre-Arab/Islamic Pharaonic roots and thus their older and more indigenous history and heritage. In response to the threat of Islamic militancy, the Coptic church experienced a revival which included its younger generation, who formed their own militant groups to preserve and defend their identity and community. However, the death of Sadat brought a brief cooling off period during the early Mubarak years.

The reemergence of extremist groups in the late 1980s brought a new round of Muslim-Christian conflict, as the battle between clandestine extremists and the government intensified. As the Islamic Group spread not only in large cities but also to small towns (Biba, Sennouris, and Qena) and villages, bombings of churches, homes, and shops; beatings and murders; and attempts to impose dress and behavior codes increased. Although police and security guards protecting churches were shot and killed, Coptic Christians, caught in the battle between militants and the government, charged that government officials have downplayed the number of incidents and their significance, often attributing such incidents to personal conflicts and vendettas rather than religiously motivated attacks. However, the Egyptian Organization for Human Rights condemned the "actions of the organization known as Gamaa Islamiyya [the Islamic Group], which has persisted in its recourse to violence, in its advocacy of the hatred of citizens of the Christian faith, in its incitement to various forms of discrimination against them and in actively taking part in such acts of discrimination."[31] Thus, for example, the Egyptian Organization for Human Rights in May, 1994, found that despite the use of indiscriminate firepower, killings, and arbitrary arrests by the government, militant Islamists were responsible for the bulk of human-rights abuses (including the deaths of Christians, police, and a foreign tourist) in Upper Egypt.[32]

CONCLUSION

Islamic activism in Egypt, as in much of the Muslim world, has not receded; rather, it has rooted itself more deeply and pervasively in Egyptian society. Its variety and diversity, its many faces and postures, have long been overshadowed by its equation with a monolithic radical fundamentalist threat. The broader significance and impact of Islamists can be seen by the extent to which they have gained cultural legitimacy, have become part of mainstream Muslim life and society and are not solely members of marginalized and alienated groups. Secular institutions are now complemented or challenged by Islamically oriented counterparts that provide much-needed educational and social services and underscore the limitations and continued failures of government. The Muslim Brotherhood and other activists became dominant voices in professional organizations and syndicates of lawyers, doctors, engineers, and journalists.

Islamic awareness and activism has grown among the lower and middle classes, the educated and uneducated, professionals, students, and laborers, young and old, women and men. The emergence of modern, educated but more Islamically oriented professionals in society offers a political and social alternative elite that challenges the Western, secular presuppositions and lifestyles of many in the establishment. Members of this alternative elite presented their criticisms and demands within the context of a call for greater democratization, political representation, and respect for human rights.

Contemporary Islamic activism provides an alternative system or infrastructure, an implicit critique of the failure and inability of the state to adequately respond to the needs of its citizens. This, combined with the remarkable growth of Sufism and other nonpolitical religious organizations and societies, creates a potential pool of politically and nonpolitically oriented Muslims. Given the right conditions (failure of the system, lack of viable political or Islamic alternatives), they can be politically mobilized to vote for those who proclaim "Islam is the solution."

The fact that Islamists are specific in their indictment of the government but general in terms of their own programs tends to work in their favor. They are able to criticize the failings of the government, from employment and housing to corruption and maldistribution of wealth, without having to offer their own specific solutions to seemingly intractable problems. They employ Islamic rhetoric and symbols, call for an Islamic solution and the implementation of the Sharia, but do not delineate precisely what these would mean in terms of specific policies. Moreover, although at the macro level, they often only offer general prescriptions and promises; the source of their credibility and success is that at the micro level. Their educational and social programs demonstrate to ordinary people the concrete, tangible meaning and impact of an Islamic order. In contrast, the government is often seen as offering promises but failing to effectively deliver at the macro and the micro levels.

The major accomplishment of the Islamic movement, and the Muslim Brotherhood in particular, and the source of its strength and credibility is the extent to which, motivated by religion as well as political, social, and economic considerations, it has created an alternative, normative order. Its alternative order provides an ideological worldview based on and legitimated by religion and an alternative social system of services that demonstrates the relevance and effectiveness of religion to social realities and problems. As a result, the Islamic factor is regarded as both an effective change agent and challenge or threat. While many Muslims find meaning, direction, assistance and a sense of empowerment, others (in particular the government and many elites) see Islamic movements as an indirect critique of the government's failures, a challenge to its legitimacy, and a direct threat to the stability of the Egyptian government and society.

The reality of Egyptian society, as indeed of many Muslim societies, today contributes to a climate in which the influence of Islam and activist organizations on sociopolitical development will increase rather than diminish. Egypt continues to exist in a climate of socioeconomic crisis and cultural alienation in which many experience the failure of the state and of secular ideologies. The government and ruling elites or classes possess tenuous legitimacy in the face of mounting disillusionment and opposition, among whom Islamic activists remain the most vocal, best organized, and most effective. The extent to which the government fails to meet socioeconomic needs, restricts political participation, proves insensitive to the need to effectively incorporate Islam and moderate Islamists, or appears exceedingly dependent on the West contributes to the continued appeal of an Islamic political alternative. Resorting to past patterns of repression, whatever its apparent short-term gains, will only contribute to further radicalization and long-term instability. Opening up the system and fostering the growth of a strong civil society will have its difficulties in the short term but serve Egypt's long-term interests and development: "the future development of the Islamic movement depends on how it is treated (or mistreated) by those in power and not on any inherent conflict between Islam and freedom . . . Egypt's rulers can expect to see an Islam that faithfully reflects the skill or folly of their own statecraft."[33]

Conclusion

Throughout much of the Muslim world, the 1990s have witnessed the impact and interaction of the forces of resurgent Islam and democratization. Issues of religious and cultural identity, authenticity, and legitimacy have been intertwined with those of political participation, empowerment and civil society. The post-independence drift along a more Western, secular path of development has been challenged if not rejected. Both governments and political and social movements have often reappropriated religious symbols and vocabulary; they have used and abused, implemented and manipulated religion in politics and society.

Muslim experiences, however, have not occurred in isolation. Today, we are witnessing a global movement of religious and communal (ethnic, linguistic, and cultural) resurgence and democratization. The global tendency toward desecularization has challenged the presuppositions of modernization, the progressive Westernization and secularization of societies which had often been articulated as inevitable evolutionary principles of development. Nations and religious traditions, political and religious leaders, have had to contend with religious and ethnic/nationalist forces who reassert their identity and seek empowerment. The many forms of this postmodern transformation can be seen not only in Muslim societies, but also in the disintegration of the former Soviet Union and of Yugoslavia, communal confrontations between Hindus and Muslims in India, and the revolt of Sikh nationalists in the Punjab, Muslims in Kashmir, Tamils in Sri Lanka, and confrontations between militant Jewish religious groups and their more secular counterparts in Israel. For some observers, the reassertion of age-old religious and ethnic identities has led to talk of a clash of civilizations, of a post–Cold War period or New World Order in which the threat of global confrontation will no longer be between superpowers or nation-states but civilizations.

All major world religions have witnessed a reassertion of religious themes and issues reflected in mainstream as well as more marginal religious organizations. Their voices and names are many; they are often characterized as fundamentalist, reformist, revolutionary, or liberation movements, depending on the ideological and political vantage point of the observer. Despite vast differences of geography, history, doctrine, culture, and experience, increasingly many people throughout much of the world have become more disillusioned with and critical of a modernity run wild or out of control; they are more concerned with issues of identity, meaning, and values, particularly family and community values, and political participation and social justice. Most do not cling mindlessly to the past, nor do they espouse an anachronistic religious vision or utopia, but instead advocate a reconceptualization or reapplication of formative religious principles and values to contemporary life. Thus, their concerns address issues of political, economic, social, and religiocultural identity and empowerment.

The demand for democracy, the growth of prodemocracy movements, is now evident throughout much of the Muslim world. While some Muslim religious leaders and rulers, such as King Fahd of Saudi Arabia, and some Islamists have maintained that democracy is foreign to Islam and that Islam has its own specific traditions for political participation and governance, many others have embraced the rhetoric and politics of democratization. However, this has not been without differences and problems. As discussed earlier in this volume, although this fact is often overlooked, democracy is in reality a contested term. There may be a dominant discourse, but multiple discourses have existed and can continue to exist or be formulated. The term "democracy" is capable of multiple interpretations and applications. Contrary to the belief or presuppositions of some, the Western experience of democracy reveals a rich mosaic rather than a single paradigm. Similarly, the history and implementation of democracy in the West reveals the extent to which the emergence and development of democracy, of democratic values and institutions, was itself a "messy" process fraught with the tensions and conflicts that accompany all great periods of historical and social transformation; it was the subject of great debates and great revolutions, of rhetoric and bloodshed, championed by democrats and demagogues. Acceptance of the contested nature of democracy, its diversity and dynamics of development, enables the recognition that there can be alternative and rival uses of the term. Thus, democratization need not simply be the adoption of Western democracy (in some monolithic form) but can equally be the adaptation of Western democratic forms or the formulation of indigenously rooted forms of political participation and empowerment. Similarly, recognition of the extent to which the formulation and legitimacy of western democracy was not only the creation of something new but also the product of a reinterpretation or reformulation of older concepts, beliefs, and institutions opens up the possibility of other cultural and religious traditions generating and accommodating democratic forms of governance.

However different their understanding and usages, calls for democratization, political participation, and Islamic democracy demonstrate the contemporary currency of democracy in many Muslim societies. While some remain convinced that democracy is un-Islamic or anti-Islamic, or that it is simply another attempt by the West in the post–Cold War era to achieve ideological and political hegemony in the name of a New World Order, many Muslims have made advocacy of democracy the political litmus test for the credibility and legitimacy of regimes and for political parties and opposition. As Muslim rulers and politicians, whatever their degree of religiosity or ideological orientation, have always had to contend with the political sensitivity of Islam, so too many today, like it or not, must contend with popular support for democratization.

As our case studies have demonstrated, for many in the Muslim world from North Africa to Southeast Asia, recent decades have been a time to take stock of several decades of independence, to question the political, economic, and social failures of their societies, and thus to challenge the established order. While some have chosen a path of rejection and revolution, many others, in diverse ways ranging from governments to populist movements, have combined a renewed awareness and sensitivity to religious identity and values with politics. The results have been diverse and mixed. Whatever the accomplishments of the Iranian revolution and the establishment of Islamic republics in Iran, Sudan, and Pakistan, they have been offset by the replacement of secular authoritarianisms with religiously legitimated authoritarianisms which have severely restricted political and religious minorities and opposition parties. Both self-styled Islamic republics and their secular counterparts in Algeria, Tunisia, and Egypt, for example, would identify themselves with political participation, pluralism, and human rights, even as they found excuses (the defense of Islam or the defense of the state against religious fanatics) to circumscribe the rights of any significant opposition.

Malaysia, under Prime Minister Mahathir, offers an alternative example of a nation in which Islam is the official religion and Muslims dominate the political system, but a nation with a substantial and economically significant non-Muslim minority. The government has attempted to coopt or counter Islamic opposition, and balances greater emphasis on Malay Muslim identity and modern economic development with an affirmation of Asian rather than Western values in an attempt to respond to its domestic as well as regional pluralistic realities. Government advocacy of a democratization process that, like its value orientation, is more indigenously rooted has played well despite some setbacks in national electoral politics. At the same time, the government's greater Islamic profile has raised concerns among non-Muslim minorities and become a means for the government to silence or restrict its Islamic opposition in the name of defending true Islam.

The religious landscape of the contemporary Muslim world reveals the growth and proliferation of modern Islamic movements and groups who engage in social and political activism. While some, such as Egypt's Gamaa Islamiyya, have directly threatened regimes and espoused violent revolution, many others, such as the Muslim Brotherhood, the Jamaat-i Islami, and the Islamic Salvation Front have demonstrated a willingness to participate within the system.

Although the 1970s and 1980s seemed dominated by fears of revolutionary Islam, from Iran's export of revolution to the hostage-taking and hijacking in the Middle East, the 1990s have revealed a more multilayered and nuanced religiopolitical landscape. Images of gun-toting Islamists and clandestine terrorists bent upon carrying their jihad to the West, blowing up the World Trade Center and plotting other acts of urban terrorism, are accompanied by the clear and public image and record of Islamic activists and organizations that have become mainstream political and social actors. They are part of a quiet revolution; they function in civil society, creating their own social and political organizations or parties, forming alliances with other political parties or unions, and participating in national professional associations.

The economic and political failures of many regimes in the late 1980s and the fall of the Soviet Union have produced a more open political climate that not only enabled radicals to threaten governments but also provided opportunities for some Islamic organizations and parties in the late 1980s and early 1990s to demonstrate the extent to which they constituted viable social and political alternatives. They offered educational and social welfare services in Egypt and Algeria which often proved effective and efficient alternatives to faltering governments hampered by failed economies and corruption, bloated and inefficient bureaucracies, and entrenched elites. Politically, Islamist candidates also proved a viable alternative in local and national political elections as well as those of professional organizations and associations. Islamic activists have been elected mayors, parliamentarians, heads of professional associations (doctors, lawyers, engineers, and university faculty), and have served as government ministers in countries as diverse as Egypt, Israel, Pakistan, Algeria, Sudan, Lebanon, Turkey, Jordan, Kuwait, Pakistan, and Malaysia.

The experiences and track records of Islamic movements with political participation and democratization have indeed varied. The Jamaat-i Islami of Pakistan has participated within the political system since the creation of Pakistan. Although often in opposition, it has also agreed to serve in government, as in the early days of Zia ul-Haq's rule. Ideologically and politically, the Jamaat has proven both pragmatic and flexible, moving from opposition to the creation of Pakistan to acceptance and participation, from opposition to nationalism and democracy to full participation within the political system and dual advocacy of both an Islamic and a democratic state. Ironically, although the ability of the Jamaat and other Islamic parties to participate in politics strengthened their influence and enhanced the Islamic character and profile of Pakistan's politics and political culture, severely limiting secular ideologies, it has never translated into significant numbers of votes. Neither the Jamaat nor any other Islamic group has come close to achieving governance through the ballot box. The more open political scene in Pakistan has weakened Islamic parties or organizations like the Jamaat-i Islami. Indeed, the appeal to Islam in politics and in mass mobilization, although at times producing transient united opposition movements, has in the long run divided societies. The divisions have occurred not only between secular and "Islamic" sectors of society but among Islamic activist leaders and organizations themselves, from the ayatollahs of Iran to Islamic leaders and organizations in Sudan and Pakistan. More open political systems, as have existed in Malaysia and at times in Pakistan along with alternative secular and Islamic organizations, have generally made for greater ideological and political flexibility and prevented any one Islamic group from emerging as the dominant opposition party. Conversely, as the recent histories of Algeria, Tunisia, and Egypt demonstrate, Islamist groups are more likely to emerge as the major opposition party when they are "the only game in town," that is, when they function in political environments in which they become the sole credible voice of opposition and thus attract the votes of those who simply wish to vote against the government or system, as well as the votes of their members.

If the 1980s were dominated by fears of export of Islamic radicalism through violent revolution, the mainstreaming of Islamic activism and the electoral successes of Islamists in the 1990s has triggered new concerns. Is the participation of Islamic organizations in electoral politics simply tactical—a stratagem for coming to power and then imposing their Islamic system of governance? After more than a decade in which many governments in the Muslim world and the West had charged that "Islamic fundamentalism" was a radical revolutionary threat with little public support, the emergence of Islamists in elections as the leading opposition in Tunisia, Egypt, Jordan, and Turkey, and the specter of their coming to power through elections in Algeria, has led some to charge that Islamists are out to hijack democracy. This charge has provided the excuse for governments such as those of Tunisia, Egypt, and Algeria to slow down or curtail their democratization process and to crack down on and repress their Islamic critics or opposition. While some warn of Islamists' hijacking democracy, others charge that many regimes have demonstrated that they only believe in risk-free democracy or democracy without dissent. Although repression has appeared to be successful in the short term in Tunisia, in Algeria it has produced a bloody civil war and unleashed a spiral of violence and revenge, and increasingly threatened the stability of Egypt.

Given the political and economic realities of many Muslim societies, the future of democratization remains in doubt. Some continue to question the degree to which democracy, which grew up in the West, can be transported to other cultures, while others more directly question whether Islam and democracy are compatible. The question is compounded if we use terms such as Islam or democracy in an essentialist or monolithic manner rather than acknowledging their flexibility and adaptability and the diversity of actual experience. It is also useful to recall that when they penetrated Muslim societies, nationalism and socialism became less the preserve of more Westernized secular elites and more indigenously rooted and transformed and thus Islamized. So, too, democratization tends to lose its secular dimensions as it becomes a more popular, more truly democratic movement, reinforcing and strengthening a resurgent political Islam.

Beyond these questions lies an equally vexing set of issues. How do authoritarian governments, with problems of legitimacy and authority, become persuaded to build strong civil societies? To what extent will rulers be willing to look beyond the short-term retention of power and be prescient enough to realize the importance of fostering conditions that will foster the values and institutions that support and sustain civil society and democratization? The political situation is compounded by the economic realities of the post–Cold War and post–Gulf War period. Developing nations in the Muslim world, as elsewhere, can no longer count on the substantial aid and assistance which often resulted from the superpower rivalry. The Soviet Union is gone, and the United States is no longer in a position or of a mind to provide substantial assistance. Similarly, the Gulf states, with their own economic problems, no longer provide the aid to Muslim states or jobs to foreign workers that they formerly did. Countries with faltering economies and escalating populations, a high percentage of which are people under the age of twenty-five, face a future in which it is extraordinarily difficult to deal with the issues of popular empowerment and identity.

POLICY ISSUES

Many in the Muslim world and the West charged during the 1980s that Islamic organizations were simply radical fringe groups that were not representative and would simply be repudiated by the electorate. The justification for the condemnation and suppression of Islamic movements had been that they were violent extremists, small nonrepresentative groups on the margins of society, who refused to work within the system and as such were a threat to society and regional stability. However, their participation and proven electoral strength in the late 1980s and early 1990s challenged these assumptions. The vision of Islamic organizations working within the system ironically made them an even more formidable threat to regimes. Those who once dismissed Islamist claims as unrepresentative and who denounced Islamic radicalism as a threat to the system now accused Islamist organizations that wished to participate within the system of an attempt to "hijack democracy." The electoral successes of the FIS in Algeria in the early 1990s, and likelihood that it might actually come to power through the ballot box, proved a nightmare that alarmed many Muslim and Western governments.

Concerns that Islamic movements might use the ballot box to come to and then, in effect, seize power are rooted in a realistic possibility. Certainly the examples of the Islamic republics of Iran, Pakistan (under Zia ul-Haq) and the Sudan (under the NIF-backed regime of Omar al-Bashir) show that Islamists in power will work to alter the political system significantly. At the same time, this issue must be balanced by an equal awareness that more secularly oriented or non-Islamist governments are themselves far from democratic. However liberal Egypt may have appeared relative to other countries in the region, it has been and continues to be an authoritarian state. Its rulers, like most in the Muslim world, have been far more dependent on the military and security apparatus for legitimacy and stability than the popular support of an electorate. The Egyptian government remains a one-party dominated state that "tolerates" and controls its opposition and the institutions of civil society. Its commitment to political liberalization or to the democratic process must be seen within this context, a context carefully crafted and guided to prevent the development of any powerful opposition parties. Similarly, the examples of Tunisia and Algeria, where governments first promised political liberalization and then reneged on their promises and attempted to crush Islamists when electoral results demonstrated they were the only substantial political opposition, should be remembered. Many rightfully question whether the liberal political statements of Islamist leaders like Rashid Ghannoushi represent an actual party program that would be translated into action if it came to power. Will his deeds match his words? Yet few note that President Ben Ali's track record is well documented, a record in which promises of political liberalization when he took power proved a brief flirtation in an otherwise decades-long identification with authoritarian rule.

The threat of authoritarianism comes less from religious doctrine than politics and power, history and political culture. Identifying governments as regimes committed either to implementating religious law or Westernization provides no prediction as to whether or not the regime will be authoritarian or democratic. Commitment to Westernization is no guarantee of democracy, nor is application of Islamic law a proof of an inherent authoritarianism in Islam. In fact, the active debates and contests in the elections of the Iranian Republic and in the deliberations of the parliament, however strictly the limits are set, show a higher degree of political disagreement than was publically possible during the last decade of the Shah's rule. Islamist and secular leaders alike in the Islamic world face strong historical heritages of political authoritarianism in their efforts to create greater political participation in an era when affirmation of historic identities is also of great popular concern.

While the threat of radicalism and terrorism must be countered, failure to distinguish between extremists who are avowedly committed to the violent overthrow of the prevailing system and those organizations that have demonstrated a willingness to participate within the system has led to indiscriminate state repression of both kinds of Islamic organizations. This approach runs the risk of setting in motion a spiral of state violence and movement toward counter-violence and revenge that can lead to the creation of self-fulfilling prophecies: the radicalization, terrorism, and polarization of society. The general attempt to suppress or "decapitate" Islamic movements can in fact lead not only to the breakup of violent movements across the board but also to the radicalization of moderates, as has occurred in Algeria and is increasingly a risk in Egypt. It would be more productive to discriminate between moderates and violent extremists and thus drive a wedge between them rather than create conditions that will cause them to close ranks.

As we have seen, the history of the Muslim Brotherhood in Egypt and the Jamaat-i Islami in Pakistan are instructive. Gamal Abdel Nasser's repression of the

Muslim Brotherhood, and the subsequent violence and counter-violence, spawned the more militant ideological interpretation of Sayyid Qutb and the ascendance of a radical wing within the Muslim Brotherhood. The ultimate suppression of the Brotherhood in the 1960s led many to conclude that it had been effectively eradicated. In fact, prison experience and repression led more than a decade later to the formation of violent extremist splinter groups like Takfir wal Hijra and the Jamaat al-Jihad, the assassins of Anwar Sadat, and their offshoots today, many of whom are clustered under the umbrella of the Gamaa Islamiyya.

In contrast, Islamic movements such as the Jamaat-i Islami in Pakistan (or Jordan's Muslim Brotherhood and ABIM and PAS in Malaysia) have been able to function within the system. The Jamaat has been politically influential but never an electoral or violent revolutionary threat. Indeed, while Pakistan, like Malaysia, has been a theater for significant Islamic political activity, the Jamaat-i Islami and major Islamic parties such as the JUI and JUP have generally functioned within the system, and have both been coopted into government and have participated as opposition parties. Over time, they have incorporated significant ideological and political changes. Indeed, as Pakistan and Malaysia demonstrate, in a more open atmosphere without a common enemy and repression to unite them, many Islamic organizations, like other political parties, fall victim to the personality and ideological factors and differences that weaken and divide rather than strengthen and unite. This phenomenon can be seen in Sudan, where Sadiq al-Mahdi's Ummah party and Hasan al-Turabi's National Islamic Front have often been in contention, and in the competition between PAS and ABIM in Malaysia, the rivalry between Pakistan's Jamaat-i Islami and other Islamic parties, and differences among religious leaders in Iran.

In contrast, while massive repression in Syria in the early 1980s and in Tunisia in the early 1990s, and in Iraq throughout the decades, have in the short term silenced and driven underground domestic Islamist opposition, Algeria and Egypt demonstrate the extent to which measures which restrict political parties and professional associations reinforce the image of an intrusive, authoritarian government interested only in power and severely weaken civil society. They contribute to a growing polarization in society in which citizens are for all practical purposes forced to choose sides between the government and a "radical fundamentalist threat," as the middle ground erodes in a world in which one is either "for or against." A militant government no longer distinguishes between radical surgery to counter violent extremists and accommodation of nonviolent opposition but instead perceives a broad-based Islamic threat to society. This results in an Islamic movement in which moderates are increasingly driven to the margins, convinced by their experience that participation in the system is no longer a viable option.

Too often the lessons of history have been forgotten. Authoritarian governments in the Muslim world regard effective opposition by populist movements, whether in the name of nationalism, socialism, liberal democracy, or Islam, as a threat. They challenge the power and privilege as well as way of life of rulers and entrenched elites. This reality can be seen in recent years not only in Egypt but also, and more graphically, in Tunisia and Algeria, where the relatively successful electoral showing of Islamic movements resulted in government repression, military courts and show trials, and repression and torture which have been documented and criticized in reports by major international human-rights organizations and the U.S. Department of State. At the same time, Islamic governments in Iran and Sudan have engaged in their own brand of authoritarianism and repression, and organizations such as Egypt's Gamaa and Jihad and Algeria's Armed Islamic Group commit brutal acts of terrorism and attempt to destroy any who disagree with their particular interpretations of Islam. The successes and failures of the Islamist governments and organizations should be viewed within the broader context of the contemporary world and standards of judgment should be consistently applied. Suppression of opposition, torture and terror should be condemned with equal vigor, whether the perpetrators are self-proclaimed Islamists or secularists. In the same way, active efforts to create institutions for effective popular participation in politics should be encouraged, even if those efforts involve perspectives and approaches that are not identical to those used in democracies in Western Europe or North America.

At the start of the twenty-first century, governments that are genuinely interested in the political and social development of their countries and not simply in retaining power at any cost will be challenged to demonstrate a commitment to political liberalization and human rights by fostering the development of those institutions and values that support democratization and strengthen civil society. They must implement policies that discriminate between organizations, secular or Islamic, that directly threaten the freedom and stability of society and those that are willing to participate in a process of gradual change from within the system. Even actually functioning democracies are at present engaged in major efforts to reshape institutions of power and to "re-invent government."

Islamic movements, in light of examples from Iran, Sudan, and Zia ul-Haq's Pakistan, as well as the activities of radical extremist groups, will be challenged to prove by their actions as well as their promises that if elected they will honor the very rights of opposition groups and minorities that they now demand for themselves. Islamic activists today are challenged to be as vociferous in their denunciation of extremism and terrorism done in the name of Islam as they are of government repression and Western imperialism. Like governments, Islamist movements must demonstrate an awareness that authoritarianism, whether religious or secular, in the name of God or the state, is counterproductive and dangerous.

The United States and other Western governments that advocate the promotion of self-determination and democracy should demonstrate by their policies that they respect the right of any and all, religious as well as secular, movements and parties to participate within the political process. Some western officials have taken a sober stance. Edward Djerejian, the former American assistant secretary of state, on several occasions pointed out that the United States did not regard Islam or Islamic movements as the enemy and that it recognized the right of any movement to participate within the electoral process provided that it, like any other movement, did not use democratic elections to seize power, that is, that it come to power motivated by a belief in "one man, one vote, one time."[1] However, the test came in Algeria when FIS electoral victories raised the specter not of an Islamic movement emerging as the chief political opposition, as had occurred in Egypt, Tunisia, or Jordan, but of a movement actually coming to power through the ballot box.

The intervention of the Algerian military tested the democratic commitment of Muslim and Western governments alike. The policy failures evident in American and European responses toward the subversion of the electoral process and indiscriminate repression of the FIS in Algeria and of the Renaissance party in Tunisia, like their impotence in the face of the genocide of Muslims in Bosnia or seeming indifference to the plight of Muslims in Chechnya and Kashmir, discredit, in the eyes of Islamists and many other Muslims, the democratic commitment of the West. They reinforce the perception and charge that the U.S. and European governments are guilty of employing a "double standard," a democratic one for the West and selected allies and another for the Middle East and Islamic movements. Respect and support of the democratic process and human rights must be seen as truly universal and consistent.

The thwarting of a participatory political process by governments encourages the radicalization of more moderate Islamists. Many of those who experience regime violence (harassment, imprisonment, or torture, or see their colleagues languish and die in prison) conclude that seeking "democracy" is a dead end. They will be driven to withdraw from participation in the political process and become convinced that force or violence is the only recourse against repressive regimes.

Islamically oriented political actors and groups should be evaluated by the same criteria as any other potential leaders or opposition party. While some are rejectionists, most Islamically oriented leaders or governments that might come to power through the electoral process will be critical and selective in their relations with the United States. However, like their secular counterparts, on most issues, many would operate on the basis of national interests and demonstrate a flexibility that reflects acceptance of the realities of a globally, politically and economically, interdependent world. Iranian efforts to be more actively involved in trade with the West illustrate this possibility. American policy should be carried on in the context in which ideological differences are recognized and accepted or at least tolerated where U.S. interests are not directly threatened.

Muslim governments will continue to be challenged to become governments of inclusion, whose legitimacy is built upon representation and political participation. The challenge is one of incorporation and power-sharing, of creating conditions that will allow strong alternative parties and opposition groups to develop and have access to power. The membership of Islamic organizations generally constitutes a numerical minority, *not* a majority of the population. The electoral strength of the Egyptian Muslim Brotherhood, Tunisia's Renaissance Party, Algeria's FIS, or Jordan's Muslim Brotherhood has come not only from a hard core of dedicated followers but also from the fact that they were the most credible and effective alternative "game in town." Thus, their support includes members, sympathizers or supporters, and other Muslims who simply wish to vote for an Islamic agenda, as well as those who wish to cast a vote against an ineffective or discredited government and try any alternative.

Finally, the realities of a more open marketplace, of having to compete for votes or of coming to power and having to rule amid diverse interests, force Islamic groups, as they do more secular political parties, to adapt or broaden their ideology and programs in response to domestic realities and diverse constituencies and interests. Success in these efforts, for all major political actors, increasingly involves an affirmation of the long-term religio-cultural identities of their peoples and societies. Even the most secularized political systems, as in Turkey, have seen the gradual Islamization of political discourse. The two great developments of the late twentieth century—growing demand for popular political participation and the Islamic resurgence—have come together, creating new realities that affect the relationship between Islam and democracy. The cases of Egypt, Iran, Algeria, Sudan, Pakistan, and Malaysia reveal this process of ideological and political development or transformation. They demonstrate that the historic situation of the present cannot be understood in monolithic terms but must be seen as a complex, multifaceted reality in which both complementarities and contradictions can be seen.

Notes

Introduction

1. See, for example, the presentation in a widely used textbook, Arthur Goldschmidt, Jr., *A Concise History of the Middle East*, 3rd ed. (Boulder, Co.: Westview Press, 1988), p. 49, and the presentation in widely read books by Muslims, Suzanne Haneef, *What Everyone Should Know about Islam and Muslims* (Chicago: Kazi Publications, 1982), p. 83; and Syed Qutb, *Milestones*, trans. S. Badrul Hasan (Karachi: International Islamic Publishers, 1981), pp. 46–48.

2. See, for example, Ira M. Lapidus, "The Separation of State and Religion in the Development of Early Islamic Society," *International Journal of Middle East Studies* 6, no.4 (Oct. 1975): 363–385.

3. Important studies of these two movements are Richard P. Mitchell, *The Society of the Muslim Brothers* (New York: Oxford University Press, 1969; reprinted 1993), and Seyyed Vali Reza Nasr, *The Vanguard of the Islamic Revolution: The Jama'at-i Islami of Pakistan* (Berkeley, Calif.: University of California Press, 1994).

4. This process is more fully discussed in James P. Piscatori, *Islam in a World of Nation-States* (Cambridge: Cambridge University Press, 1986), and John Obert Voll, *Islam: Continuity and Change in the Modern World* (Syracuse, N.Y.: Syracuse University Press, 1994), especially chapter 4.

5. The closest approximation would be the articles on the various movements which appear in John L. Esposito, ed., *The Oxford Encyclopedia of the Modern Islamic World* (New York: Oxford University Press, 1995).

CHAPTER ONE. *Islam and Democracy*

1. *New York Times*, 29 March 1993.

2. Samuel Huntington, *The Third Wave: Democratization in the Late Twentieth Century* (Norman, Ok.: University of Oklahoma Press, 1991), p. xiii.

3. Zbigniew Brzezinski, *Between Two Ages: America's Role in the Technotronic Era* (New York: Viking Press, 1970), p. 55.

4. W. B. Gallie, *Philosophy and the Historical Understanding* (London: Chatto and Windus, 1964), p. 158.

5. Ibid, pp. 187–188.

6. For a discussion of this perception of the "end of the melting pot" from the context of the 1990s, written by one of the scholars involved in the analyses of the 1960s, see Daniel Patrick Moynihan, *Pandaemonium: Ethnicity in International Politics* (New York: Oxford University Press, 1993), pp.22–23.

7. Roland Robertson and JoAnn Chirico, "Humanity, Globalization, and Worldwide Religious Resurgence: A Theoretical Exploration," *Sociological Analysis* 46, no. 3 (1985): 222.

8. Ibid, 233.

9. Ibid, 240.

10. H. A. R. Gibb, *Modern Trends in Islam* (Chicago: University of Chicago Press, 1947), p. 119.

11. Giovanni Sartori, "Democracy," in David L. Sills, ed., *International Encyclopedia of the Social Sciences* (New York: Macmillan, 1968), 4:118.

12. Ibid, 4:118, 120.

13. See, for example, Enrique Krauze, "England, the United States, and the Export of Democracy," in Brad Roberts, ed., *The New Democracies: Global Change and U.S. Policy* (Cambridge, Mass.: M.I.T. Press, 1990).

14. Barry Munslow, "Why Has the Westminster Model Failed in Africa?" *Parliamentary Affairs* 36, no.2 (1983):

15. J. L. Talmon, *The Origins of Totalitarian Democracy* (New York: Frederick A. Praeger, 1960), pp. 201–221.

16. David Held, *Models of Democracy* (Stanford, Calif.: Stanford University Press, 1987), pp. 113, 130.

17. Secretary [of State, James] Baker, "Democracy's Season," *U.S. Department of State Dispatch* 2, no. 37 (16 September 1991): 679–680. This approach and the five principles were then frequently repeated by Secretary Baker and other U.S. officials as they traveled throughout the former Soviet Union and on other occasions. See, for example, testimony given before the Subcommittee on Europe and the Middle East of the House Foreign Affairs Committee and reprinted in Robert B. Zoellick, "Relations of the United States with the Soviet Union and the Republics," *U.S. Department of State Dispatch* 2, no. 40, (7 October 1991): 740–748.

18. Herman J. Cohen, "Democratization in Africa," *U.S. Department of State Dispatch* 2, no. 43 (28 October 1991): 796.

19. Herman J. Cohen, "Africa and Democracy," *U.S. Department of State Dispatch* 2, no. 48 (2 December 1993): 872.

20. Vice-president [J. Danforth] Quayle, "African Democracy and the Rule of Law," *U.S. Department of State Dispatch* 2, No.38 (23 September 1991): 698.

21. For an analysis of these two types in the context of American society, see Jane J. Mansbridge, *Beyond Adversary Democracy*, rev. ed. (Chicago: University of Chicago Press, 1983).

22. Warren Christopher, "U.S. Foreign Relations: International Peace," *Vital Speeches of the Day* 59:13 (15 April 1993): 387.

23. Ibid, 389.

24. *Washington Post*, 5 May 1993.

25. Mamoun Fandy, "Clinton: More Fulbright than Rhodes?" *Christian Science Monitor*, 14 January 1993.

26. Mansbridge, *Beyond Adversary Democracy*, p. 32.

27. John Burnham, *Is Democracy Possible? The Alternative to Electoral Politics* (Berkeley, Calif.: University of California Press, 1985), p. 9.

28. Michael Levin, *The Spectre of Democracy: The Rise of Modern Democracy as Seen by Its Critics* (New York: New York University Press, 1992), p. 4.

29. Paul E. Corcoran, "The Limits of Democratic Theory," in *Democratic Theory and Practice,* ed. Graeme Duncan (Cambridge: Cambridge University Press, 1983), pp. 13, 15.

30. Corcoran, "Limits of Democratic Theory," p. 14.

31. Steven Muhlberger and Phil Paine, "Democracy's Place in World History," *Journal of World History* 4:1 (Spring 1993): 26, 28.

32. Hugh Chisholm, "Parliament," *Encyclopaedia Britiannica, 11th* ed. (1911), vol. 28, p. 837.

33. Sayyid Abul A'la Maududi, *Islamic Way of Life,* trans. Khurshid Ahmad (Delhi: Markazi Maktaba Islami, 1967), p. 40.

34. Ismail Raji al Faruqi, *Tawhid: Its Implications for Thought and Life* (Herndon, Va.: International Institute of Islamic Thought, 1402/1982), pp. 5, 10–11. While al-Faruqi was a relatively "fundamentalist" Sunni Muslim, the importance of *tawhid* in the full spectrum of Islamic faith can be seen by looking at the Sunni modernist (and nonfundamentalist) Fazlur Rahman, *Major Themes of the Qur'an* (Minneapolis: Bibliotheca Islamica, 1980), who on page 83 says that this doctrine "is central to the Qur'an—without which, indeed, Islam is unthinkable." In addition, the centrality of *tawhid* is emphasized by major Shi'i thinkers. See, for example, *Islam and Revolution: Writings and Declarations of Imam Khomeini,* trans. Hamid Algar (Berkeley, Calif: Mizan Press, 1981), pp. 300–301.

35. Abu'l A'la Mawdudi, "Political Theory of Islam," in Khurshid Ahmad, ed., *Islam: Its Meaning and Message,* (London: Islamic Council of Europe, 1976), pp.159–160.

36. Ibid, pp. 160–161.

37. Ibid, p. 161.

38. Ayatullah Baqir al-Sadr, *Introduction to Islamic Political System,* trans. M. A. Ansari (Accra: Islamic Seminary/World Shia Muslim Organization, 1982), pp. 78–79.

39. *Imam Khomeini's Last Will and Testament* (English trans. distributed by Interests Section of the Islamic Republic of Iran in the Embassy of Algeria, Washington, D.C.), pp. 36–37.

40. Ibid, p. 82.

41. Ibid, p.79.

42. See, for example, the discussion in Bernard Lewis, *The Political Language of Islam* (Chicago: University of Chicago Press, 1988), pp. 53–55.

43. Ali Shari'ati, *On the Sociology of Islam,* trans. Hamid Algar (Berkeley, Calif.: Mizan Press, 1979), p.87.

44. Ayatullah Sayyid Mahmud Taleghani, *Society and Economics in Islam,* trans. R. Campbell (Berkeley, Calif.: Mizan Press, 1982), p. 129.

45. E. I. J. Rosenthal, *Political Thought in Medieval Islam* (Cambridge: Cambridge University Press, 1962), p. 3.

46. A good discussion of this process of change is Bernard Lewis, *The Emergence of Modern Turkey* (London: Oxford University Press, 1961), chapters 8 and 11.

47. See, for example, the discussions in Jacob M. Landau, *The Politics of Pan-Islam: Ideology and Organization* (Oxford: Clarendon Press, 1990), chapter 4; Martin Kramer, *Islam Assembled: The Advent of the Muslim Congresses* (New York: Columbia University Press, 1986), chapter 9.

48. Maududi, *The Islamic Way of Life,* p. 42.

49. Ibid, pp. 43–44.

50. *Universal Islamic Declaration* (London: Islamic Council of Europe, 1400/1980), p. 6.

51. Gulzar Haider, "Khilafah," in Ziauddin Sardar and Merryl Wyn Davies, eds., *Faces of Islam: Conversations on Contemporary Issues* (Kuala Lumpur: Berita Publishing, 1989), p. 86.

52. Ibrahim M. Abu-Rabi', ed., *Islamic Resurgence: Challenges, Directions and Future Perspectives—A Round Table with Khurshid Ahmad* (Tampa, Fl.: World and Islam Studies Enterprise, 1994), p. 62.

53. John L. Esposito, *Islam and Politics*, 3rd ed. (Syracuse, N.Y.: Syracuse University Press, 1991), p. 149.

54. Muhammad Hamidullah, *Introduction to Islam* (Gary, In.: International Islamic Federation of Student Organizations, 1970), pp. 116–117.

55. Fazlur Rahman, "The Principle of Shura and the Role of the Ummah in Islam," in Mumtaz Ahmad, ed., *State, Politics, and Islam* (Indianapolis, In.: American Trust Publications, 1406/1986), pp. 90–91.

56. Ibid, p.95.

57. Ayatullah Baqir al-Sadr, *Islamic Political System*, pp. 81–82.

58. John L. Esposito, *Islam: The Straight Path*, expanded ed. (New York: Oxford University Press, 1991), pp. 45, 83.

59. Hamidullah, *Introduction to Islam*, p. 130.

60. Louay M. Safi, "The Islamic State: A Conceptual Framework," *The American Journal of Islamic Social Sciences* 8, no. 2 (September 1991): 233.

61. Khurshid Ahmad, "Islam: Basic Principles and Characteristics," in Khurshid Ahmad, ed., *Islam: Its Meaning and Message* (London: Islamic Council of Europe, 1976), p. 43.

62. Altaf Gauhar, "Islam and Secularism," in Altaf Gauhar, ed., *The Challenge of Islam*, (London: Islamic Council of Europe, 1978), p. 307.

63. Allama Muhammad Iqbal, *The Reconstruction of Religious Thought in Islam* (Lahore: Sh. Muhammad Ashraf, 1968, reprint), pp. 173–174.

64. Ibid, p.157.

65. Taha J. al Alwani, "Taqlid and Ijtihad," *The American Journal of Islamic Social Sciences* 8, no.1 (March 1991): 141.

66. Ibid, 142.

67. Fazlur Rahman, "Shurah and the Role of the Ummah," p. 94.

68. A good discussion of these and other such writings can be found in Hamid Enayat, *Modern Islamic Political Thought* (Austin, Tex.: University of Texas Press, 1982), pp. 130–134.

69. Enayat, *Modern Islamic Political Thought*, p. 135.

70. Khurshid Ahmad, as quoted in John L. Esposito and John O. Voll, "Khurshid Ahmad: Muslim Activist-Economist," *The Muslim World* 80, no.1 (January 1990): 31.

71. A book that is widely quoted by leaders in the administration of President Clinton is David Osborne and Ted Gaebler, *Reinventing Government: How the Entrepreneurial Spirit Is Transforming the Public Sector* (Reading, Mass.: Addison-Wesley, 1992).

72. Osborne and Gaebler, for example, place great emphasis on decentralized participation and one of their frequently cited principles is "Decentralized government: From hierarchy to Participation and Teamwork." (*Reinventing Government*, chapter 9.)

73. Samuel P. Huntington, "The Coming Clash of Civilizations Or, the West against the Rest," *New York Times*, 6 June 1993.

CHAPTER TWO. *State and Opposition in Islamic History*

1. Rober A. Dahl, "Introduction," in Robert A. Dahl, ed., *Regimes and Oppositions* (New Haven: Yale University Press, 1973), p. 1.

2. Rodney Barker, "Introduction," in *Studies in Opposition*, ed. Rodney Barker (London: Macmillan, 1971), p. 2.

3. Ibid., pp. 15–20.

4. Barbara N. McLennan, "Approaches to the Concept of Political Opposition: An Historical Overview," in Barbara N. McLennan, ed., *Political Opposition and Dissent* (New York: Dunellen Publishing, 1973), pp. 4–5.

5. Dankwart A. Rustow, "The Military in Middle Eastern Society and Politics," in Syndey Nettleton Fisher, ed., *The Military in the Middle East* (Columbus, Oh.: Ohio State University Press, 1963), p. 4.

6. Quoted in Barker, "Introduction," p. 8.

7. Giovanni Sartori, "Opposition and Control: Problems and Prospects," in Rodney Barker, ed., *Studies in Opposition* (London: Macmillan, 1971), p. 33.

8. David Held, *Models of Democracy* (Stanford, Calif.: Stanford University Press, 1987), pp. 38–39.

9. J. L. Talmon, *The Origins of Totalitarian Democracy* (New York: Frederick A. Praeger, 1960), p. 1.

10. Chantal Mouffe, "Democratic Politics Today," in Chantal Mouffe, ed., *Dimensions of Radical Democracy: Pluralism, Citizenship, Community* (London: Verso, 1992), p. 12.

11. Sheldon Wolin, "What Revolutionary Action Means Today," in Chantal Mouffe, ed., *Dimensions of Radical Democracy*, p. 249.

12. Morton H. Halperin, "Guaranteeing Democracy," *Foreign Policy* 91 (Summer 1993): 107.

13. Ibid.

14. David Osborne and Ted Gaebler, *Reinventing Government* (New York: Penguin, 1992), p. xv. This whole book explains this position.

15. Chantal Mouffe, "Democratic Politics Today," p. 13.

16. Francis Fukuyama, "Entering Post-History," *New Perspectives Quarterly* 6, no. 3 (Fall 1989): 50. This article is a summary of Fukuyama's widely read article "The End of History?" *The National Interest*, no. 16 (Summer 1989): 3–18. He later expanded and, to some extent, moderated his positions in *The End of History and the Last Man* (New York: The Free Press, 1992).

17. Fukuyama, "Entering Post-History," pp. 51–52.

18. A thorough discussion of the Constitution of Medina can be found in W. Montgomery Watt, *Muhammad at Medina* (Oxford: Clarendon Press, 1956), chapter 7.

19. For example, Hasan al-Turabi regularly cites this constitution of Medina, as he did in a speech to the American Muslim Council in Washington, D. C., in April 1992.

20. Fouad Al-Farsy, *Modernity and Tradition: The Saudi Equation* (London: Kegan Paul International, 1990), p. 39. This book was also published in 1990 by the Ministry of Information, Kingdom of Saudi Arabia.

21. Abdullahi Ahmed An-Na'im, *Toward an Islamic Reformation: Civil Liberties, Human Rights, and International Law* (Syracuse, N.Y.: Syracuse University Press, 1990), p. 100.

22. From the text of a letter addressed to King Fahd by forty-three leading Saudi people, in Foreign Broadcast Information Service reports, FBIS-NES-91-082 (29 April 1991).

23. Analysis of the Quranic use of the term can be found in L. Gardet, "Fitna," *Encyclopaedia of Islam*, rev. ed., 2:930–931; and Fazlur Rahman, *Major Themes of the Qur'an* (Minneapolis: Bibliotheca Islamic, 1980), pp. 158–159.

24. Gardet, "Fitna," p. 931.

25. E. I. J. Rosenthal, *Political Thought in Medieval Islam* (Cambridge: Cambridge University Press, 1962), p. 44.

26. Muddathir Abdal-Rahim, "The Roots of Revolution in the Qur'an," *Dirasat Ifriqiya* 3 (Rajab 1407/ April 1987): 14.

27. Abdal-Rahim, 14.

28. Abdal-Rahim, 14.

29. Mohammad H. Kamali, "Freedom of Expression in Islam: An Analysis of *Fitnah*," *The American Journal of Islamic Social Sciences* 10, no. 2 (Summer 1993): 178.

30. Kamali, 181.

31. Kamali, 197–198.

32. Joseph Schacht, "The Schools of Law and Later Developments of Jurisprudence," in Majid Khadduri and Herbert J. Liebesny, eds., *Law in the Middle East* (Washington: Middle East Institute, 1955), p. 70.

33. Fazlur Rahman, *Islam*, 2nd ed. (Chicago: University of Chicago Press, 1979), p. 81.

34. Schacht, "The Schools of Law," p. 70. See also Joseph Schacht, *The Origins of Muhammadan Jurisprudence* (Oxford: Clarendon Press, 1950), pp. 95–97.

35. See, for example, the discussion in G. N. Jalbani, *Teachings of Shah Waliyullah of Delhi* (Lahore: Sh. Muhammad Ashraf, 1967), chapter 3. A translation of the full text of Wali Allah's analysis will be available when the annotated translation by Marcia Hermansen of *al-Insaf fi Bayan Sabab al-Ikhtilaf* is published. The work by Muhammad Haya, *al-iqaf ala sabab al-ikhtilaf*, is now less well-known and exists in manuscript in Dar al-Kutub in Cairo (172 Mujami' Taymur).

36. Abul A'la Mawdudi, *Towards Understanding Islam*, 6th ed. (Kuwait: International Islamic Federation of Student Organizations, 1402/ 1982), p. 146.

37. Yusuf al Qaradawi, *Islamic Awakening between Rejection and Extremism*, Issues of Islamic Thought Series No. 2 (Herndon, Va.: International Institute of Islamic Thought, 1401/1981), pp. 86–87.

38. Quoted in Qaradawi, p.86.

39. Saeed Hawwa, *The Muslim Brotherhood: Objective, Stages, Method*, trans. Abdul Karim Shaikh (Delhi: Hindustan Publications, 1403/1983), p. 197.

40. Qaradawi, *Islamic Awakening*, p. 82.

41. Qaradawi, *Islamic Awakening*, p. 83.

42. Arthur L. Lowrie, ed., *Islam, Democracy, the State and the West: A Round Table with Dr. Hasan Turabi*, (Tampa, Fl.: World and Islam Studies Enterprise, 1993), pp. 42–43.

43. Lowrie, ed., *Islam, Democracy*, p. 42.

44. Ibid., p. 44.

45. Article 12, Constitution of the Islamic Republic of Iran, of 24 October 1979, as amended 28 July 1989, in Albert P. Blaustein and Gisbert H. Flanz, eds., *Constitutions of the Countries of the World* (Release 92–8; Dobbs Ferry, New York: Oceana Publications, 1992), pp. 21–22. The schools listed are the four Sunni law schools plus the school of the Zaydi Shii tradition.

46. H. A. R. Gibb, "Some Considerations on the Sunni Theory of the Caliphate," in Stanford J. Shaw and William R. Polk, eds., *Studies on the Civilization of Islam* (Boston: Beacon Press, 1962), p. 148.

47. Claude Cahen, "Dhimma," *The Encyclopaedia of Islam*, rev. ed., 2:227.

48. Maurice Duverger, *Political Parties*, trans. Barbara and Robert North (New York: John Wiley & Sons, 1954), p. 413.

49. Ibid.

50. Ira M. Lapidus, "The Separation of State and Religion in the Development of Early Islamic Society," *International Journal of Middle East Studies* 6:4 (October 1975): 384–385.

51. H. A. R. Gibb, "Constitutional Organization," in Majid Khadduri and Herbert J. Liebesny, eds., *Law in the Middle East* (Washington, D. C.: Middle East Institute, 1955), p. 24.

52. See, for example, Emmanuel Sivan, *Radical Islam: Medieval Theology and Modern Politics* (New Haven: Yale University Press, 1985), pp. 95–101.

53. See, for example, the helpful discussion of the Ottoman legal system in Stanford J. Shaw, *History of the Ottoman Empire and Modern Turkey*, vol. 1 (Cambridge: Cambridge University Press, 1976), pp.134–138.

54. The best available English translation of this is in *Islam and Revolution, Writings and Declarations of Imam Khomeini*, trans. Hamid Algar (Berkeley, Calif.: Mizan Press, 1981). The translation done by the Joint Publications Research Service of the U.S. government is less reliable. It is available as Ayatollah Ruhollah Khomeini, *Islamic Government* (New York: Manor Books, 1979).

55. *Islam and Revolution*, p. 60.

56. *Islam and Revolution*, p.63.

57. Article 5, Constitution of the Islamic Republic of Iran, in Blaustein and Flanz, p. 19.

58. See, for example, the coverage in the *New York Times*, 17 December 1992.

59. Unnamed official, quoted in "Choice or Confrontation," *Sudan Focus* 1:4 (June 1994): 2.

60. See, for example, Jane Perlez, "A Fundamentalist Finds a Fulcrum in Sudan," *New York Times*, 29 January 1992, and "Islam's Star," *The Economist*, 1 February 1992.

61. "Interview," *Sudan Focus* 1:6 (15 August 1994): 11.

62. Hassan al-Turabi, "The Islamic Awakening's New Wave," *New Perspectives Quarterly* 10:3 (Summer 1993): 43.

63. Abdallah al-Salih Al-Uthaymin, *al-Shaykh Muhammad ibn Abd al-Wahhab: Hayatuhu wa Fikruhu* (Riyadh: Dar al-Ulum, n.d.), p. 62.

CHAPTER THREE. *Iran*

1. Richard W. Cottam, "Inside Revolutionary Iran," *The Middle East Journal* 43:2 (Spring 1989), p. 168.

2. See, for example, Juan R. I. Cole and Nikki R. Keddie, eds., *Shiism and Social Protest* (New Haven: Yale University Press, 1986), and Martin Kramer, ed., *Shiism, Resistance, and Revolution* (Boulder, Colo.: Westview 1987).

3. This chapter draws on the previous study, "The Iranian Revolution: A Ten Year Perspective," in John L. Esposito, *The Iranian Revolution: Its Global Impact* (Miami: Florida International University Press, 1990), chapter 1.

4. Said Amir Arjomand, *The Turban for the Crown: The Islamic Revolution in Iran* (New York: Oxford University Press, 1987), p. 79.

5. Ibid., p. 78.

6. Shahrough Akhavi, "Iran: Implementation of an Islamic State," in John L. Esposito, *Islam in Asia: Religion, Politics, and Society* (New York: Oxford University Press, 1987), p. 29.

7. H. E. Chehabi, *Iranian Politics and Religious Modernism: The Liberation Movement of Iran under the Shah and Khomeini* (Ithaca, New York: Cornell University Press, 1990), p. 37.

8. For an analysis of the political relationship of the ulama to the state, see Shahrough Akhavi, *Religion and Politics in Contemporary Iran: Clergy-State Relations in the Pahlavi Period* (Albany, N.Y.: State University of New York Press, 1980).

9. James A. Bill, *The Eagle and the Lion: The Tragedy of American-Iranian Relations* (New Haven: Yale University Press, 1988), pp. 186–192.

10. Ruhollah Khomeini, *Islam and Revolution*, trans. Hamid Algar (Berkeley, Calif.: Mizan Press, 1981), pp. 182, 183, 185.

11. Ibid., pp. 249–250.

12. Hamid Algar, "The Oppositional Role of the Ulama in Twentieth Century Islam," in Nikkie R. Keddie, ed., *Scholars, Saints, and Sufis* (Berkeley, Calif.: University of California Press, 1972), pp. 250, 255.

13. Shireen T. Hunter, *Iran After Khomeini* (Washington, D. C.: CSIS, 1992), p. 7.

14. Chehabi, *Iranian Politics*, p. 38.

15. Eric Hoogland, "Iranian Populism and Political Change in the Gulf," *Middle East Report* no. 174, vol. 22, no. 1 (January/February 1992): 21.

16. Ervand Abrahamian, *Iran between Two Revolutions* (Princeton: Princeton University Press, 1982), p. 259.

17. Chehabi, *Iranian Politics*, 39.

18. Jalal-Al-e-Ahmad, *Gharbzadegi* [Weststruckness], trans. John Green and Ahmad Alizadeh (Lexington, Ky.:Mazda Press, 1982), pp. 11, 59.

19. Ali Shariati, *On the Sociology of Islam* (Berkeley, Calif.: Mizan Press, 1979), p. 17.

20. Ervand Abrahamian, "Ali Shariati: Ideologue of the Iranian Revolution," MERIP Reports 102 (Jan. 1982): 25.

21. R. K. Ramazani, "Iran's Foreign Policy: Contending Orientations" *The Middle East Journal* 43:2 (Spring 1989): 203.

22. Shaul Bakhash, *The Reign of the Ayatollahs* (New York: Basic Books, 1984), p. 11.

23. Hunter, *Iran After Khomeini*, p. 1.

24. Richard Cottam, *Nationalism in Iran* (Pittsburgh: University of Pittsburgh Press, 1964), chapters 2–3.

25. As quoted in Hamid Enayat, "Iran: Khumayni's Concept of the 'Guardianship of the Jurisconsult,'" in James P. Piscatori, ed., *Islam in the Political Process*, (Cambridge: Cambridge University Press, 1983), p. 170.

26. Ruhollah Khomeini, *Islam and Revolution*, p. 170.

27. Ibid., p. 60.

28. Bakhash, *The Reign of the Ayatollahs*, p. 86.

29. "Islamic Republic of Iran," in Albert P. Blaustein and Gisbert H. Flanz, eds., *Constitutions of the Countries of the World* (Release 92–8; Dobbs Ferry, N.Y.: Oceania Publications, 1992), p. 8.

30. *New York Times*, 17 December 1992.

31. Eric Hoogland, "Iranian Populism and Political Change in the Gulf," 20.

32. Akhavi, "Iran: Implementation of an Islamic State," p. 38.

33. Arjomand, *The Turban for the Crown*, p. 164.

34. Ibid.

35. Shahrough Akhavi, "State Formation and Consolidation in Twentieth Century Iran,"

in Myron Weiner and Ali Banuaziz, eds., *The State, Religion and Ethnic Politics*, (Syracuse, N.Y.: Syracuse University Press, 1986), p. 212.

36. Dilip Hiro, *Iran Under the Ayatollahs* (London: Routledge & Kegan Paul, 1985), p. 256.

37. Azar Tabari, "The Enigma of the Veiled Iranian Woman," *MERIP Reports* (no. 103), 12:2 (February 1982): 22–27.

38. The situation described here draws on material from the *Christian Science Monitor*, 28 March 1995, and the *New York Times*, 21 December 1994.

39. Geraldine Brooks, *Nine Parts of Desire: The Hidden World of Islamic Women* (New York: Anchor Books, Doubleday, 1995), p. 233.

40. Barry Rubin, *Iran's Future: Crises, Contingencies, and Continuities* (Washington, D.C.: The Johns Hopkins Foreign Policy Institute, 1987), p. 10.

41. Hiro, *Iran under the Ayatollahs*, p. 242–243.

42. Akhavi, "Iran: Implementation of an Islamic State," p. 37.

43. As quoted in Robin Wright, *In the Name of God* (New York: Simon & Schuster, 1989), p. 196.

44. *Amnesty International 1994* (London: Amnesty International Publications, 1994), p. 163.

45. Ibid.

46. Ali Banuaziz, "Iran's Revolutionary Impasse, Political Factionalism, and Societal Resistance," *Middle East Report* no. 191, vol. 24, no. 6 (Nov.–Dec. 1994): 7.

47. Homa Hoodfar, "Devices and Desires, Population Policy and Gender Roles in the Islamic republic," *Middle East Report* (no. 190), vol. 24, no. 5 (Sept.–Oct. 1994): 17.

48. "Reporter's Notebook: Jewish Lifestyle Under Ayatollahs Isn't So Bad Now," *The Wall Street Journal*, 22 April 1992, p14.

49. Judith Miller, "Islamic Radicals Lose Their Tight Grip in Iran," *New York Times*, 8 April 1991,

50. *Middle East Matters*, vol. III, no. 1, 1.

51. "Bishop's Killing Puts Focus on Persecution in Iran," *New York Times*, 6 February 1994, 20.

52. Eric Hooglund, "Iran 1980–85: Political and Economic Trends," in Nikki R. Keddi and Eric Hooglund, eds., *The Iranian Revolution and the Islamic Republic* (Syracuse, N.Y.: Syracuse University Press, 1986), pp. 24–25.

53. Muriel Atkin, "The Islamic Republic and the Soviet Union," *The Iranian Revolution and the Islamic Republic*, p. 201.

54. "Bishop's Killing," 20, and "Death Sentences for the Bahai," *New York Times*, 31 December 1993, A 28.

55. "Iran's Nuremburg Trials," *New York Times*, 27 February 1993, A 18.

56. "Iran: Walk in Fear," *The Economist*, (23 July 1994): 40.

57. Miller, *New York Times*, 8 April 1991.

58. Fouad Ajami, "Iran: The Impossible Revolution," *Foreign Affairs*, 67, no. 2 (Winter 1988/89): 136.

59. Ibid., 144.

60. Shireen T. Hunter, "Post-Khomeini Iran," *Foreign Affairs* 68, no. 5 (Winter 1989/90): 138.

61. "Rafsanjani Gives Revolution Day Speech," Foreign Broadcast Information Service FBIS-NES-95-030 (February 14, 1995).

62. "Militant Clerics Issue Revolution Anniversary Statement," FBIS-NES-95-030 (February 14, 1995).

63. "Mohtashami on Perpetuation of Revolution Objectives," and "Berates Officials for Deviating," FBIS-NES-95-029 (February 13, 1995.)

64. Statement by Daryush Foruhar of the Party of the People of Iran, in "Opposition Group Calls for Democracy on Anniversary," FBIS-NES-95-029 (February 13, 1995).

65. Farzin Sarabi, "The Post-Khomeini Era in Iran: The Elections of the Fourth Islamic Majlis," *The Middle East Journal* 48, no. 1 (Winter 1994): 89.

66. Hoogland, "Iranian Populism and Political Change in the Gulf": 21.

CHAPTER FOUR. *Sudan*

1. Karol Jozef Krotki, *First Population Census of Sudan 1955/56: 21 Facts about the Sudanese* (Khartoum: Ministry for Social Affairs, 1958), p. 26.

2. Na'um Shuqayr, *Tarikh al-sudan al-hadith* (Cairo: n.p., 1903): 3: 40–48.

3. Richard Hill, *Egypt in the Sudan, 1820–1881* (London: Oxford University Press, 1959), p. 108.

4. Albert Hourani, "Ottoman Reform and the Politics of Notables," in *Beginnings of Modernization in the Middle East: The Nineteenth Century*, ed. William R. Polk and Richard L. Chambers (Chicago: University of Chicago Press, 1968), p. 45.

5. Ibid, p. 46.

6. R. C. Mayal, "Recent Constitutional Developments in the Sudan," *International Affairs* 28, no. 3 (July 1952): 318–319.

7. See, for example, Mayal, "Recent Constitutional Developments," p. 320.

8. Peter K. Bechtold, *Politics in the Sudan* (New York: Praeger, 1976), pp. 177–178, 180.

9. al-Sadiq al-Mahdi, ed., *Jihad fi sabil al-istiqlal* (Khartoum: al-Matba'ah al-hukumah, n.d.), p. 128.

10. See, for example, al-Sadiq al-Mahdi, ed., *Jihad fi sabil al-dimuqratiyyah* (Khartoum: al-Matba'ah al-hukumah, n.d.).

11. Bechtold, *Politics in the Sudan*, pp. 229–239.

12. Peter Woodward, *Sudan, 1898–1989: The Unstable State* (Boulder, Co.: Lynne Rienner, 1990), p. 104.

13. The positions of the SPLM and John Garang are presented in Mansour Khalid, ed., *John Garang Speaks* (London: KPI, 1987).

14. For the broader historical context of these developments, see John O. Voll, "The Evolution of Islamic Fundamentalism in Twentieth Century Sudan," in *Islam, Nationalism, and Radicalism in Egypt and the Sudan*, ed. Gabriel Warburg and Uri Kupferschmidt (New York: Praeger, 1983), pp. 113–131.

15. The description of the early years of the Islamic movement is based primarily on Abdelwahab El-Affendi, *Turabi's Revolution: Islam and Power in Sudan* (London: Grey Seal, 1991), chapter 3, and Hasan Makki Muhammad Ahmad, *Harakah al-ikhwan al-muslimin fi al-sudan, 1944 m.- 1969 m.* (Khartoum: Dar al-fikr, n.d.), Part I.

16. El-Affendi, *Turabi's Revolution*, p. 53.

17. Hasan al-Turabi, *al-Harakah al-Islamiyyah fi al-sudan, al-tatawwur wa al-kasab wa al-minhaj* (Cairo: al-Qari' al-arabi, 1991), p. 30.

18. El-Affendi, *Turabi's Revolution*, p. 57.

19. al-Turabi, *al-Harakah al-islamiyyah*, p. 31.

20. Quoted in El-Affandi, *Turabi's Revolution*, p. 60.

21. El-Affandi, *Turabi's Revolution*, p.62.

22. Turabi, *al-Harakah al-Islamiyyah*, p. 32.

23. Ibid, pp. 33–34.

24. These are the figures presented in El-Affendi, *Turabi's Revolution*, pp. 77 and 84. Bechtold gives a lower total of five seats in 1965 and and three in 1968 (Bechtold, *Politics in the Sudan*, pp. 232 and 249). The difference may be in the way that some independents are identified by the two scholars.

25. El-Affendi, *Turabi's Revolution*, p. 76. Specific aspects of the program defined in the charter can be found in Hasan Makki, *Harakah al-ikhwan*, pp. 107–110.

26. El-Affendi, *Turabi's Revolution*, p. 111. Turabi provides his own description of the organizational evolution of the movement in *al-Harakah al-Islami*, pp. 63–67.

27. This point was made, for example, by Hasan al-Turabi in a discussion of the history of the movement. Interview with John L. Esposito and John O. Voll in Khartoum, March, 1992.

28. al-Turabi, *al-Harakak al-islamiyyah*, pp. 35–36.

29. Hasan al-Turabi, *al-Mar'ah bayn ta'alim al-din wa taqalid al-mujtama'* (Jiddah: al-Dar al-Sa'udiyyah, 1984). An English translation of this is Hasan Turabi, *Women in Islam and Muslim Society* (London: Milestones, 1991).

30. Hasan al-Turabi, *Tajdid usul al-fiqh al-islami* (Khartoum: Dar al-Fikr, 1980).

31. Turabi interview with Susan Bridge, Independent Broadcasting Associates, for the radio series *The World of Islam*, 14 January 1982.

32. Ibid.

33. The lack of involvement in the process leading up to the promulgation of the decrees and the reservations about some aspects of the decrees was emphasized in interviews with a number of Ikhwan leaders, including Hasan al-Turabi, and officials in the President's office who were responsible for drafting the decrees by John L. Esposito and John O. Voll in August 1984.

34. Turabi, *al-Harakah al-islamiyyah*, p. 37.

35. Both Umar Hasan al-Bashir and Hasan al-Turabi affirmed this in March 1993, when there was no particular reason for them to deny prior association. Interviews with John L. Esposito and John O. Voll, March 1993.

36. Mohamed Omer Beshir, *The Southern Sudan, From Conflict to Peace* (New York: Barnes & Noble, 1975), p. 17.

37. Muhammad Asad, *Islam and Politics* (Geneva: Islamic Centre, November 1963), p. 7.

38. Beshir, *The Southern Sudan, from Conflict to Peace*, p. 124.

39. Turabi, *al-Harakah al-islamiyyah*, p. 36.

40. El-Affendi, *Turabi's Revolution*, p. 149.

41. An example of Turabi's discussion of the early Medina experience is Hassan al-Turabi, "The Islamic State," in John L. Esposito, ed., *Voices of Resurgent Islam* (New York: Oxford University Press, 1983), p. 250.

42. Francis Deng and Prosser Gifford, *The Search for Peace and Unity in the Sudan* (Washington: The Wilson Center Press, 1987), p. 86. The full text of the charter is reprinted in this book, pp. 78–89.

43. Deng and Gifford, *The Search for Peace*, p. 80.

44. The quotations are from a newsletter published in Great Britain which is sympathetic to the NSR regime, *Sudan Focus* 2, no. 11 (15 January 1995): 2.

45. Deng and Gifford, *The Search for Peace*, p. 85.

46. *Sudan Focus* 1, no. 9 (15 November 1994): 3.

47. See, for example, the discussion of non-NIF trade unions in "'In the Nme of God': Repression Continues in Northern Sudan," *Human Rights Watch/ Africa Newsletter* (A609) 6 (November 1994): 32–33.

48. A description of some of this suppression presented from an antigovernment perspective can be found in *Sudan Democratic Gazette* no. 49 (June 1994): 6.

49. *Sudan Focus* 1, no. 9 (15 November 1994): 3.

CHAPTER FIVE. *Pakistan*

1. For my analysis, I have drawn on my previous work, in particular John L. Esposito, *Islam and Politics*, 3rd rev. ed. (Syracuse, New York: Syracuse University Press, 1991), and John L. Esposito, "Islam: Ideology and Politics in Pakistan," in Ali Banuazizi and Myron Weiner, eds., *The State, Religion, and Ethnic Politics* (Syracuse, N.Y.: Syracuse University Press, 1986), chapter 12.

2. Hamza Alavi, "Ethnicity, Muslim Society, and the Pakistan Ideology," in Anita M. Weiss, ed., *Islamic Reassertion in Pakistan* (Syracuse, N.Y.: Syracuse University Press, 1986), p. 41. See also Muhammad Munir, *From Jinnah to Zia* (Lahore: Vanguard Books, n.d.), p. 32ff.

3. G. W. Choudury, ed., *Documents and Speeches on the Constitution of Pakistan* (Dacca: Green Book House, 1967), p. 25.

4. Ibid., p. 30.

5. Munir, *From Jinnah to Zia*, p. 36.

6. Alavi, "Ethnicity, Muslim Society, and the Pakistan Ideology," p. 44.

7. Anita Weiss, "The Historical Debate on Islam and the State in South Asia," in *Islamic Reassertion in Pakistan*, p. 8.

8. Esposito, *Islam and Politics*, p. 115.

9. Freeland Abbott, *Islam and Pakistan* (New York: Cornell University Press, 1968), p. 196.

10. *Criterion* 5, no. 4 (1970), as cited in H. Mintjes, "The Debate on Islamic Socialism in Pakistan," *Al-Mushir* (Rawalpindi) 20, no. 4 (Summer 1978): 70.

11. Wayne Wilcox, *Pakistan: The Consolidation of a Nation* (New York: Columbia University Press, 1963), p. 195.

12. Shahid Javed Burki, *Pakistan Under Bhutto, 1971–1977* (New York: St. Martin's Press, 1980), p. 93.

13. Ibid., p. 181.

14. Ibid., p. 183.

15. Ghafoor Ahmad (minister of commerce), Mahmud Azam Faruqi (Minister of Information), and Khurshid Ahmad (Deputy Chairman of the Planning Commission).

16. *Manifesto*, Jamaat-e-Islami Pakistan (Lahore, Pakistan, 1970).

17. Rashida Patel, *Islamization of Laws in Pakistan* (Karachi: Faiza Publishers, 1986), chapters 5–9.

18. Ibid., p. 60.

19. "The Muslim Community," *News from the Country, 1980–84* (Rawalpindi, Pakistan: Christian Study Center, 1985), p. 182.

20. Ibid., p. 182–83.

21. *Pakistan Affairs* 35, no. 1 (1 January, 1982): 1.

22. Hafeez Malik, "Martial Law and Islamization in Pakistan," *Orient*, vol. 27, no. 4 (1986): 602.

23. Abbas Rashid, "Pakistan: The Politics of 'Fundamentalism,'" *Special Bulletin on Fundamentalism and Secularism in South Asia* (Lahore: Shirkat Gah, June 1992): 21.

24. *Gallup Political Weather Report* (Islamabad: Gallup Pakistan, June 1991), p. 18.

25. Munir, *From Jinnah to Zia*, p. 172.

26. *al-Mushir* (Rawalpindi, Pakistan: Christian Study Center), vol. XXVII, no. 3 (Autumn 1985): 162–63, and no. 1 (Spring 1985): 50–51.

27. *News from the Country, 1980–84*, pp. 146–47.

28. *News from the Country, 1980–84*, p. 149.

29. Ahmed Rashid, "The Great Divide: Shias and Sunnis Battle It Out in Pakistan," *Far Eastern Economic Review* (9 March 1995): 24.

30. Ibid.

31. Rashid, "The Great Divide: Shias and Sunnis Battle It Out in Pakistan": 24.

32. Salamat Ali, "Pakistan: The Great Ethnic Divide," *Far Eastern Economic Review* (January 14, 1988): 28.

33. Benazir Bhutto's interior minister, Aitzaz Ahsan, as quoted in *Dawn Overseas Weekly*, 12 April 1989.

34. See, for example, John F. Burns, "A Network of Islamic Terrorism Traced to a Pakistani University," *New York Times* (20 March 1995), and Burns, "Pakistan Asks for U.S. Help in Crackdown on Militants," *New York Times* (22 March 1995).

35. Ahmed Rashid, "Schools for Soldiers: Islamic Schools Mix Religion and Politics," *Far Eastern Economic Review*, 9 March 1995: 25.

36. Ibid., and Burns, "Pakistan Asks for U.S. Help in Crackdown on Militants."

37. I. A. Rehman, "Rout of the Mullahs," *Newsline* (October 1993): 44.

CHAPTER SIX. *Malaysia*

1. Gordon P. Means, "Malaysia: Islam in a Pluralistic Society," in Carlo Caldarola, ed., *Religion and Societies: Asia and the Middle East* (Berlin: Mouton, 1982), p. 470.

2. Fred R. von der Mehden, "Malaysia: Islam and Multiethnic Polities," in John L. Esposito, ed., *Islam in Asia: Religion, Politics, and Society* (New York: Oxford University Press, 1987), chapter 8.

3. For a discussion of the introduction of Islam in Southeast Asia, see M. B. Hooker, "The Translation of Islam into Southeast Asia," in Hooker, ed., *Islam in Southeast Asia* (Leiden: E. J. Brill, 1983), chapter 1.

4. von der Mehden, "Malaysia: Islam and Multiethnic Polities," p. 448.

5. Fred R. von der Mehden, "Islamic Resurgence in Malaysia," in John L. Esposito, ed., *Islam and Development: Religion and Sociopolitical Change* (Syracuse, N.Y.: Syracuse University Press, 1980), p. 164.

6. *Malayan Constitutional Documents*, vol. I (Kuala Lumpur: Government Press, 1962), p. 124.

7. Means, "Malaysia: Islam in a Pluralistic Society," pp. 471–472.

8. von der Mehden, "Islamic Resurgence in Malaysia," p. 164.

9. Chandra Muzzafar, *Islamic Resurgence in Malaysia* (Selangor, Malaysia: Penerbit Fajar Bakti, 1981), pp. 23ff.

10. von der Mehden, "Malaysia: Islam and Multiethnic Polities," p. 179.

11. For this discussion, see John L. Esposito, "Trailblazers of the Islamic Resurgence," in Yvonne Yazbeck Haddad, John Obert Voll, and John L. Esposito, eds., *The Contemporary*

Islamic Revival: A Critical Survey and Bibliography (Westport, Conn.: Greenwood Press, 1991), pp. 47–52.

12. Fred R. von der Mehden, "Islamic Resurgence in Malaysia" in John L. Esposito, ed., *Islam and Development: Religion and Sociopolitical Change* (Syracuse, N.Y.: Syracuse University Press, 1980), p. 169.

13. See Judith Nagata, *The Reflowering of Malaysian Islam: Modern Religious Radicals and Their Roots* (Vancouver: University of British Columbia Press, 1984), and Muhammad Syukri Sallaeh, *An Islamic Approach to Rural Development — The Arqam Way* (London: ASOIB International Limited, 1992).

14. "Premier vs. Power," *Far Eastern Economic Review* (15 September 1994): 15.

15. Mohamed Jawhar, "Malaysia in 1994," *Asian Survey* 35, no. 2 (February 1995): 190.

16. Siddiq Fadil, as quoted in Muzaffer, *Islamic Resurgence in Malaysia*, p. 48.

17. Ibid., p. 49.

18. Ibid., pp. 12–13.

19. Ibid., p. 16.

20. Anwar Ibrahim, as quoted in Muzaffer, ibid., p. 50.

21. von der Mehden, "Islamic Resurgence in Malaysia," pp. 174–175.

22. Ibid., p. 174.

23. Delair Noer, "Contemporary Political Dimensions of Islam," in Hooker, ed., *Islam in Southeast Asia*, p. 200.

24. Jomo Kwame Sundaram and Ahmad Shabery Cheek, "The Politics of Malaysia's Islamic Resurgence," *Third World Quarterly*, vol 10. no. 2 (April 1988): 852–853.

25. Zainah Anwar, *Islamic Revivalisms in Malaysia: Dakwah Among the Students* (Selangor: Pelanduk Publications, 1987), p. 29.

26. Ibid., p. 52.

27. von der Mehden, "Malaysia: Islam and Multiethnic Polities," p. 195.

28. Fred R. von der Mehden, *Two Worlds of Islam: Interaction Between Southeast Asia and the Middle East* (Gainesville, Fl.: University of Florida Press, 1993).

29. von der Mehden, *Two Worlds of Islam: Interaction Between Southeast Asia and the Middle East*, p. 97.

30. "Back to English: Government Promotes Bilingualism as a Business Asset," *Far Eastern Economic Review* (11 November 1994): 18.

31. Mahathir Mohammad, "Islam and Justice," in *Islam and Justice*, ed. Aidit bint Hj. Ghazali (Kuala Lumpur, Malaysia: Institute of Islamic Understanding, 1993), p. 2.

32. Ibid.

33. H. E. Dato Seri Dr. Mahathir Mohamad, "A Muslim Perspective on the New World Order," United Nations Forty-sixth Session, New York, 24 September 1991 (Washington, D.C.: American Muslim Council, 1991), pp. 3, 6.

34. Ibid., p. 7.

35. Ibid.

36. Ibid.

37. Ibid.

38. Mahathir, "Islam and Justice," p. 2.

39. Ibid., pp. 2–7.

40. Mahathir Mohamad, "Religion Has Pertinent Role To Play in Society," *Perspektif IKIM* no. 5 (December 1993): 16.

41. "Malaysia Raps Rap," *The Economist*, 18 June 1994: 39.

42. Michael Vatikiotis, "The Golden Mean: Faith in Religion Invoked to Cope with Modern Pressures," *Far Eastern Economic Review* (14 October 1993): 23.

43. Mahathir Mohamad, "A Muslim Perspective on the New World Order," p. 8.

44. Michael Vatikiotis, "Value Judgments: Younger Leaders Search for New 'Asian' Directions," *Far Eastern Economic Review* (10 February 1994), p. 28.

45. Mustaf Ali, "Malaysia," in Azzam Tamimi, ed., *Power Sharing Islam?* (London: Liberty Publications, 1993), p. 109.

46. "National Front Issues Election Manifesto," *New Straits Times* (13 April 1995), p. 4, as quoted in *FBIS* (19 April 1995): 41.

47. "Mahathir Warns Islamic Party on Behavior," *FBIS* (8 May 1995): 54–55.

48. "Panel Set Up to Monitor PAS Activities," *The Star* (15 May 1995): 2, as quoted in *FBIS* (16 May 1995): 42.

49. von der Mehden, "Malaysia: Islam and Multiethnic Politics," p. 197.

50. Maria Luisa Seda-Poulin, "Islamization and Legal Reform in Malaysia," *Southeast Asian Affairs 1993* (Singapore: Institute of Southeast Asian Studies, 1993), p. 226.

51. Means, "Malaysia: Islam in a Pluralistic Society," p. 486.

CHAPTER SEVEN. *Algeria*

1. Robert Mortimer, "Islam and Multiparty Politics in Algeria," *The Middle East Journal* vol. 45, no. 4 (Autumn 1991): 575.

2. Jean Claude Vatin, "Religious resistance and State Power in Algeria," in Alexander S. Cudsi and Ali E. Hillal Dessouki, eds., *Islam and Power* (Baltimore: Johns Hopkins University Press, 1981), p. 146.

3. Ibid., p. 575.

4. Mahfoud Bennoune, *The Making of Contemporary Algeria, 1830–1987: Colonial Upheavals and Post-Independence Development* (Cambridge: Cambridge University Press, 1988).

5. *Charte Nationale* (Republique Algerienne, 1976), pp. 21–22.

6. David Ottoway and Marina Ottoway, *Algeria: The Politics of a Socialist Revolution* (Berkeley, Calif.: University of California Press, 1970), p. 30.

7. Vatin, "Religious Resistance and State Power in Algeria," p. 135.

8. Francois Burgat, *The Islamic Movement in North Africa*, trans. William Dowell (Austin: Center for Middle Eastern Studies, University of Texas, 1993), p. 261.

9. *Middle East Watch*: vol. 4, no. 2 (February 1992): 11.

10. Daniel Brumberg, "Islam, Elections, and Reform in Algeria," *Journal of Democracy* vol. 2, no. 1 (Winter 1991): 59. See also Saad Eddin Ibrahim, "Crises, Elites, and Democratization in the Arab World," *The Middle East Journal* vol. 47, no. 2 (Spring 1993): 292–305.

11. "Algeria's Facade of Democracy," *Middle East Report* (March–April, 1990): 17.

12. "Algeria's Brush with Freedom," *The Economist* (15 June 1991): 40.

13. John Reudy, *Modern Algeria: The Origins and Development of a Nation* (Bloomington, Ind.: Indiana University Press, 1992), p. 242.

14. Ibid., p. 243.

15. Burgat, *The Islamic Movement in North Africa*, p. 276.

16. "Transcript: Interview With Abassi Madani" (Los Angeles: Pontifex Media Center, 1991), p. 4.

17. Ibid., p. 5.

18. Ibid.

19. Ibid., p. 6.

20. Ibid., p. 8.

21. Ibid., p. 10.

22. Ibid.

23. Ibid., p. 11.

24. Ibid.

25. Ibid., p. 14.

26. Ibid., p. 16.

27. Burgat, *The Islamic Movement in North Africa*, p. 279.

28. Mohamed Esseghir, "Islam Comes to Rescue Algeria," *The Message International* (August 1991): p. 13.

29. Burhan Ghalyoun, in *Al-Yawm Al-Sabi*, "Algeria: Democratization at Home, Inspiration Abroad," quoted in *The Message International* (August 1991): 19.

30. For an example of this kind of activity, see "Taking Space in Tlemcen: The Islamist Occupation of Urban Algeria," *Middle East Report*, vol. 22, no. 6 (November/December 1992): 12–13.

31. "Amid Praise for Algerian System: Hopes for an Islamic Government," *The Message International* (August 1991): 17.

32. John P. Entelis and Lisa J. Arone, "Algeria in Turmoil: Islam, Democracy, and the State," *Middle East Policy*, 1:2 (1992), p. 29.

33. John P. Entelis, as quoted in *Maghreb Report* (March/April, 1993): 6.

34. Entelis and Arone, "Algeria in Turmoil," p. 31.

35. Brumberg, "Islam, Elections, and Reform in Algeria," p. 69.

36. "Human Rights in Algeria Since the Halt of the Electoral Process," *Middle East Watch*, vol. 4, no. 2 (February 1992): 2.

37. "Amid Praise for Algerian System: Hopes for an Islamic Government": 16.

38. David Hirst, "Algiers Militants Urge Care at the Gates of Victory," *The Guardian*, 18 January 1992.

39. "Human Rights in Algeria": 13.

40. *Middle East Times*, 19–25 June, 1990 and "Human Rights in Algeria": 13.

41. John L. Esposito and James P. Piscatori, "Democratization and Islam," *The Middle East Journal* vol. 45, no. 3 (Summer 1991): 440.

42. Vandewalle, "Ben Ali's new Tunisia," *Field Staff Reports: Africa/Middle East* 1989–90, no. 8, p. 3.

43. Jonathan C. Randal, "Algerian Elections Cancelled," *The Washington Post*, 13 January, 1994.

44. Alfred Hermida, "Algeria: Democracy Derailed," *Africa Report*, vol. 37, no. 2 (March–April, 1992): 15.

45. Ibid.

46. "Algeria: Dusting off the Iron Glove," *The Middle East* (April 1993): 19.

47. Entelis and Arone, "Algeria in Turmoil," p. 35.

48. Jonathan C. Randal, "Fundamentalist Leader in Algeria Is Arrested," *The Washington Post*, 22 January, 1994.

49. Randal, "Algerian Elections Cancelled."

50. "Human Rights in Algeria," p. 1.

51. "Algeria: The Army Tightens Its Grip," *The Economist*, 17 July, 1993: 37.

52. "Algeria: A Kite for Peace," *The Economist*, 5 March, 1994: p. 45.

53. "Algeria: Looking for Scapegoats," *The Middle East* (May 1994): 20.

54. Ibid., p. 21.

55. Ibid., p. 21.

56. John P. Entelis, "Political Islam in Algeria," *Current History* (January 1995), p. 17.

57. Entelis and Arone, "Algeria and Turmoil," pp. 33–35.

CHAPTER EIGHT. *Egypt*

1. See, for example, Nazih Ayubi, *Political Islam: Religion and Politics in the Arab World* (London and New York: Routledge, 1991), chapter 4; Raymond William Baker, *Sadat and After: Struggles for Egypt's Political Soul* (Cambridge, Mass.: Harvard University Press, 1990), chapter 8; John L. Esposito, *The Islamic Threat: Myth or Reality?* (New York: Oxford University Press, 1992), chapters 4–5, and idem, *Islam and Politics*, 3rd rev. ed. (Syracuse, N.Y.: Syracuse University Press, 1991), chapters 4–5; Amira El-Azhary Sonbol, "Egypt," in Shireen T. Hunter, ed., *The Politics of Islamic Revivalism* (Bloomington, Ind.: The University of Indiana Press, 1988), chapter 2.

2. Robert Bianchi, "Islam and Democracy in Egypt," *Current History* (February 1989): 93.

3. Saad Eddin Ibrahim, "Egypt's Islamic Activism in the 1980's," *Third World Quarterly* 10:2 (April 1988): 643.

4. For an analysis of this issue, see John L. Esposito and James P. Piscatori, "Democratization and Islam," *The Middle East Journal* 45 (Summer 1991); John L. Esposito, "Islam, Democracy, and U.S. Foreign Policy," in Phebe Marr and William Lewis, eds., *Riding the Tiger: The Middle East Challenge After the Gulf War*, (Boulder, Co.: Westview, 1993), *Islam and Democracy: Religion, Politics, and Power in the Middle East* (Washington, D.C.: The United States Institute of Peace, 1993).

5. Richard Mitchell, *The Society of Muslim Brothers*, 2nd ed. (New York: Oxford University Press, 1969; 1993 ed.), p. 226.

6. Ibid., p. 261.

7. Raymond Baker, "Islam, Democracy, and the Arab Future," in Tariq Y. Ismael and Jacqueline S. Ismael, eds., *The Gulf War and the New World Order* (Boulder: Westview Press, 1992), p. 485.

8. John O. Voll, *Islam: Continuity and Change in the Muslim World*, 2nd rev. ed. (Syracuse, N.Y.: Syracuse University Press, 1994), p. 116.

9. Baker, "Islam, Democracy, and the Arab Future," p. 489.

10. Ibid., p. 491. For a detailed analysis of Islamist reactions and responses to the Gulf War, see James P. Piscatori, ed., *Islamic Fundamentalisms and the Gulf War* (Chicago: University of Chicago Press, 1991).

11. Amira El-Azhary Sonbol, "Egypt," *The Politics of Islamic Revivalism*, p. 25.

12. *Irish Times*, 23 February, 1994.

13. *South China Morning Post*, 27 March, 1994.

14. Jane Freedman, "Democratic Winds Blow in Cairo," *The Christian Science Monitor*, 17 January, 1990.

15. Christopher Hedges, "Seven Executed in Egypt in Move to Suppress Islamic Rebel Group," *New York Times*, 9 July, 1993.

16. "U.S. Said to Ask Egypt About Lawyer's Death," *New York Times*, 27 May, 1994.

17. Ibid.

18. Virginia N. Sherry, "Egypt's Trampling of Rights Fosters Extremism," *New York Times*, 15 April, 1993.

19. Sami Zubaida, "Islam, the State and Democracy: Contrasting Conceptions of Society in Egypt," *Middle East Report* (November–December 1992): 8.

20. "Militants rally to lawyer's death," *Middle East Times* (16–22 May 1994): 1.

21. "Fugitive lawyer Remains defiant," *Middle East Times* (27 June–3 July, 1994): 16.

22. "Professors can not choose," *Middle East Times* (6–12 June 1992): 1.

23. Chris Hedges, "Egypt Begins Crackdown on Strongest Opposition Group," *New York Times*, 12 June, 1994: 3.

24. "Security Girds for Post-militant Political Order," *Middle East Times* (6–12 June, 1992): 2.

25. "Educating Against Extremism," *Middle East Times* (2–8 May, 1994): 1.

26. "Ministering to the 'Satanic West,'" *Middle East Times* (2–8 May 1994): p. 6.

27. Ibid.

28. Ibid., p. 2.

29. Baker, "Islam, Democracy, and the Arab Future," p. 257.

30. Nadia Ramsis Farah, *Religious Strife in Egypt: Crisis and Ideological Conflict in the Seventies* (New York: Gordon and Breach, 1986), p. 4.

31. EOHR, "A Statement of Recent [Incidents] of Communal/Religious Violence," 3 April, 1990, p. 1.

32. "Assiut bears the brunt of Islamists' human rights abuse," *Middle East Times* (16–22 May, 1994): p. 2.

33. Bianchi, "Islam and Democracy in Egypt," p. 104.

Conclusion

1. Edward P. Djerejian, "The U.S. and the Middle East in a Changing World" (Washington: D.C.: Meridian House International, June 2, 1992). The policy was reiterated by Robert H. Pelletreau, Djerejian's successor, in "Islam and U.S. Policy," an edited version of which appeared in Robert H. Pelletreau, Jr., Daniel Pipes, and John L. Esposito, "Political Islam Symposium: Resurgent Islam in the Middle East," *Middle East Policy* 3 (1994): 7–8.

Suggestions for Further Reading

It is not possible to provide a comprehensive bibliography for this subject in a short study of this nature. However, it is possible to suggest sources where the interested reader can find further information about the subjects discussed and bibliographical information for further study.

For general information and specific articles about most of the major countries and people involved in the issues of "Islam and democracy," an important source is *The Oxford Encyclopedia of the Modern Islamic World*, edited by John L. Esposito (New York: Oxford University Press, 1995). A relatively comprehensive bibliography of Islamic movements through the world is provided by Yvonne Y. Haddad, John L. Esposito, and John O. Voll, *The Contemporary Islamic Revival: A Critical Survey and Bibliography* (Westport, Conn.: Greenwood Publishing, 1991). *The Middle East Journal* provides a good continuing bibliography of books and articles on the Middle East and Islam.

Many books have been written about different aspects of democracy in the Muslim world. Good discussions of critical aspects of this subject can be found in the series, "Issues in Third World Politics," published by Lynne Rienner Publishers: Heather Deegan, *The Middle East and Problems of Democracy* (1994); Jeff Haynes, *Religion in Third World Politics* (1994); and Robert Pinkney, *Democracy in the Third World* (1994). In terms of the states and societies of the Middle East, one important line of analysis has been to examine the dimensions of "civil society" and political systems. Perhaps the most useful collection of studies from this perspective is Augustus Richard Norton, ed., *Civil Society in the Middle East* (Leiden: Brill, 1994). A continuing source of information is the journal *Civil Society*, published by the Ibn Khaldoun Center for Development Studies in Cairo.

Another important part of the literature is discussions of the nature and significance of the "Islamic Resurgence" of the late twentieth century. For more extended presentations of the views of the authors of this book on the Islamic resurgence, see John L. Esposito, *The Islamic Threat: Myth or Reality* (Revised edition; New York: Oxford University Press, 1995) and John Obert Voll, *Islam: Continuity and Change in the Modern World* (2nd ed.; Syracuse, N.Y.: Syracuse University Press, 1994). There are many discussions of this topic, but a starting point for this literature is the many essays on Muslim countries and movements in the volumes of "The Fundamentalism Project" edited by

Martin E. Marty and R. Scott Appleby, especially *Fundamentalisms Observed* (Volume 1; Chicago: University of Chicago Press, 1991) and *Fundamentalisms and the State: Remaking Polities, Economics, and Militance* (Volume 3; Chicago: University of Chicago Press, 1993). An example of the debates on the subject of Islam and democracy can be found in John O. Voll and John L. Esposito, "Islam's Democratic Essence," and the ripostes in *Middle East Quarterly* (September 1994), pages 3–19, and Voll and Esposito's reply in *Middle East Quarterly* (December 1994), pages 71–72.

Each of the countries examined as case studies in this volume is the subject of a large body of literature on Islam and politics. Some of the most useful starting points for further study of Islam and democracy in each of these countries are:

IRAN

Arjomand, Said Amir. *The Turban for the Crown: The Islamic Revolution in Iran* (New York: Oxford University Press, 1988)

Algar, Hamid, trans. *Islam and Revolution: Writings and Declarations of Imam Khomeini* (Berkeley: University of California Press, 1981)

Esposito, John L., ed. *The Iranian Revolution: Its Global Impact* (Miami, Fla.: Florida International University Press, 1990)

Wright, Robin. *In the Name of God: The Khomeini Decade* (New York: Simon and Schuster, 1989).

SUDAN

El-Effendi, Abdelwahhab. *Turabi's Revolution: Islam and Power in Sudan* (London: Gray Seal, 1991).

Voll, John O., ed. *Sudan: State and Society in Crisis* (Bloomington: Indiania University Press, 1991)

PAKISTAN

Nasr, Seyyed Vali. *The Vanguard of the Islamic Revolution: The Jamaat-i Islami of Pakistan* (Berkeley: University of California Press, 1994)

Binder, Leonard. *Religion and Politics in Pakistan* (Berkeley: University of California Press, 1963).

ALGERIA

Burgat, Francois. *The Islamic Movement in North Africa*, trans. William Dowell (Austin: Center for Middle Eastern Studies, University of Texas, 1993).

Ruedy, John, ed. *Islamism and Secularism in North Africa* (Washington, D.C.: Center for Contemporary Arab Studies, Georgetown University, 1994)

EGYPT

Baker, Raymond. *Sadat and After: Struggles for Egypt's Political Soul* (Cambridge: Harvard University Press, 1990)

Kepel, Gilles. *Muslim Extremism in Egypt: The Prophet and Pharoah* (Berkeley: University of California Press, 1986)

MALAYSIA

Anwar, Zainah. *Islamic Revivalism in Malaysia* (Kuala Lumpur: Pelanduk Publications, 1987)

Muzaffar, Chandra. *Islamic Resurgence in Malaysia* (Kuala Lumpur: Penerbit Fajar Bakti Sdn, 1987)

Index